W9-BNY-592

THE BEST OF BIRDS & BLOOMS® 2012

contents

88
Best Blooms for
Hummingbirds

from the **editor**

What a great year! I'm so happy to bring you this edition of the *Best of Birds & Blooms* because it offers so many fantastic tips, heartwarming stories and gorgeous photos from last year. Page through this keepsake and you'll discover our top picks for colorful blooms, new ways to attract hummingbirds and which feathered flyers our readers like best. In addition, we offer fun ideas to get kids into birding, share tips from nature photographers and review a few vacation hot spots for birders and gardeners alike! (Don't miss one reader's visit to a butterfly sanctuary—see page 164.) With the affordable projects, container plans and other ideas found in the *Best of Birds & Blooms 2012*, you'll have no trouble transforming your space into a backyard haven!

Stacy Tornio
Editor, *Birds & Blooms*

COVERS, FROM TOP LEFT: STEVE GREER; RICHARD DAY / DAYBREAK IMAGERY; ROLF NUSSBAUMER; STEVE GREER; BILL LEAMAN; MASLOWSKI WILDLIFE; TIM FITZHARRIS; MASLOWSKI WILDLIFE; DAYBREAK IMAGERY; RICHARD DAY; TIM FITZHARRIS; MASLOWSKI WILDLIFE

THE BEST OF
BIRDS & BLOOMS
2012

Catherine Cassidy Vice President, Editor-in-Chief
Heidi Reuter Lloyd Vice President, Executive Editor/Books
Mark Hagen Senior Editor/Books
Julie Kastello Project Editor
Edwin Robles Jr. Associate Creative Director
Raeann Sundholm Art Director
Julie Wagner Content Production Manager
Kathy Crawford Layout Designer
Deb Warlaumont Mulvey Copy Chief
Barbara Schuetz Project Proofreader
Trudi Bellin Photo Coordinator
Mary Ann Koebernik Assistant Photo Coordinator
Barb Czysz Administrative Assistant

BIRDS & BLOOMS

Heather Lamb Executive Editor
Sharon K. Nelson Creative Director
Stacy Tornio Editor
Sue Myers Art Director
Crystal Rennicke Senior Editor
Joanne Weintraub, Dulcie Shoener, Susan Uphill Copy Editors
Dena Ahlers Production Coordinator
Jamieson Hawkins Krampf Digital Editor
Danielle Calkins Assistant Digital Editor
Lorie L. West Editorial Assistant

George Harrison Birding Expert
Melinda Myers Horticulture Expert
Kenn and Kimberly Kaufman, Sally Roth, David Mizejewski Contributing Editors

Lisa Karpinski North American Chief Marketing Officer
Dan Fink Vice President/Book Marketing
Jim Palmen Creative Director/Creative Marketing

The Reader's Digest Association
Robert E. Guth President and Chief Executive Officer
Dan Lagani Executive Vice President, RDA, and President, North America

5400 S. 60th St, Greendale WI 53219

International Standard Book Number (10): 0-89821-999-X
International Standard Book Number (13): 978-0-89821-999-9
International Standard Serial Number: 1553-8400

Printed in U.S.A.

Front cover:
Baltimore Oriole/Richard Day/Daybreak Imagery;
Giant Swallowtail/Raeann Sundholm

Back cover:
Hummingbird/Larry Kimball;
Woodpecker/Sharon Stiteler;
Aster/Val Thoermer/Shutterstock

For additional copies of this book, visit ShopTasteofHome.com or call 800-344-6913 or email *rpsubscustomercare@custhelp.com*.

Be sure to visit our website at *birdsandblooms.com*.

CHAPTER 1

topflight Birds

Find out if your favorite feathered friend is among the most beloved backyard birds, meet the friendliest fliers and other winged wonders, plus delight in the best bird encounters from readers.

ROSE-BREASTED GROSBEAK, MASLOWSKI WILDLIFE

North America's favorite

Readers select their No. 1 bird picks in honor of our 100th issue.

BY STACY TORNIO, EDITOR

Baltimore oriole

birds

In the first 100 issues of *Birds & Blooms* magazine, we've featured stories and photos on just about every backyard bird in North America.

Sure, we can write about birds, give you advice on attracting them and show you beautiful photos. But it's the amazing, often funny stories from readers that help these birds really come to life and make our magazine unique.

In a recent survey, we asked readers to name their favorite backyard birds. It was a close race in many categories, but we finally came up with this diverse group of eight.

Take a look at these reader picks. And in true *Birds & Blooms* fashion, we'll show you some gorgeous photos, provide tips for drawing birds to your yard and share some entertaining reader stories.

MOST COLORFUL BIRD • BALTIMORE ORIOLE

THE BASICS: The Baltimore oriole beat out the scarlet tanager and painted bunting to earn the honor of most colorful. The males' fiery orange feathers certainly stand out in a crowd. While there are several orioles in the U.S., the Baltimore is the most widespread. Females aren't nearly as colorful, but their pale-yellow feathers are still beautiful. Orioles are known for the distinctive pouchlike nests they hide high in trees.

HOW TO ATTRACT: Orioles will come to backyard feeders for oranges, grape jelly and sugar water. If you can entice them when they first arrive in spring, you might keep them coming back all summer.

READER STORY: Paula Williams and her husband, from Stony Point, New York, had an unusual encounter with an oriole family a few years ago after a storm. Paula writes, "I saw an oriole nest on the ground and picked it up. I couldn't help but admire the detail of it, as it was finely woven. Inside I spied three hungry little bills. Quickly, my husband got his ladder to put the nest safely back in a large oak tree. Then he began climbing down the ladder. Before he could reach the bottom, two tiny oriole chicks jumped out and landed on his shirt! I gently put the chicks back into the nest, and within minutes the mother and father returned to feed them."

RICHARD DAY / DAYBREAK IMAGERY

NORTHERN CARDINAL

THE BASICS: With the males' prominent crests and brilliant coloring, it's no wonder cardinals top the songbird list. Despite the name, they're traditionally a Southern bird. They didn't move into the Midwest until the mid-1800s, expanding into the Northeast in the early 1900s. Though mostly Eastern birds, they are starting to stray into the West, with sightings in Arizona, Colorado and nearby states. Once they do find a place they like, cardinals generally stay put. So the very ones you see in your backyard now are probably the same ones that are there year-round.

HOW TO ATTRACT: Cardinals prefer to feed alone, so they often show up first and last at feeders. Offer sunflower or safflower seeds to attract these beauties. (Safflower bonus: Squirrels don't like these seeds.)

READER STORY: Debbie Richmond of Warren, Rhode Island, sent her story of a cardinal pair in her own backyard. She wrote, "I have cardinals come to my feeders every day. In spring, the female will perch herself in a tree close to the feeder. When the male arrives, he'll get a couple of seeds for himself, then bring some to the female to feed her. It's so nice to see a bird be passionate toward its mate."

PILEATED WOODPECKER

THE BASICS: While it's not the easiest woodpecker to attract to your backyard, the pileated is certainly one of the most impressive. With a length of roughly 16 inches, it dwarfs other birds in its family. (By comparison, the downy woodpecker is only 6 to 7 inches long.) Males and females look alike except for the red "mustache" males wear under their bill. They tend to stick close to mature conifers, where they look for bugs in tree trunks.

HOW TO ATTRACT: If you don't have mature trees around you, pileated woodpeckers aren't likely to call your backyard home, so go out camping or hiking to find one instead. If you do have lots of trees, be sure to offer suet in feeders about 10 feet above the ground.

READER STORY: Pileated woodpeckers love pecking dead trees, and they'll even use stumps, as Jerry Miller of Poughquag, New York, discovered: "One day I saw this enormous bird pecking away at my tree stump. The stump is about 6 inches above the ground and has always gotten in the way of the lawn mower. The bird tore away at that stump for half an hour or so. When it left, I went to take a closer look, and the stump was completely obliterated. Now if only I could convince him to come back and pull some dandelions."

CARDINAL, RICHARD DAY / DAYBREAK IMAGERY; WOODPECKERS, MIKE MATTHEWS; DANDELION, ALBO003 / SHUTTERSTOCK.COM; WARBLER, LARRY DITTO / KAC PRODUCTIONS; HUMMINGBIRD, JOE KEGLEY

YELLOW WARBLER

THE BASICS: Though there are 50-some wood-warblers in North America, they aren't exactly considered backyard birds. Since they don't eat at feeders, you're more likely to see a warbler stopping in your yard during spring migration. If you're really lucky, one might stop at your birdbath. The yellow warbler seems to be an exception, though. It's much less timid than others in its family, which is probably why it easily took the top honors. You can find this brightly colored bird all over North America in spring and summer.

HOW TO ATTRACT: Since they're not seedeaters, your best chance is to offer a birdbath, especially one with moving water. Look for yellow warblers in spring, when they're flying through for summer—and when the males are at their brightest.

READER STORY: Carol Freeman of Glenview, Illinois, a nature photographer, fondly remembers the day she saw a yellow warbler building a nest: "I was at the Magic Hedge, a great birding area near Lake Michigan in Chicago. I saw a yellow warbler building her nest. As I took a closer look, I saw that she was using pieces of discarded tissue. I smiled to myself. She was a true city bird, making do with what she had."

RUBY-THROATED HUMMINGBIRD

THE BASICS: *Birds & Blooms* readers love hummingbirds of any kind, but the ruby-throat, which has the largest range in the U.S., is the favorite. In fact, it's the only hummingbird commonly seen in the East. Hummingbirds have impressive habits, and the ruby-throat is no exception. It hovers at flowers, can fly backward, sideways and upside down, and will change directions on a dime. Its nest is about the size of half a walnut shell, and the eggs are the size of navy beans.

HOW TO ATTRACT: Plant nectar-rich flowers, offer hanging baskets and put out sugar-water feeders. (The sugar water recipe is 4 parts water to 1 part sugar.) Even if you don't attract them early in spring, put your feeders back out in late summer. Often, you'll attract those migrating south for winter.

READER STORY: An unusual photo and story came from Joe Kegley of Charlotte, North Carolina, who wrote, "I spotted a female ruby-throated hummingbird enjoying the nectar from a bee balm plant in my mother's garden. When she pulled her bill out of the bloom, the flower came with it! I grabbed my camera and snapped a photo as fast as I could. The bird quickly shook the blossom off, but I'll always have this photo to remember the moment."

SNOWY OWL

THE BASICS: Location isn't everything, at least when it comes to birding. Unless traveling to Canada, most U.S. birders will never have the chance to see a snowy owl, but that didn't stop readers from putting it at the top of their lists. The heaviest owl in North America, it measures about 23 inches long. In summer, a snowy owl sports a dark-speckled look over much of its body, but in winter it's nearly pure white.

HOW TO ATTRACT: Listen first for its deep, muffled hoot. Since snowy owls feed mostly on small animals, your best chance of seeing one is spotting it perched near a field, waiting for prey. If you do want to attract owls to your yard, put out an owl box to bring in an eastern or western screech-owl.

READER STORY: Rob Fry of Cornwall, Ontario, shares his story of a snowy owl he calls Georgette: "I work in the rural areas of eastern Ontario, and snowy owls often perch here in winter. There is one in particular that perches on a utility pole that has become a bit of a celebrity among birders and photographers. One day I stopped to see the owl when it suddenly flew toward me and brushed me with its wing. It even knocked me back a bit. I never knew snowy owls had such power!"

BLUE JAY

THE BASICS: We included a troublemaker category because birds such as jays, mourning doves and crows often get a bad rap, but many birders still love them. With blue jays, it's not hard to see why. They're some of the friendliest and most colorful birds in backyards, often eating peanuts right out of someone's hand. If you don't see this bright-blue bird right away, then you'll definitely hear its loud *jay, jay, jay* call. Males and females look alike, and at 11 inches long, they're larger than most songbirds.

HOW TO ATTRACT: Put out sunflower seeds, suet cakes and peanuts to bring in this friendly flier.

READER STORY: One night a few inches of snow fell and covered the feeders in Irene Houck's backyard in Branson, Missouri. She writes, "A blue jay was sitting about a foot from the feeder, sweeping its head rapidly from side to side, clearing off the snow with its bill. When the jay removed all the snow, it calmly walked over and started eating seeds. Now, that's using your head."

EAGLE, FRITZ POELKING / THE IMAGE FINDERS; BLUE JAY, MASLOWSKI WILDLIFE; OWL, ANTHONY MERCIECA; PEANUTS, NATTIKA / SHUTTERSTOCK.COM

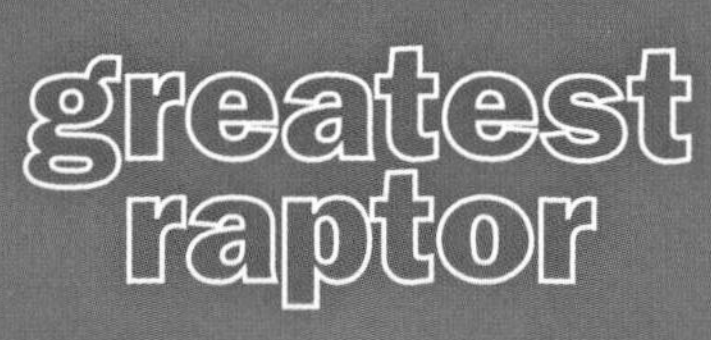

BALD EAGLE

THE BASICS: The bald eagle is one of the most beloved birds in North America. For years, it was on the endangered or threatened species lists, but it's been in the clear since 2007. Males and females often stay together for life and will go back to the same nest year after year. In fact, they keep building onto it, and some nests have been found to weigh a ton or more!

HOW TO ATTRACT: Bald eagles aren't backyard birds, but you can often spot them along rivers, where they like to fish, and other bodies of water. Since eagles return to the same areas year after year, check with local birding groups. They often know when and where to spot one.

READER STORY: Photographer Cheyenne Brenda Ware from Decatur, Illinois, was out hiking one day when she had an amazing encounter with a bald eagle family. She writes, "Suddenly a huge bird flew over me. I could see the shadow on the ground, but then I looked up into the sun and missed it. Then I heard it—two adult bald eagles were chattering back and forth. I looked up again and they were circling above me, doing a dance in the sky. I looked across the river and saw their huge nest sitting at the top of a dead tree. We hadn't had eagles nesting in our town for years, and it gave me hope that one day bald eagles will thrive here again."

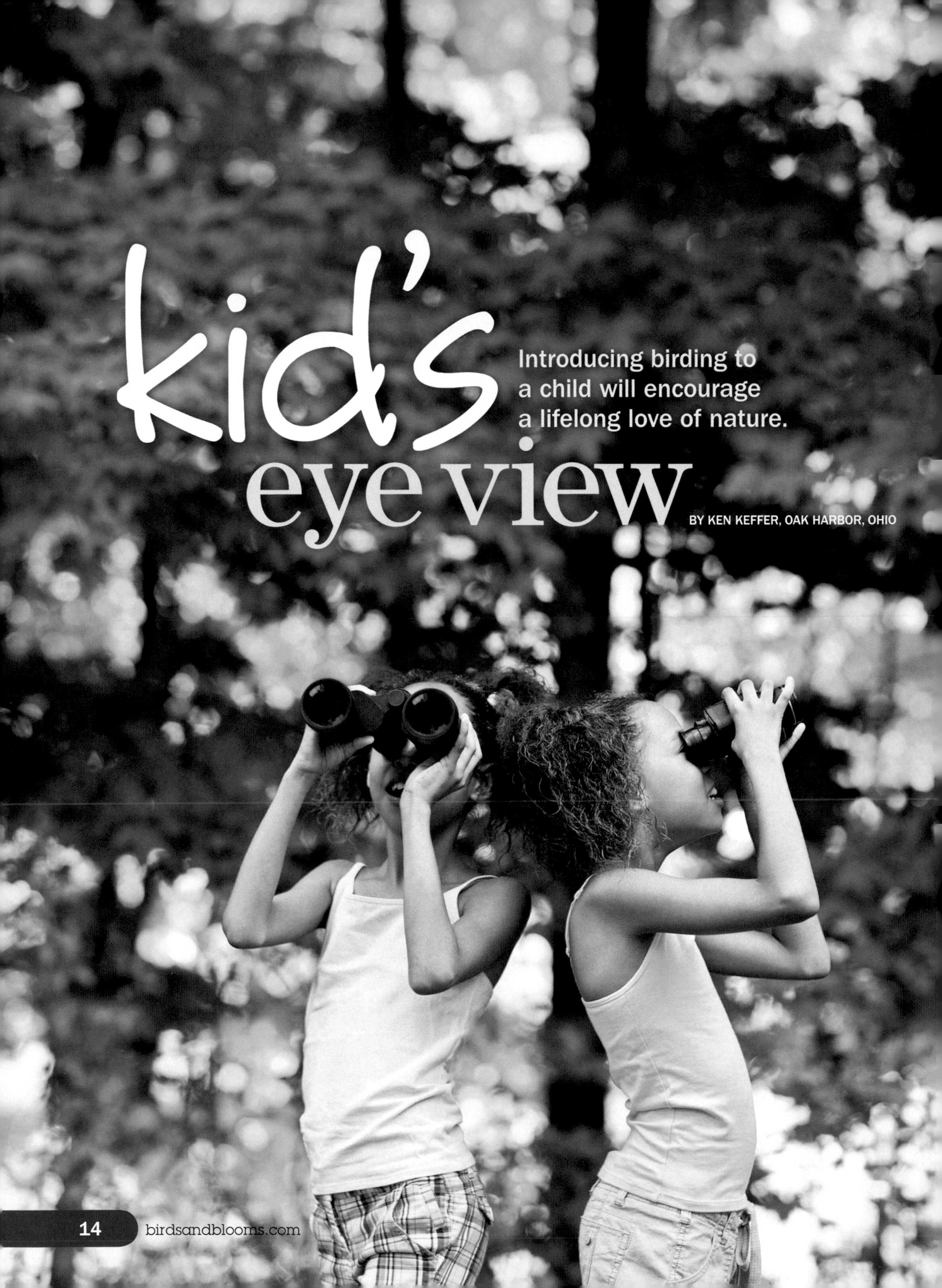

kid's eye view

Introducing birding to a child will encourage a lifelong love of nature.

BY KEN KEFFER, OAK HARBOR, OHIO

When you think back on your childhood, what do you remember most about being outside?

Perhaps a chorus of frogs resonates in your ears. Maybe the hours of fishing or splashing in the old watering hole are what you remember most. For me, it's the sweet aroma of harvested alfalfa from the fields of my grandparents' ranch near Buffalo, Wyoming.

No matter what the memory, many of us are fortunate enough to recall a time when being outside was part of being a kid. These days, it seems everyone is spending more time plugged in and tuned in and a lot less time outdoors. But nature is just as alluring now as it's ever been.

As the education director for the Black Swamp Bird Observatory in Oak Harbor, Ohio, I am privileged to share nature with thousands of people every year. And while every interaction is unique and rewarding, I'm most thrilled when I see a child's face light up with natural curiosity.

If you enjoy birds, I encourage you to reach out to the youth in your area. You don't have to be a bird or kid expert to share birding with others. Enthusiasm is the key to opening the door for the naturalists of tomorrow.

Learn where to go

Birds are the perfect hook for getting kids interested in nature, because you can find them everywhere. Just as you recruit young anglers with bluegill, you recruit birders with cardinals, chickadees and goldfinches.

Backyard bird feeders are a wonderful place to start. I remember spending countless hours at my grandparents' window watching the antics of black-billed magpies. Children are mesmerized by nature, so a window into that world is all you need to get them started on this lifelong hobby.

Neighborhood parks provide much more than a patch of green to walk in. They offer endless potential for observing birds, butterflies, dragonflies, frogs, toads, sticks, rocks, leaves and more. Many parks also have wetland areas, and since water birds are often large and conspicuous, ponds are a good place to start with beginning birders.

Go beyond the ordinary when looking for bird-watching spots. City dumps, sewer lagoons and even cemeteries provide surprising opportunities to see lots of birds. Or head out biking, hiking or kayaking for a change of pace.

GO EXPLORING. Top, the Ohio Young Birders explore their surroundings. Above and at left, because a prothonotary warbler doesn't feed at feeders but will use a nest box, sighting one is a challenging but realistic goal for kids. Above center, a killdeer nest proves you have to keep your eyes peeled at all times.

TWO GIRLS, CORBIS SUPER RF / ALAMY; BIRDERS ON ROCKS, COURTESY OF BLACK SWAMP BIRD OBSERVATORY / BSBOBIRD.ORG; EGGS, ROBIN CLARK; WARBLER, RANDY STREUFERT; BIRD HOUSE SCENE, WILLIAM LEAMAN / ALAMY

MAKE THE MOST OF IT. At right, members of the Ohio Young Birders Club didn't let a little rain stop them from enjoying a day of birding. No matter what, says Ken, there's always something in nature to see, like the green frog hiding near a waterlily below.

Ken Keffer, a lifelong naturalist (pictured above with a young birder), thinks you're never too old to learn something new. Four years ago he took up curling (yes, the kind that involves stones, brooms and ice). And recently he started taking mandolin lessons.

Share the experience

Birding isn't a solitary hobby. When you see an unusual bird or get to observe its entertaining behavior, you want to tell someone. Kids feel the same way.

Find a bird walk to attend. Many local bird clubs, nature centers, parks and wildlife refuges offer regular walks. Staff naturalists are a great source of information, and, like me, many are delighted to see families out and about in nature.

Attend a banding demo offered by a bird observatory or other nature organization. Beyond providing stunning glimpses at birds, these programs connect audiences with the joy and beauty of birds in a way no picture or video can.

Look for a young birders club to join. The Black Swamp Bird Observatory pioneered a program in 2006, and now there are similar clubs in 16 states. These clubs allow youth to interact with their peers and nature in a stimulating setting.

Keep an eye out for festivals with kid activities. Birding festivals are often looking for ways to get families involved. At the Biggest Week in American Birding (*biggestweekinamericanbirding.com*), we hold family bird walks, and they're free! Other groups are doing similar things, so be sure to take a look near you.

Don't forget to have fun

Well-meaning bird experts will sometimes do young naturalists a disservice by focusing too much on birds. It's always important to be flexible with kids.

Encourage exploration, and never pass up an opportunity to discover something in the natural world. I've led many a bird walk where the highlight of the day wasn't a bird at all. Perhaps the glimpse of a weasel—or something as simple as a caterpillar or pretty stone—became a lifelong memory.

Practice with your equipment first. Binoculars are a bit tricky to master and can be frustrating while in the field.

Skip the identification altogether. Try having a bird behavior scavenger hunt without the pressure of pinning down an exact species. Ask kids to watch for dozens of behaviors, from preening and perching to walking and hopping.

Always remember that it's about the kids. It's not about the birds, though they certainly are a hook. Nothing is more inspiring than seeing children explore nature. Embrace this, and get out there with your children, your grandchildren or perhaps the neighbor kid down the street. Together we can ensure that future generations will understand and appreciate the magical chorus of frogs and the allure of the old watering hole that keep us in tune with nature.

KEN KEFFER, RAINY BIRDING: COURTESY OF BLACK SWAMP BIRD OBSERVATORY / BSBOBIRD.ORG; FROG, WILLIAM DEATON; FATHER AND SON, ROB HOWARD / CORBIS

get equipped

While you can enjoy birds without any special tools, a few relatively inexpensive items will enhance the experience for kids.

Field guide. It helps with identifying the species of birds you encounter. And often, a colorful book will grab the curiosity of a child.

Binoculars. While not mandatory, proper binoculars are a great investment. A good pair will run you about $100. Also, many nature centers offer loaners for daily use.

Apps. You can get field guides on your phone or access birdcalls with the touch of a finger. If this kind of technology helps draw kids into nature, it's definitely worth it.

Notebook. A simple notebook or sketchbook goes a long way toward capturing the moment in the field.

Most kingfishers, like this belted kingfisher, are brightly colored, with greens, blues and patches of red, brown and white. They are chunky, compact birds with short necks and large heads. When raised, their distinctive crests make them look startled.

all hail the KING

Even the world's best angler can't beat the remarkable skill of the kingfisher.

BY GEORGE HARRISON, CONTRIBUTING EDITOR

MASLOWSKI WILDLIFE

Green kingfisher

Ringed kingfisher

Belted kingfisher feeding its young

RINGED, GREEN: LARRY DITTO / KAC PRODUCTIONS; FEEDING YOUNG, FISHING: ANTHONY MERCIECA

Any bird that can catch fish as well as this one deserves the title "king of fishers." The fishing technique of all three of our North American kingfishers is a spectacle to see, one that trumps any of Grandpa's best fishing stories.

"Fly" Fishing

One summer I watched a male belted kingfisher feed from a dead tree above the lake on which I live. Though kingfishers commonly hover above water before diving, my bird often sits on a branch some 30 feet above the water, waiting and watching below until he spots a fish.

Then, with wings folded, the bird drops headfirst off the limb into the water like a torpedo, zeroing in on the quarry. The bird snatches the fish with his bill, then leaps out of the water flapping his wet wings and returns to the tree. While holding the wriggling fish between his feet, the wet bird then hammers his unlucky catch with his bill before tossing it into the air and swallowing it whole.

I once mistakenly believed that the dramatic feeding behavior of the North American species was unique among the 86 kingfishers worldwide. Imagine my surprise when, on the other side of the globe in Kenya, I watched a malachite kingfisher catch, clobber and devour a fish in exactly the same way.

I had to ask myself: How is it possible for kingfishers around the world, thousands of miles apart, to duplicate feeding behaviors? I have no answer other than genetics.

Raising Young Fishers

Of the three kingfisher species in North America, the belted is by far the most common, ranging from Alaska across Canada and south throughout the lower 48 states. The other two, the ringed and the green, live in the Southwest, mostly in Texas, along the Rio Grande border with Mexico. All three species nest at the ends of tunnels they dig in earthen banks.

My first real encounter with a kingfisher was on my grandfather's Pennsylvania farm. At the bend of a creek, where spring floods had torn away the bank until it stood high above the

Belted kingfisher doing what it does best: fishing

fishy facts

- Some of the Old World kingfishers don't eat fish at all. Dwelling in the woodlands, they thrive on termites, ants and other insects. The six species in the New World, including our three, are all true fishers and live near water. Males and females have similar coloring, but the female belted kingfisher has two bands across her breast, one gray and one orange-brown, compared to the male's single gray band.

- The belted kingfisher's species name is *alcyon*, derived from the Greek legend of Halcyon, who, along with her husband, was turned into a kingfisher for incurring the wrath of the gods. The story had it that no wind blew during the days of their brooding, hence the expression "halcyon days."

- Kingfishers are related to motmots, bee-eaters, rollers, hoopoes, hornbills and the Australian kookaburra.

water, a pair of belted kingfishers had dug a nesting burrow.

I spotted the bird carrying small fish into a 4-inch round hole, presumably to feed the young at the end of the 6-foot tunnel. Though I knew the belted kingfisher by its rattling call and fast flight along creeks and rivers, I had never before found a nest.

Years later, my father and I went back to the farm after nesting season and dug out a burrow to photograph the nest chamber at the end of the tunnel. The chamber was dome-shaped, higher and wider than the tunnel, and smelled strongly of rotting fish.

Both parents dig this burrow with their heavy bills and push the sand out with their feet. It takes two to three weeks to complete the excavation. They incubate the six or seven pure-white eggs for 24 days. After hatching, the young remain in the tunnel for another three to four weeks before the fully feathered miniatures of their parents emerge. The youngsters follow their elders on fishing forays for several more weeks before learning to fish for themselves.

In northern areas of the continent, belted kingfishers migrate south to open water for the winter. They return to their nesting territories early in the spring, soon after the frozen lakes and streams melt.

Often, the first bird of spring for me is not the robin or bluebird, but the belted kingfisher as it rattles its call around the melting edges of my lake.

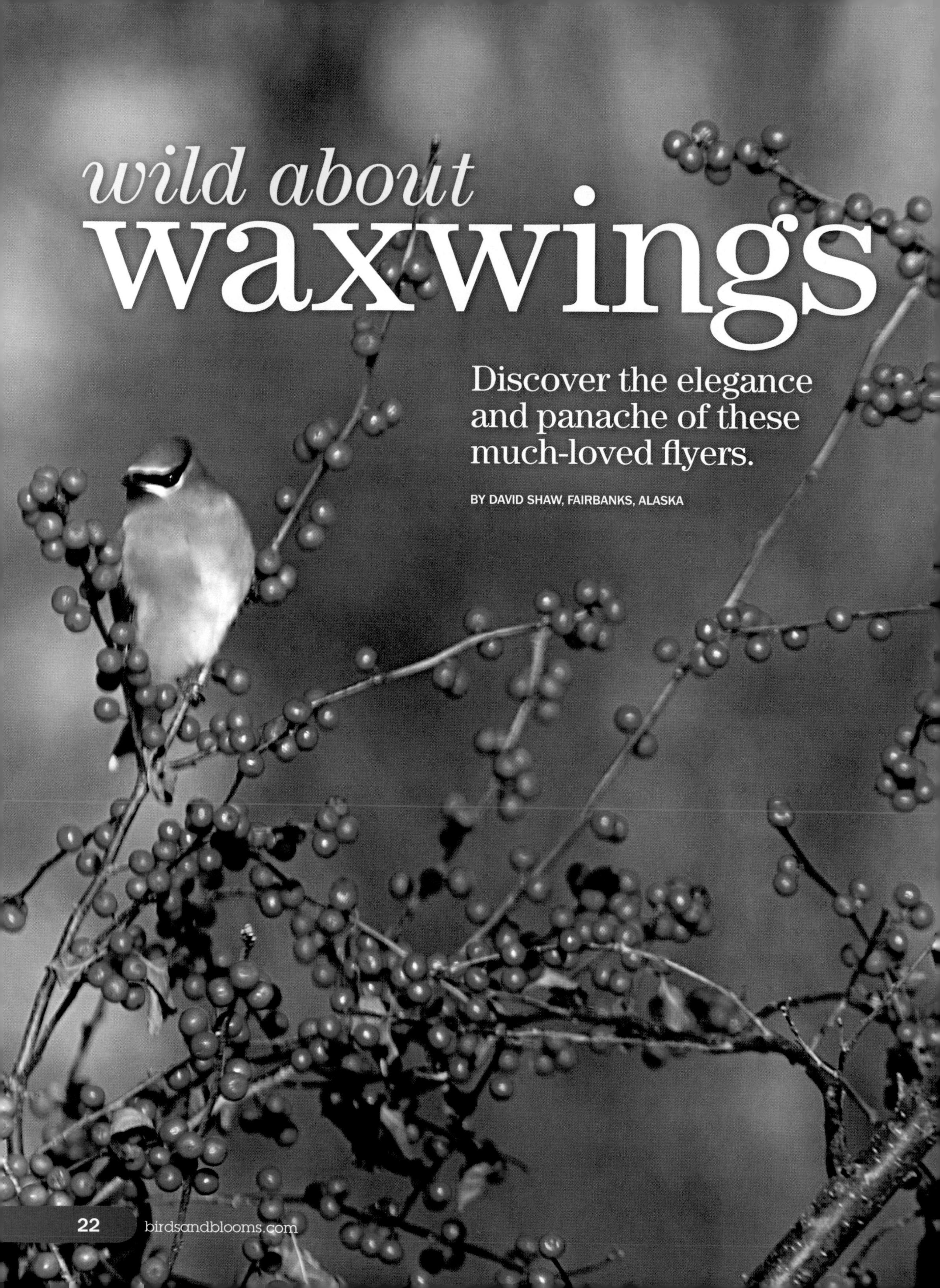

wild about waxwings

Discover the elegance and panache of these much-loved flyers.

BY DAVID SHAW, FAIRBANKS, ALASKA

RICHARD DAY / DAYBREAK IMAGERY

BERRY BINGEING. These winterberries provide a satisfying treat for cedar waxwings during the fall and winter months.

Through my freezing binoculars, the bird's feathers looked so smooth they seemed molded from clay. A small crest rose from the back of its head, and yellow patches adorned the wings and tip of the tail. But the strangest thing about this already odd and beautiful bird was the red teardrops hanging from the bars of the wings.

Brutally cold winter air and icy fog swirled around me. I fled back to the relative warmth of my vehicle, where the radio announced that the temperature outside was a punishing minus 20. Yet beyond the frosty glass of my windshield, perched on an ornamental chokecherry tree in a parking lot, a small flock of Bohemian waxwings devoured the dried fruit clinging to the branches.

ELEGANT MASKED FLIERS. The sleek feathers, masked faces and bright pops of red and yellow of the Bohemian waxwing (above) are a sight to see. But since Bohemians breed only in the far northern part of the continent, many birders are more familiar with cedar waxwings (opposite page) flocking to berry-laden backyard trees and shrubs.

A Living Sculpture

In my work as a field biologist, I've had the great pleasure of handling Bohemian waxwings only a few times. In the hand, the birds are surprisingly docile, their extraordinary form even more compelling. Up close, they look more like sculptures than living birds, as each detail from the tail tip to the black and white in the wing becomes more obvious and lovely.

Bohemian waxwings reach the top of my list for most elegant birds. They breed only in the far northern part of the continent, in the boreal and mountain forests of Canada and Alaska. Each year I get a dozen calls and emails from birders visiting my home state of Alaska, wanting to find Bohemians.

Often I can direct them to the right places, but sometimes not. The birds aren't always easy to find during the breeding season, when they scatter across the wet and swampy forests. In fact, few people venture into the breeding habitat of old burns and stands of forested wetlands.

Probably because of this inaccessibility, few major biological studies have even looked at the species. But in winter, when they congregate to eat berries in backyard ornamentals, Bohemian waxwings are much easier to find.

Family Favorite

Most birders in the lower 48 are acquainted with the similar cedar waxwing. Clearly a sibling of its northern counterpart, the cedar has almost all the elegance and charm of the Bohemian. The species is aptly named, as it replaces the gray feathers of the Bohemian with a warm cedar brown. Like their neighbor to the north, cedars sport yellow tail tips and waxy teardrops on the wings.

I recall my first peek at a cedar waxwing. I was a high school birder living in the southern Great Plains of Oklahoma. One green spring morning, as I walked through a parking lot, a small flock of the birds flew overhead, making a buzzing call. The group alighted in a tree at the lot's edge.

I'd seen pictures of the birds in my field guide but was astonished to see them in real life. They looked like a painting, so smooth and sleek. I had no binoculars with me, but the birds allowed me within a few feet of their foraging spot, and I was treated to a perfect view. Moments later, as quickly as they appeared, the flock was off again, disappearing behind a nearby building—searching, I suppose, for another fruit-laden tree.

Unlike its northern counterpart, the cedar waxwing is widely distributed, with growing numbers. Populations of cedars have boomed in recent years, and the species' range is expanding. They prefer shrubby areas, overgrown farms and even backyards for their nesting sites. Cedar waxwings can be found at one time of year or another

in every state except Hawaii. Their summer range just sneaks into the far southern tip of Alaska's panhandle.

Following the Order

Both species derive their name from the waxy droplets on the tips of their greater coverts, the short feathers that slightly overlap the main flight feathers of the wings. The purpose of those little pendants is to indicate maturity in the birds' social order. Older, more successful birds have more and larger droplets, which makes them more appealing to prospective mates.

Both cedars and Bohemians eat insects almost exclusively during the summer, switching to sugary fruits for the autumn and winter. Species dependent on fruit during the winter are rare in the temperate zone, making waxwings even more intriguing.

Before the days of ornamental shrubs in Alaskan backyards, the Bohemian waxwings I see on cold winter days would have fled farther south. Now, I revel in their presence. Few species are hardy enough to survive a winter in the bitter cold of Alaska's interior, and I feel warmly toward each of them. The Bohemian waxwings, however, with their colors, elegance and panache, are the debutantes at the ball, brightening the most cheerless winter day.

the third waxwing

Worldwide, there are only three species of waxwings: our two North American species, the cedar and the Bohemian waxwing; and the Japanese waxwing of northeast Asia. While the first two species are stable or increasing, the Japanese waxwing is simply not so fortunate.

Despite its name, the species breeds in far eastern Russia, visiting Japan only in the winter.

This beautiful bird, which looks like a flashy combination of the cedar and Bohemian waxwings, is listed as "near threatened" by BirdLife International, a worldwide conservation group. Its preferred breeding habitat in coniferous forests is under threat from logging and development, and its striking plumage has made it desirable in the illegal pet trade.

friendly fliers

Discover why these four birds top our list when it comes to congeniality.

BY DAVID SHAW, FAIRBANKS, ALASKA

As a scientist, I dislike anthropomorphizing the birds I study. Most of the time I can easily argue away their near-human behavior. But there are a few species that, for their intelligence, appealing behavior and association with humans, are just exceedingly likable. Lacking a good scientific term for this group of birds, I think I'll just call them friendly.

Cheery Chickadees

The first group of friendly species is the chickadees. They frequent our yards and feeders so often that they would be impossible not to include. Seven species of chickadees are found in North America. One, the gray-headed chickadee, occurs only in Alaska, and even there requires so much searching that most Alaskan birders, including me, have never seen one.

Five species are regional. Carolina chickadees occur in the Southeastern United States. Boreal chickadees are limited to the boreal forest that covers the northern portion of the continent. Mountain chickadees are found in the Rocky Mountains, Mexican chickadees occur only in the far southern tip of Arizona and New Mexico, and chestnut-backed chickadees are found in the Northwest. Only black-capped chickadees occur across the whole of North America.

All the chickadee species share some traits, the most notable being their bold and inquisitive nature. They do not seem to fear, well, anything. I've watched a chickadee on a cold winter day fly down and land atop my ski pole as I paused along the trail. That bird eyed me with some curiosity before letting loose a scolding *Chick-a-dee-dee!* and returning to the branches above.

I've watched chickadees dive-bomb and harass a goshawk that outweighed them more than a hundred times. When I've captured black-capped chickadees during research projects, they—unlike every other of the hundreds of species I've handled—will fight every step of the way.

CHICKADEE, RICHARD DAY / DAYBREAK IMAGERY

SOCIAL BIRDS. Though many birds display humanlike behavior at times, birds such as the white-breasted nuthatch (above, left), the Clark's nutcracker (above) and the white-crowned sparrow (above, right) are especially well-known for their bold, friendly antics that make them so endearing to humans.

They will peck at the hands of the bander as the measurements are taken, bite as hard as they can at the sensitive spots between fingers, and often, before flying off after release, will pause to administer one more painful peck.

A friend who helped teach me about birds many years back told me, "If chickadees were as big as jays, nobody would go into the woods." He may well be right. Yet I consider them friendly. It seems counterintuitive, but to me, it's their boldness and courage—traits I find admirable in humans—that make them seem so friendly.

Neighborly Nuthatches

Nuthatches are just too endearing not to be included in this group of friendly birds. North America has four species: the brown-headed nuthatch of the Southeastern U.S., the pygmy nuthatch of the pine forests of the mountain West, the red-breasted nuthatch of the boreal forest and the higher elevations of the western part of the country, and the white-breasted nuthatch, which is distributed across most of the Lower 48.

As a group, they are as bold as chickadees, but without the attitude, often flying right up to a feeder even as it's being loaded with seeds or peanut butter. They will perch vertically, upside down, on a tree trunk and wait patiently for their chance at the treat. In fact, it is this trait—their ability to perch head down on a vertical surface—that distinguishes them from all other species of birds. When not visiting feeders, they derive a good portion of their food from the insects hiding beneath the scales of tree bark. Their unique ability to scale up and down the trunk of a tree is a perfect strategy for such a search.

Nutty Nutcrackers

While several species of corvids—the family that includes crows, ravens and jays—are friendly, one group has earned the nickname of camp robber. Clark's nutcrackers are the

quintessential avian thieves. If you've picnicked or camped in the high conifer forests of the Rockies, you've probably encountered a Clark's nutcracker. They appear almost magically from the forest, somehow knowing where there's food to be found.

They are large gray jays with black wings, white outer tail feathers and intelligent dark eyes. Their main food source, apart from the opportunistic theft from camper's backpacks, is the seeds of pines. In fact, they are so closely tied to pines that several species of trees, including the whitebark pine and the southwestern white pine, depend almost entirely on the Clark's nutcracker for seed dispersal.

They have an uncanny memory that can store the locations of thousands of seeds, which they cache as the pinecones ripen. That memory and the ability to acquire food are attributes I'd choose in any friend.

Splendid Sparrows

The last species, the white-crowned sparrow, I include for personal reasons. In Alaska, they are among the most abundant songbirds during the spring and summer. I conduct a lot of field research, and whether I'm searching for nests in the boreal forest or surveying birds in the high alpine ridgetops, I am rarely out of earshot of a singing white-crowned sparrow. I've had them sing from the top of my tent as I camped in the tundra, and had juveniles land on my boot while I rested during a hike. It must be their constant presence in my life that strikes me as friendly.

These species, more than many others, have chosen to associate with humans. They seem to like us. And, for me, that feeling is mutual. Their antics, courage and intelligence are striking, memorable and entertaining. And, like good friends, they are always around when I need them.

NUTHATCH, NUTCRACKER: MASLOWSKI WILDLIFE; SPARROW, MARIE READ

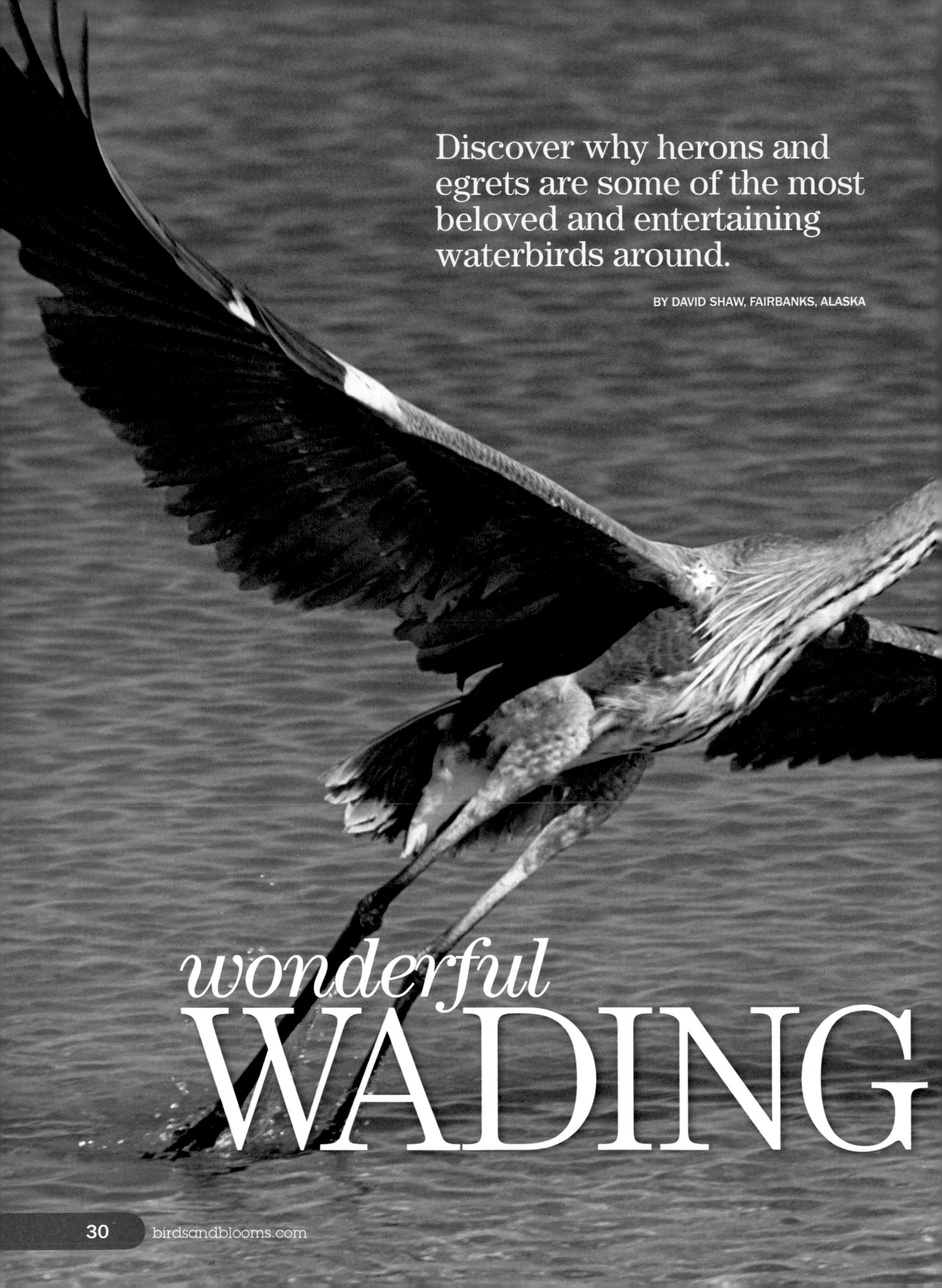

wonderful WADING

Discover why herons and egrets are some of the most beloved and entertaining waterbirds around.

BY DAVID SHAW, FAIRBANKS, ALASKA

A cold, spitting mist hit my face as I walked along the dikes at the Nisqually National Wildlife Refuge near Olympia, Washington. The winter rains were falling, as they always do in that part of the world. Everything was gray and green.

I pulled up the hood of my rain jacket and walked on, peering every now and then through my water-spotted binoculars at the flocks of wintering waterfowl, paddling easily in the flooded fields and ponds. Along a side stream, I jumped as a great blue heron lifted with surprising grace from the creekside vegetation.

The bird gave a few easy flaps, then croaked a loud call that echoed against the hillside. I heard a gasp behind me and then a child's voice: "Dad, is that a dinosaur?"

I laughed aloud when the father responded, "Yes. Yes, that is a dinosaur." I thought, *It really doesn't take a great leap of the imagination to jump from great blue heron to pterodactyl.*

BIRDS

JACK ZATZ / ALAMY

Family Favorites

While the enormous and beautiful great blue is probably the best-known heron in North America, 13 species of herons, egrets and bitterns make their home north of the border. I include all three groups because the differences among them are entirely semantic.

For example, the great blue heron's Latin name is *Ardea herodias*, while the great egret is *Ardea alba*. They are members of the same genus, very close relatives. The same is true for the little blue heron and the reddish egret, both members of the genus *Egretta*.

All the herons and egrets are long-legged, long-necked wading birds. And while the species differ in color and behavior—some, like the strange night-herons, are primarily nocturnal—they have a very similar diet of fish, frogs and large aquatic invertebrates. They live all across the continent, from the windblown coastline of southern Alaska to the steamy swamps of the Southeast.

When it comes to breeding, many species share some behaviors, such as colony nesting. One's first view of a heron or egret colony is a strange sight indeed.

These tall, gangly birds, perched by the dozens in the tops of trees, look downright weird. Their large nests of sticks are arranged in the uppermost branches, with neighboring nests almost within reach. While it seems odd, nesting in these clusters has a very important purpose: With more birds, there are more eyes on the lookout for predators.

MAJESTIC MOVEMENTS. Herons and egrets have graceful movements. Above, a great egret shows off its plumes, likely during a courtship. At left, this least bittern (part of the heron family) moves slowly and steadily through marshes. Birders say that they are more easily heard than seen.

A Group Effort

During a summer job as an undergraduate, I monitored a colony of great blue herons for several hours a day near Tacoma, Washington. Watching the birds come and go from their nests through a spotting scope, I noticed that while there were always some birds napping on their nests or on nearby branches, there were many other herons constantly peering about, watchful.

And with good reason: Bald eagles were constantly on the hunt. An eagle swooping into the colony, searching for an unguarded nestling, would be met with a terrifying response. All the adult herons would let loose a great roaring call, sounding for all the world like a room full of screaming people. It was eerie and frightening, the birds' panic palpable as they rose to defend their nests.

GROWING UP. At right, this great blue heron parent checks on its two young, which look as if they're almost ready to fledge. Herons nest in large groups called rookeries so the birds are more safe.

Eagles and other wild predators were not always the only threat to the herons and egrets of North America. For a time, a much deadlier hunter lurked around the birds' colonies. During the early 20th century, fashionable women sought great feathers with which to decorate their hats.

This demand led to the wholesale slaughter of herons and egrets by so-called "plume hunters." During the breeding season, birds like the snowy egret develop long downy plumes on their backs, necks and heads. For these elegant feathers, market hunters killed the birds right off their nests by the tens of thousands, leaving untold numbers of chicks to starve.

Interestingly, it was the outrage over this atrocity that led to the formation of the National Audubon Society and the eventual legal protection of all native birds. Now herons and egrets are abundant throughout the former hunting grounds; their recovery is one of America's great conservation success stories.

Long-Legged Legends

I now live in Fairbanks, Alaska, one of the few areas in North America with no herons, and I look forward to my travels to places where these wonderful birds live. On trips to the southern part of the state, I'm on the lookout for great blues foraging along salmon streams or on the rocky beaches of Prince William Sound.

Outside Alaska, their diversity skyrockets, and I take every opportunity to look for the long-legged birds. To me, these species feel almost as rare and exotic as the prehistoric creatures they resemble.

cattle egret invasion

In 1876, there were no cattle egrets in the Western Hemisphere. But a year later, this Old World species appeared in northeastern South America, probably blown over in a storm from Africa. Preferring land to water and insects for food, they avoided competition with the native herons and egrets, taking well to the New World, where they rapidly spread across South America and then northward.

By 1941 the species had reached the southern U.S., and by 1953 they were breeding. Now, just a few decades after arriving within our borders, the cattle egret is one of the most abundant wading birds in the country. It's been quite a journey for this accidental invader.

LEAST BITTERN, CATTLE EGRETS: ROLF NUSSBAUMER; GREAT EGRET, MARIE READ; NESTING HERONS, BARBARA MAGNUSON / LARRY KIMBALL

bird tales

Readers share close encounters of the feathered kind.

May Surprise

Spring was the first time I'd ever seen a lazuli bunting at my house. They came and then they were gone, just visiting for May. I spent many happy hours on my patio, watching them at my feeder and taking pictures.

—**JUDY WATSON,** *Layton, Utah*

Tufted Daredevil

My grandmother, sister and I were filling our bird feeders when a tufted titmouse on a low branch startled me. I froze, expecting it to fly away, but it merely chirped at me and hopped back and forth. Curious to see how friendly it was, I held out a handful of seed. The bird swooped down, nabbed some and flew back to its branch.

I called my sister over to try it. The titmouse came to her but landed on her head instead of her hand. She shrieked, and the startled bird flew to my grandmother, perching on the waistband of her pants.

Grandma did a little dance of alarm, turning in frantic circles while this little bird clung to her pants for dear life. When I managed to compose myself and explain to Grandma what was happening, she stood still. The titmouse shook its head a couple of times, then fluffed its feathers and flew back to the tree. To this day, we still laugh about the little gray daredevil that took a ride on Grandma's trousers.

—**EMILY BUCHANAN**
Mint Hill, North Carolina

Dancing with the Cranes

On a trip to Florida, we were on our way back to my sister-in-law's home in Crystal River when I spotted four sandhill cranes in a grassy area beside the road. I pulled over, grabbed my camera and snapped a few photos.

As I watched, two of the birds separated from the others and began the most amazing dance. Since it was spring, we imagined it was their mating dance.

—**BARBARA FRANKENFIELD**
Hillsborough, New Jersey

Battle for The Brood

While I was photographing a pileated woodpecker pair feeding their three young, a snake slithered up and into their nest hole! My pulse raced so fast I could hardly hold the camera.

The mama tried fighting from the outside, pulling the snake out, but that didn't work, so she dived in. I could see her fighting—a few times she stuck her head out as if gasping for air. Then the snake came out of the hole and halfway down the tree, only to flip back up and go in again! Finally, the mother drove the snake out for good, and the pair pecked at it all the way down the trunk.

The woodpeckers returned to the nest, taking turns going in and out, but there was no sight or sound of the young that had been so vocal before the snake appeared. When I left for home, the daddy bird just sat, his head sticking out of the nest hole. It was so sad.

A few days later, I just had to go back and check, and I got a wonderful surprise. All three nestlings peeped out of the tree, looking whole, healthy and bright-eyed! Hooray!

—**LUANNE BROOKER**
Sandersville, Georgia

A Song of Thanks

Several years ago, I noticed that a beautiful cardinal had decided to build its nest on a blue spruce limb that hung over my door. I started talking to it as it built its nest, thanking it for building where I could see its pretty eggs and babies.

One day, while I was babysitting my two great-granddaughters, we heard the mother cardinal screech. The wind was blowing very hard that day, and when we looked out, we saw that the nest had almost blown out of the tree. The babies were just a few days old at the time, and they were clinging to the nest for their lives. My daughter ran to get a ball of twine, and she quickly tied the nest back to the tree limb.

Soon after, the mama bird was sitting on the porch railing, singing and looking in the window at my great-granddaughters and me as if to say thank you with its beautiful song.

—**HELEN ROBERTSON**
Arkansas City, Kansas

Counting Owls

My most memorable owl experience happened late one December. I was having a hard time falling asleep, so I tiptoed down to the family room to hang out for a bit.

As I settled onto the couch, I heard an eerie woo-hoo-hoo coming from the patio window. Immediately, I heard another call answering back. I peeked through the blinds and saw two huge birds sitting at the top of our willow tree, not more than 15 feet from the deck.

The full moon was bright enough to reveal perfect silhouettes of two great horned owls. They sat on the top branches calling to each other for 10 or 15 minutes. Their soft, fluting hoots were eerie at first, but then sounded like a friendly conversation between buddies.

I felt guilty for not waking my husband and children to witness this wonderful exchange, but I knew that as soon as I moved, the magic moment would have passed. The owls eventually flew away, and I was finally able to fall asleep. I was excited to share the story at breakfast the next morning.

—**CAROL BROST**
Noblesville, Indiana

bird tales

A Lesson From a Martin

We wait in anticipation for the purple martins to arrive around Feb. 1 every year. Their constant racket while they're nesting and guarding their habitat gives us such joy.

One evening I noticed a male martin carrying a stick about 5 or 6 inches long. He was determined to get that large stick into his tiny apartment. He would fly around his house and then aim for the hole at great speed, only to hit the opening and bounce right off. He tried this over and over again, but to no avail.

Not only was I watching a comical sight, I was learning from this remarkable bird, too. He reminded me not to give up if something I want seems out of reach.

Eventually, the little martin dropped the stick and chose a small piece of moss instead. He adjusted his focus, but I'll never forget his will and determination.

—LINDA LEHMANN
Warda, Texas

A Peach of a Pose

California's extra winter rain produced even more blossoms than usual on our peach tree one year. House finches are common here year-round, flying back and forth between the feeders and the trees. I enjoy standing in front of the window, hoping to photograph birds in the peach tree without being noticed. One morning in early March, I caught this finch (above) among the pretty blossoms.

—MARCIA HERRMANNSFELDT
Los Altos, California

Remembering Mom

My mother and I were best friends and next-door neighbors. We always watched the birds together, and bluebirds were her favorite. When she passed away, it was a very difficult time for me.

A week after she passed, I went outside and heard baby birds chirping on my front porch. I had hung a decorative birdhouse there, and the noise was coming from inside! I saw the parents bringing food repeatedly to the nest. I was pleased to see that they were bluebirds (below).

I ran to get some mealworms. As soon as I put them out, the parents landed at my feet and scooped them up. They took turns bringing the worms to the babies. These bluebirds have been a gift to me at a very sad time in my life.

—BEVERLY MILLER
New Port Richey, Florida

Splish-Splash

Our birds always perched on this little tree before visiting my birdbath, so I moved the bath close to the tree. Then I placed a sprinkler head in the bowl. The birds love it, especially the yellow warblers.

—MONA DOEBLER
Hinsdale, Montana

Protecting the Nest

One spring, my wife and I were fascinated by a pair of robins trying to build their nest on a small board attached to our deck railing. To the birds' frustration, the wind blew away every piece of grass as quickly as they put it in place.

To help them out, I built a small box that fit in the narrow opening, hoping they wouldn't reject the location. It took just one day for them to get used to it and to continue building their nest.

One of the things that really caught our attention was the protective way the male robin acted during rainstorms. He would stand on the deck railing next to his mate, totally exposed to the elements. Talk about a faithful, supportive mate.

—REV. JOHN SCHAUER
Carroll, Iowa

The Friendliest Oriole

Every spring, my husband, Homer, puts grape jelly in an orange half and places it on our deck railing. Various birds stop by for a treat, and the orioles in particular love it.

One oriole was exceptionally crazy for the jelly. He'd sit and devour it, almost as if he were famished. Maybe his migration was a little more difficult than anticipated?

Since Homer loves his backyard birds, he wondered if he could get close enough to hold this oriole. He slowly slid his hand closer and closer to the bird, and it finally climbed on. Soon enough, he had the oriole eating grape jelly right out of a spoon he held!

We even had our grandkids stop by and feed the bird by hand (left). After a week, the oriole was still around, but as time went on, he wouldn't let us get as close to him. Still, he provided us with an experience we'll never forget!

—KATHY TEITSMA
Sparta, Michigan

Play Ball!

We've never seen a western scrub-jay as friendly and playful as our little friend. After fledging, it investigated everything in our yard, including the dog's toys, and as you can see, it seems to like the mini basketball best. Our jay comes when called, even now, a year later. It's so fun—especially the time I called and suddenly the scrub-jay was on my head! Talk about a feathered hat!

—JEAN OEDEWALDT
Palo Alto, California

White-breasted nuthatch, Carolina chickadee and northern cardinal at feeder.

birds in an instant

Short on time and space? These fast and fun ideas make attracting birds easy!

BY GEORGE HARRISON, CONTRIBUTING EDITOR

To attract wild birds to any backyard, you need to provide the three basics for survival: food, water and cover. The most important of these is cover, which is natural vegetation in which birds can hide from predators.

Natural Cover Is Key

A friend told me that her neighbor is envious because no birds come to her feeders, while a few feet away in my friend's yard, the birds arrive in flocks. The neighbor finally asked my friend what was up. "You don't have any kind of natural cover in your backyard," my friend replied.

It's that simple. Apparently, the neighbor has her feeders out in the open, with no trees or bushes nearby into which the birds can flee when threatened. My friend has only a cherry tree, but it's enough to make the birds feel safe.

The idea of planting trees, shrubs and bushes just to attract birds is too daunting—or is too long to wait—for some people. But there's a handy, inexpensive alternative: a homemade habitat that you can complete in a couple of hours some weekend.

Installing an Instant Bird Habitat

With these five simple steps, you can have a bird habitat right outside your window!

- Select a favorite window that looks out onto your yard.
- Go outside and, a few feet from the glass, place a potted evergreen on each side of the window. You can buy these small pines or arborvitae at a nursery. Or, if you have access to a woodland where you can legally transplant a couple of small evergreens into pots, they'll cost you nothing but a little work.
- A few feet beyond the potted trees, stack a pile of twigs, several branches and a log.
- Inside the semicircle made by the trees and the brush, place a small birdbath on a pedestal and a feeder on a post or shepherd's hook. With suction cups, attach a small tray feeder to the window glass.
- Fill the feeders with sunflower seeds and the bath with clean water—and then stand back and wait for the first chickadee to arrive. It will happen quicker than you'd think.

SUCCESS IN SECONDS. Hang a feeder near your window (above left) or attach a window feeder (below) to attract birds to any size yard. A potted evergreen (above right) provides instant natural cover.

Carolina chickadee and northern cardinal

A small conifer goes a long way in creating a bird-friendly habitat.

Apartment Birders

This same procedure can be used to establish a bird habitat on an apartment balcony. Using potted trees, with feeders and a birdbath on stands, you can offer passing birds food, water and cover, even if you live on the second or third floor or higher.

Even a windowsill has adequate space for a bird habitat. Simply select potted vegetation, a vine or flowers small enough to fit on the sill, a dish of water and a feeder. Maintaining the habitat is as simple as raising the window and adding food and water.

If you build a natural habitat, even a small one, where the birds feel safe, they will find it and return to it time and time again.

BIRD FEEDERS, MASLOWSKI WILDLIFE; POTTED EVERGREEN, MARK TURNER; GARDEN OWNER, FONDA & RON DOWNS

glad you asked!

Clearing Up Confusion

I have read conflicting advice about different kinds of birdseed. One source said safflower is good, while another said it's unpalatable to birds. One said millet is good; the other said it is a waste. What mix do you suggest?

—**SUE LYONS,** *Asheville, North Carolina*

George: All the recommendations you have received are true. Safflower seeds are well received after the birds learn that they're edible. It took my cardinals more than a decade to learn that. But once they got hooked on safflower seed, most of the other common species, such as chickadees, learned to like them.

There are several kinds of millet, including red and white. The white millet seems to be more popular among finches.

But the best all-around food for birds in the backyard is sunflower seeds, in any form—in the shell or hulled (cracked), black-oil sunflower or striped sunflower seeds—the birds love them all. I would caution against cheap mixes, which contain few sunflower seeds and lots of fillers such as cracked corn and red millet. Birds will sometimes kick the fillers out of the feeders, and other critters will eat those discards on the ground.

Feeders With Flair

For my birthday, my husband and son built me this bird feeder (above right). We used stain and paint to finish it. The birds don't seem to use it as much as the old one it replaced. Why not?

—**SUZY RANDLE**
Hamburg, New York

George: What a nice feeder! I would look at the way the seed fills the trough. If the glass is too near the tray, the seed won't flow in and the birds will soon have eaten all they can reach. Another

possibility is that the birds are frightened by their reflections in the glass. Try soaping or covering reflections; the feeder should soon be visited by hungry birds.

Housing Requirements

In spring I would like to put up as many birdhouses as I can. Do I need to leave a lot of space in between them?

—**ERIC NUESKE,** *Wittenburg, Wisconsin*

George: If you have the space, 100 yards between houses is ideal. At least 50 yards is required by the feeding territories of each pair. The houses should be facing open fields where the birds can find insects to feed their young. The best time to put your birdhouses up is in early March.

Zen Birdhouses

What is the correct direction for a birdhouse to face?

—**JIM ESHELBY,** *Burns, Oregon*

George: In the case of most house-nesting birds, it does not matter which direction they face. Bluebirds seem to prefer houses that face open fields, regardless of the direction.

My recommendation is that backyard birdhouses should face your best bird-watching window or your porch or patio, so you get maximum enjoyment from watching them raise their young.

Downy woodpecker
Photo by Richard Day / Daybreak Imagery

White-winged dove
Grand Prize Winner in our Backyard Photo Contest
Photo by Howard Creek

Meadowlark
Photo by Maslowski Wildlife

Indigo bunting
Photo by Richard Day / Daybreak Imagery

Red-breasted nuthatch
Photo by Francis & Janice Bergquist

CHAPTER 2

penny-wise Projects

Make the most of your backyard dollar with these inexpensive ideas, including creating a low-cost, bird-friendly landscape, building birdhouses and feeders on the "cheep," and crafting garden accents from recycled items.

More than a dozen solutions to get the most bang for your buck while creating a haven for birds and butterflies.

BY DAVID MIZEJEWSKI, WASHINGTON, DC

BACKYARD HABITAT *on*

With the continued poor state of the economy, gardeners everywhere are feeling the pinch. When it comes down to it, paying the bills and putting food on the table will always win out over buying new plants or bags of birdseed. The good news is that cultivating a wildlife-friendly garden doesn't have to break the bank. In fact, it's one of the best and least expensive ways to garden.

BLOOMS WITH POWER. Goldfinches just love flowers with seeds. At right, ruby-throated hummingbirds enjoy nectar from columbines. Below right, a cabbage white butterfly and bees share a sweet treat at a hawkweed bloom.

GOLDFINCH, MASLOWSKI WILDLIFE; HUMMINGBIRDS, RICHARD DAY / DAYBREAK IMAGERY; BEES & BUTTERFLY, OJPHOTOS / ALAMY

a budget

Find Plants for Cheap

Let's face it—purchasing plants from the nursery can get expensive. You can cut your gardening costs by avoiding the nursery altogether and getting your plants from other sources.

It's not too late to start herbaceous plants from seeds, either those you've already saved from last season or from store-bought seed packets that cost just a few bucks. For woody plants, take cuttings of mature non-patented plants and, with the help of some rooting hormone, you can start a forest for pennies.

Admittedly, it can take a bit longer to get garden gratification when you start plants from seeds or cuttings.

SMART SELECTIONS. When you choose the right plants, you really get a lot of bang for your buck. Milkweed (with the monarch caterpillar at left) is a good option, as are black-eyed Susans and bee balm (right). In this photo, a Townsend's warbler stops at a feeder smeared with peanut butter. Far right, a tiger swallowtail stops to feed.

Some perennials don't bloom in their first year, and it will take longer for plants to reach mature landscape size than if you bought them from the nursery. But annuals will give you same-year benefits to tide you over—and the money you save will be worth it.

By joining a gardening club, native plant society, arboretum or botanical garden, you can get special discounts at plant sales. Other members can be a great source of cuttings, divisions and even mature plants. Many such groups host plant swaps, and some even coordinate plant rescues from development sites where wild native plants would otherwise be destined for the bulldozer.

Plant choice is another way to get the most for your dollar. By buying only plants that offer multiple benefits to wildlife, you'll spend less. Choose plants that have nectar-rich blooms and also produce seeds, nuts or berries, or provide shelter or places to raise young.

Milkweed is a great example. In the spring and summer, milkweed flowers provide pollen and nectar to bees, butterflies and other pollinators. Later, small mammals and birds such as orioles, goldfinches and bluebirds use the silky tufts attached to the seeds as nesting material. And, of course, milkweed is the only larval food source for monarch butterflies.

Spicebush is another excellent example. In the spring, its yellow flowers offer nectar to pollinators (notably beetles); in the fall, birds relish its red berries. Spicebush foliage feeds the caterpillars of tiger and spicebush swallowtails, as well as the stunning promethea moth, but it's unpalatable to deer.

Finally, keep in mind that sometimes just doing nothing is the best way to attract wildlife and save money. Stop mowing and let a corner of your yard grow wild, and all sorts of creatures will show up to feed, nest and find shelter there. Just be careful to monitor such wild patches for invasive exotics, which you should always remove.

Make Your Own Feeders

Remember, wildlife relies primarily on food supplied by native plants, but if you still enjoy having a bird feeder to attract your winged friends to one spot, simply grow your own seed feeders by planting a patch of sunflowers. The bright flowers will attract pollinators, and you can cut and dry the flower heads once seeds form, saving and hanging them in the garden throughout the fall and winter.

Or make your own bird feeders by spreading inexpensive peanut butter

CATERPILLAR, RICHARD DAY / DAYBREAK IMAGERY; WARBLER, MASLOWSKI WILDLIFE; PRAIRIE, RADIUS IMAGES / ALAMY; SWALLOWTAIL, RALF BROSKVAR / SHUTTERSTOCK.COM

on a pinecone or a piece of stale bread and hanging it outside. Bagels work well, too, because their density helps them hold up well outside, and their holes make it easy to attach a string for hanging.

In winter, you can save by making your own suet. Simply save bacon drippings or render beef, lamb or pork fat in a pot over medium heat until liquefied. Strain out any bits of meat, let solidify and melt again. (Warning: Rendering animal fat can be a smelly process.) You can mix cupboard staples such as seeds, nuts, fruits or peanut butter into the cooling suet, but it's not necessary.

This twice-rendered fat will form a hard cake just like the kind you buy and can be stored the freezer for later use. To save even more, ask your local grocer, baker or butcher for stale bread and fat trimmings that would otherwise be thrown away.

For hummingbirds, don't spend money on commercial nectar. Make your own by mixing 1 cup of white sugar and 4 cups of hot water. When the sugar is completely dissolved, let the nectar cool and use it to fill your hummingbird feeders. There's no need to add red food coloring.

Beyond Plants And Feeders

Remember, ecologically friendly gardening is also economically friendly. Plants native to your region will need little or no maintenance in the form of fertilizers, pesticides and supplemental watering once established, which means you keep harmful chemicals out of the environment, conserve water and save money all at the same time.

Mulching your garden beds to help retain soil moisture and using a rain barrel to collect rainwater will also help you save money and water. Many municipalities even offer free mulch and rain barrels to residents, so be sure to look into those possibilities.

Composting your kitchen and yard waste keeps lots of organic matter out of the landfill, cutting down on the potent greenhouse gas methane. Meanwhile, your garden benefits from the nutrient-rich compost.

Similarly, switching to a push mower will reduce the carbon dioxide you send into the atmosphere and save you money on gasoline. You can even build nesting and roosting boxes for birds by recycling scrap lumber.

It's as easy as that! With a little planning and creativity, you can have a beautiful garden that attracts wildlife, protects the environment and saves your hard-earned cash.

create a living wall

Turn a pair of salvaged shutters into an instant planter for your garden. BY ALISON W. AUTH, RICHMOND, VIRGINIA

I've been recycling materials for years. I enjoy seeing everyday things differently and love alley treasures and architectural salvage. For this project, I revamped a pair of old shutters into a new home for plants. This living wall makes a striking focal point in the backyard, and it barely costs a thing! Here's how to make your own.

1. Assemble your wall. Screw two matching shutters together at all four corners and at the middle. Be sure the slats are facing in the same direction on each side.

2. Seal or paint it. If you find shutters with peeling paint or a faded finish, all the better! For a rustic look, just seal them with shellac or varnish. Another option is to paint them a gorgeous apple red or sunflower yellow. I chose a subdued brown, because I have lots of chocolate-brown deck accents, and I love the way the chartreuse color of my succulents really becomes the focal point.

3. Make a kickstand. For added stability, or if you'd like your shutter garden to be freestanding without a base, screw a drawer handle horizontally in the middle of the back, where there's solid wood. Then look for an interesting stick or slender tree limb. Slide one end of it into the handle, tilt the wall back a bit, and use the stick as a kickstand to support it.

4. Add a base. Adding feet or another base will give your wall added elegance and presence. I used some old andirons. Try cabinet knobs, short candlesticks, wooden feet from a discarded nightstand or even interesting branches you find in your yard. It's amazing what you find when you start looking around. So have fun treasure hunting! Depending on what you choose, you can attach your base with screws, straps or glue.

5. Plant your wall. I planted succulents in my shutters, since they're drought-resistant and don't need a lot of fussing. They also come in such beautiful textures and colors and have interesting trailing habits. I added some small ornamental grasses and drought-tolerant perennials to fill out the mix. For planting, remove plants from their pots and use a hose to lightly rinse off all the soil and bark clinging to the roots. Next, put a little soil between the slats of the shutters and firmly tuck in each plant, adding more soil as needed after the plants are in place.

6. Find a home.
Place your wall near an entry for a natural welcome, or in a sunny corner of the patio to enjoy its shade.

7. Water your wall. Turn your hose on a light spray setting and water both sides of the shutters to settle the soil. If you choose drought-tolerant plants, you will need to water less often than with other plants. Just make sure you monitor the soil's moisture.

HEIDI HESS

What You Will Need

- Two identical shutters
- Wood screws
- Drawer handle
- Stick
- Base of your choice (optional)
- Paint (optional)
- Shellac or water-based varnish (optional)
- Plants
- Soil

preserve

Save money by freezing your veggies now for great eating later!

BY KIRSTEN SWEET, MILWAUKEE, WISCONSIN

your garden

There's nothing quite like fresh, crisp vegetables straight from the garden. But at harvesttime, you may be up to your ears in peppers, broccoli or beans. So what to do with all those extras? Freeze 'em! It's easy, fast and can lower your grocery bill. All you need is a little freezer space to enjoy tasty veggies year-round.

Time is of the essence.

Make sure you're ready to freeze your harvest immediately after you pick it. The longer it sits, the more flavor and nutritional value it loses.

If you can't freeze your vegetables right away, store them in the refrigerator until you're ready to start the freezing process.

Be prepared.

Even though your crop isn't going directly into your mouth, it should be washed before you get started.

After the vegetables are washed, cut them into small pieces. Think about how you'll use each veggie and cut it accordingly. Prepare it for freezing just as you would if you were going to put it on the table. Turn the page for more details on specific veggies.

Blanch away.

Think you can just throw your veggies into the freezer? Not so fast. Raw vegetables need to be blanched first.

Blanching stops the active enzymes that determine the color and flavor of the vegetables. All it takes is putting your produce in boiling water for a bit.

Generally, a gallon of water per pound of prepared vegetables is sufficient. Use a blancher, or find a wire basket that fits in a large pot with a lid. Fill the basket with the prepared veggies and plunge into boiling water.

The length of blanching time varies with each vegetable. See guidelines for common veggies on the next page.

Cool down.

Immediately after the veggies are done blanching, plunge them into a bowl of ice water to cool. Keep them in there for the same amount of time they were in the boiling water. Drain them once they're cooled, and get ready to pack them away.

Use the right container.

It may not seem important, but the container in which you freeze your precious bounty is actually crucial. For best results, the container should be smaller than a half-gallon. For a top-notch thawed product, smaller is ideal.

Your best bet is to use plastic containers or resealable freezer bags. Plastic containers are handy because they stack well in the freezer. For vegetables with odd sizes or shapes, a freezer bag works like a charm.

No matter what container you choose, make sure it's firmly sealed and tightly packed. Freezer burn can damage food that hasn't been properly wrapped. And don't forget to label the package with the date.

Eat it while it's fresh.

Food in the freezer doesn't last forever. It's best to use your frozen harvest within eight to 12 months for the best flavor and highest level of nutrients. And by that time, you'll have a whole new harvest!

VEGETABLES, ERSLER DMITRY / SHUTTERSTOCK.COM; PEPPERS, ISTOCKPHOTO.COM / AJAYKAMPANI

at-a-glance guide to freezing vegetables

VEGETABLE	PREPARATION/ STORAGE	BLANCHING TIME	COOKING TIME (FROM FROZEN)
ARTICHOKES, GLOBE	Cut off coarse outer leaves and stems; trim off tops and remove central hairy chokes. Wash artichokes thoroughly, and blanch with a few drops of lemon juice in the water. Cool and drain upside down; store in rigid containers.	7 to 9 minutes	About 10 minutes (or until leaves pull out easily)
ASPARAGUS	Wash thoroughly, cut off woody parts and grade by thickness. Trim to even lengths; blanch, cool in ice water for 5 minutes and drain. Tie in bundles and store in rigid containers, laying adjacent bundles tips to stalks. Separate layers with parchment paper.	Thin stems: 2 minutes Thick stems: 4 minutes	5 to 8 minutes (depending on thickness)
BEANS	Remove tops and tails. Wash and cut into 1-inch pieces. Blanch, cool in ice water for 5 minutes, drain thoroughly and dry. Store in plastic bags.	3 to 4 minutes	5 minutes
BEETS	Freeze only young, small beets about 3 inches across. Wash carefully without breaking skins; boil in water until tender. Cool under cold running water, then rub off skins. Slice or dice, then store in rigid, lined containers with ¼-inch headspace.		Store for no more than eight months. Thaw at room temperature in containers and drain. Heat to desired temperature.
BROCCOLI	Trim off leaves and woody stems; wash thoroughly in salted water. Divide into florets. Blanch, cool in ice water for 5 minutes, drain and dry. Store in cartons, tops to tails, and separate layers with parchment paper.	3 minutes	5 to 8 minutes
BRUSSELS SPROUTS	Choose small, firm heads of uniform size. Remove outer leaves, wash and blanch. Cool in ice water for same amount of time as blanching, then drain and dry. Store in plastic bags.	3 to 4 minutes (according to size)	8 minutes
CABBAGE (GREEN AND RED)	Freeze only young, crisp cabbages. Discard outer leaves. Wash and shred roughly. Blanch, cool, drain and dry. Store in plastic bags.	1½ minutes	8 minutes (use within six months)
CARROTS	Use young carrots for best results. Remove tops, trim roots and wash. Peel if necessary. Blanch whole or sliced, cool, drain and dry. Place in rigid containers with ¼-inch headspace.	Small whole: 5 minutes Diced, sliced or lengthwise strips: 2 minutes	8 minutes
CAULIFLOWER	Choose only firm, white cauliflowers. Break into small florets of uniform size, wash and blanch; add several drops of lemon juice to water to preserve color. Cool, drain and dry thoroughly. Store in rigid containers, separating the layers with parchment paper.	3 minutes	8 to 10 minutes (use within six months)
PEAS	Shell young garden peas and grade according to size. Blanch, cool quickly in ice water for 5 minutes, drain and dry. Leave sugar snap peas in pods and blanch. Store garden peas in plastic bags; store sugar snap peas in rigid containers with ¼-inch headspace.	Peas: 1 to 2 minutes Sugar snap peas: 2 to 4 minutes	7 minutes

VEGETABLE	PREPARATION/ STORAGE	BLANCHING TIME	COOKING TIME (FROM FROZEN)
PEPPERS (BELL AND SWEET)	Select crisp, tender fruits. Wash, cut in half, remove stems and seeds; if desired, cut into ¼-inch-wide strips or rings. Blanch, cool, drain and seal in plastic bags.	Halves: 3 minutes Strips or rings: 2 minutes	Several minutes
POTATOES	Freeze only small new potatoes, either blanched or cooked. Scrape the potatoes, blanch (unless cooked), cool quickly and dry. Store in plastic bags. For chips, peel and wash firm potatoes, cut into uniform chips and partially deep-fry in oil for about 3 minutes. Drain thoroughly and cool quickly. Store in plastic bags.	3 to 4 minutes	15 minutes if blanched; if already cooked, heat in hot water. Partially thaw chips; fry for 3 minutes.
SPINACH	Trim stalks, wash thoroughly and drain. Blanch in small portions, cool quickly and squeeze out surplus moisture. Store in rigid containers with ¼-inch headspace.	2 minutes	7 minutes
SQUASH, WINTER (INCLUDING PUMPKINS)	Wash, peel and cut in half. Scrape out seeds and strings; cut flesh into cubes. Steam, bake or boil until tender. Drain and leave in chunks or mash to a puree. When cool, store in rigid containers, leaving 1-inch headspace.		Thaw at room temperature for about two hours. Heat to desired temperature.
SWEET CORN	Freeze only young cobs with pale yellow kernels. Strip off husks and tassels, and trim the stalks close. Blanch a few cobs at a time. Cool, drain and dry. Wrap each cob in aluminum foil, then pack in plastic bags or containers and freeze. Alternatively, scrape the kernels from the blanched cobs and store in rigid containers with ¼-inch headspace.	Small: 4 minutes Medium: 6 minutes	Thaw completely, which takes 3 to 4 hours at room temperature, then boil for 5 to 10 minutes.
TOMATOES	May be frozen whole, but only if used for cooking later. Best frozen as a puree or juice. To freeze whole, wipe small, firm, ripe tomatoes and store in plastic bags. To make into a puree, wash and quarter the tomatoes, simmer for 5 minutes and rub through a nylon sieve. Cool and place in rigid containers with ¼-inch headspace. To prepare juice, wipe and core the tomatoes, cut in quarters and simmer for 10 minutes. Peel and put through a sieve, season with salt and store in rigid containers with 1-inch headspace.		Thaw whole tomatoes in container, slip off skins and use in cooked dishes. Use puree in frozen form in sauces, soups and casseroles. Thaw juice in container and serve chilled.
TURNIPS	May be frozen blanched or cooked and mashed. Trim roots and tops from young turnips. Peel, dice and blanch. Alternatively, cook peeled and quartered turnips until tender, then drain and mash. Cool and store in rigid containers with ¼-inch headspace.	2 minutes	Cook frozen diced turnips for 8 minutes. Heat partially thawed mashed turnips in a double boiler with butter.
ZUCCHINI	Trim ends from firm young zucchini, wash and cut into ¼-inch-thick slices. Blanch, cool, drain and dry. Alternatively, fry slices in a little butter and cool quickly. Store in rigid containers, separating the layers with parchment paper and leaving ¼-inch headspace.	1 minute	Thaw partially and fry in butter.

let's go

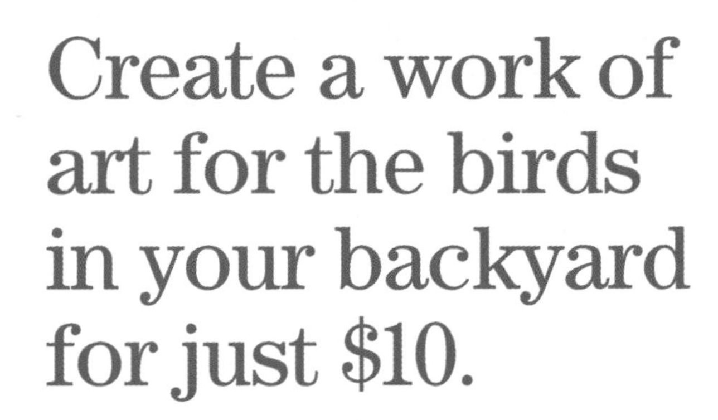

birdtiquing

STORY BY ALISON W. AUTH, RICHMOND, VIRGINIA

Birdhouses are made to be adorned—at least, that's my philosophy. I love repurposing vintage knobs, candlesticks and other odds and ends into accessories for birdhouses. I call the finished products "birdtiques," and they look fantastic in the garden.

Best of all, these birdtiques don't cost a lot of money. All you need are a simple $10 birdhouse kit, a junk pile and a little imagination. Get ready to have the most stylish birdhouse on the block—that is, if you can bear to put it outside!

Designing a Divine House

I think of each house as having four elements that make it distinctive: the base, the roof, the perches and the predator guards. You can customize each one depending on the supplies you have on hand. Here's how:

Bases. Old coat hooks, ceiling light canopies, tree branches, discarded candleholders, antique sink or shower faucet handles, ashtray stands—these items and more make wonderful birdhouse bases.

Roofs. Metal, rubber or fabric—use any kind of flexible, water-impervious material as a roof. Even if all you have is a faded scrap of Sunbrella fabric, you can glue it over the roof, seal it and then add moss for a living roof. The birds will love pulling the moss out for their nests!

Predator guards. Predator-guard options come in all shapes and sizes. Just

HEIDI HESS

adding an inch can keep squirrel and raccoon paws from scooping out the eggs. And even more will protect bluebirds from crows, cats and snakes. When selecting a guard, keep in mind what size hole you need to attract certain birds. You don't want it too big, or that will assist predators. Old porcelain light sockets, chrome radiator flanges and big rubber gaskets are a few options.

Perches. While charming in appearance, perches give predators a leg up on stealing eggs and disrupting a nest. It's always best to remove perches from store-bought birdhouses. Instead, think about using a perch on the side of the house, where it will double as a handle. Discarded cabinet knobs, tin wings and spigot handles from sinks all make interesting side perches.

first things first

MATERIALS
- Birdhouse kit
- Wire
- Base
- Roofing material
- Glue
- Paint
- Sealer
- Accessories (odds and ends, junk, etc.)

TOOLS
- Needle-nose pliers
- Assorted screws, roofing nails, finishing nails
- Cordless drill
- Coping saw (for clean-out door)
- Tin snips or sharp scissors
- Vegetable peeler or paring knife

PREPARE YOUR BIRDHOUSE

STEP 1: Assemble and glue the house, excluding the bottom. (You can also recycle an old birdhouse.) Lightly sand and smooth the inside and outside using medium- to fine-grit sandpaper. Pay special attention to the hole where birds enter and exit.

STEP 2: Drill holes in the bottom panel of the house for drainage and ventilation. Sand both sides of the bottom with a medium- to fine-grit sandpaper. Add the bottom to your house but don't glue it yet. It will be easier to attach your base if the bottom stays free.

STEP 3: Prime your house with exterior or interior-exterior primer. I like the eco-friendly low-VOC paints. Don't paint the inside, though: Keep it natural for the birds. After the primer is dry, sand your house lightly with fine-grit paper to prepare the surface for the final coat(s) of paint. Now you're ready to attach your base of choice.

Here's how you can fashion each of these birdhouses from the same $10 model

◀ GRETEL

The base of this Hansel and Gretel house was made out of an iron candlestick, which gives it a bit of panache. Before gluing the bagged moss to the roof, I made sure to fill the roof seam with caulk so little birdies would stay dry. The big, round predator guard lends a modern feel to an otherwise woodland cottage style. The tin flowers provide a delicate birds-only perch, keeping predators at bay.

SUNNY ▶

It's time to go for a walk in the woods! The legs of this fun house are sticks from the backyard. You can leave the bark on or whittle it away with a vegetable peeler, as shown here. Sunny has roof flashing that is thin and bendable enough to form a roof, wings and "feathers." The result is a very birdlike house, with the wings doubling as a safe resting spot for feathered friends. A fun paint job and tin flowers add whimsy and color.

◀ LIZA

This dainty pink house takes advantage of several workshop castoffs. Coat hooks salvaged from old closets make wonderful birdlike feet, while a piece of orange rubber belting provides a water-impervious cover for the roof. Finally, an old blue spigot handle does double duty as a side perch.

MARGARET ▶

Margaret is a little more tidy and together. A handsome copper roof, elegant copper flowers and a nicely proportioned light canopy for the base lend an air of refinement. I tinted the final coat of shellac to lend an antique quality to the finish. The front perch is a wooden button that's dainty enough for a bird but not too much to help a squirrel.

HEIDI HESS

finishing touches

You never know what odds and ends will end up making distinctive birdhouse accessories. Here's an idea for recycling tin or copper:

how to make a tin flower

1. Cut a strip of aluminum, tin, roof flashing or thin copper into strips about ½ in. high x 2½ in. long. (Be sure to wear gloves and goggles for safety.)
2. Using snips or sharp scissors, cut "fringe" along the length of the metal strip.
3. Take a sturdy wire cut to about 6 in. long and bend the tip into a U shape.
4. Hook the wire at one end of the strip and cinch the wire down in the gap between the last two fringes so that the length of the wire extends below the base of the fringe.
5. Using your fingers, wrap the strip of metal tightly in a circle.
6. Peel the cut pieces down as pictured.
7. Use needle-nose pliers to curl the petals if desired.

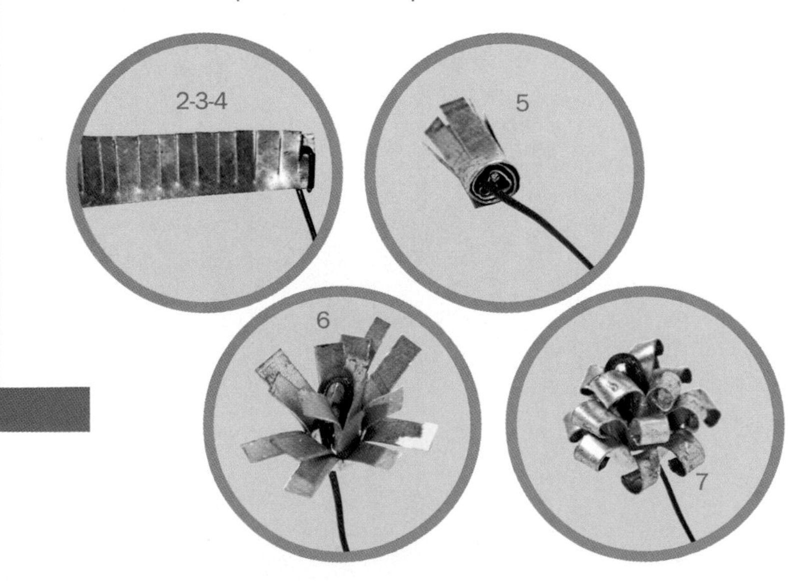

Alison's Secrets to Great Birdtiques

- Seal your house with shellac, a natural, nontoxic varnish that will protect the structure from everyday wear without poisoning a pecking bird.
- For rubber or other pliable roofing materials, use spray adhesive on both the roof and the material you're sticking it to. For a sheet-moss roof, paint Elmer's Glue over the roof, and then press on the sheet of moss, taking care to bend it over the glued edges. You can clean up the edges after the glue dries.
- Metal roofs are easy and sturdy. For tin, copper and other metals, cut a sheet of paper and fold it over the roof. Fold under the ends until you like the way it looks. Then you'll just need some snips to cut your metal to the right size and pliers to bend it.
- When working with material for the base, remember that most birdhouse kits usually use thin wood. So be careful that you don't drill all the way through the bottom of the house when attaching your material.
- To attach the base, try predrilling the holes for added security and to avoid splitting the birdhouse.

best budget *bird* HINTS

Clever readers rely on everyday items to make backyard birding easy and economical.

- You can make a great winter bird feeder with a plastic colander. (It has built-in drainage!) Simply string a few lengths of wire through its top holes or handles and hang it from a branch or shepherd's hook. Then fill with seed! —**KATHY SCARBRO,** *Mount Hope, West Virginia*

- Hollow out your pumpkins and fill them with cracked corn and birdseed to give ground-feeding birds a special treat. —**GLORIA MEREDITH,** *Harrington, Delaware*

- To squirrel-proof our feeders, we cut the neck off a 2-liter soda bottle and slipped it on the pole below the feeder. —**LENORE MATHER,** *Waverly, New York*

- A less expensive way to satisfy a bird's suet appetite is simply to spread lard on the bark of trees. They love it! —**BRUCE SCHAFFNER,** *Cochrane, Wisconsin*

- Here's an easy and inexpensive way to make your birdbath sparkle. Toss a handful of sand into the basin and scrub it with a brush. —**MARILYN CLANCY,** *Englewood, Florida*

- To combat hot birdbath water in the summer, I fill a clean cottage cheese container with water and freeze it overnight. I place it in the birdbath in the morning. It keeps the water cool for hours. —**BERNADINE PAWELEK,** *Peterborough, Ontario*

- After I brush my dog, I save the hair for nesting season. I place it in my yard so the birds can use it for nests. —**CATHLYN RAMSEY,** *Wichita, Kansas*

- I like to empty my hanging flower baskets and then turn them into "birdie hotels" for roosting on cold nights. —**KAREN COFER,** *Gainesville, Georgia*

- When cobs of sweet corn are too ripe to eat, I place them on my tray feeder. The birds love feasting on the kernels. —**GARY CLARK,** *Knowlton, Quebec*

- Bluebirds love my homemade coffee can birdhouses. I drill a 1-1/2-inch hole in the plastic lid and mount the house on a tree through the can's metal bottom. —**SUE MCKEE,** *Iuka, Mississippi*

- Place a terra-cotta saucer on a flowerpot and you'll have a simple and effective birdbath. —**SHERYL NEAL,** *Carrollton, Ohio*

- A snowman can make an excellent winter bird feeder. Just replace the traditional stick arms with coneflower stalks and sprinkle birdseed on and around the snowman. —**LORI QUALLS,** *Midland, Michigan*

- Use sunflower heads and evergreen trimmings to make all-natural wreaths for the birds. Then decorate them with edible garland and other treats. —**JUSTINE MORRIS,** *Ravenna, Ohio*

- A long-handled windshield scraper makes a handy tool for cleaning bird feeders in the winter. —**LYNNE MCLERNON,** *Lake Geneva, Wisconsin*

- Place a few pennies in your birdbath. They slow down algae buildup. —**PATTY LOWNEY,** *Appleton, Wisconsin*

BIRDBATH, HAMIZA BAKIRCI / SHUTTERSTOCK.COM; PENNIES, CRAIG WACTOR / SHUTTERSTOCK.COM

did you know?

Learn more about one of gardening's greatest values—seeds.

$40

You can save $40 or more if you grow your own zinnias from seed instead of buying plants. Pick up a pack of seeds for less than $1 instead of buying plants at the peak of the season.

10

Cucumbers, melons and tomatoes are among the veggies with the longest seed life, good up to 10 years.

3

According to major seed supplier Burpee, the top three ornamental seed varieties are:

Zinnias
Marigolds
Sunflowers

$2.75

Packets of rare heirloom tomato seeds average around $2.75 each at *seedsavers.org*.

68°

Most seeds won't germinate until the soil's temperature reaches 68°. Keep this in mind when starting seeds indoors as well. (This is why seed-starting heat mats are so popular.)

26

In fall 2010, there were 26 posts in the *Birds & Blooms* Seed Swap forum about exchanging seeds. Go to the Community section of *birdsandblooms.com* to start exchanging with fellow readers today!

1975

Seed Savers Exchange was started as a nonprofit in 1975 in an effort to save and share heirloom seeds. It's still going strong today and is one of the most respected seed sources in gardening.

SEED PACKETS, ANTIQUES & COLLECTABLES / ALAMY

thrifty *garden* TIPS

Cost-conscious contributors use household goods to help plants and flowers flourish.

- I recycled my mother's mailbox by placing it in my garden, where it serves as a handy little shed. I keep a trowel, clippers and extra gardening gloves inside.
  —**TAMALA BIGGER**, *St. Clair, Michigan*

- Use a turkey baster to water plants that you have started from seeds indoors. It prevents you from overwatering or flattening tender plants.
  —**VALERIE EVANSON**, *Phoenixville, Pennsylvania*

- I save all my old shoestrings and soft fabric belts. Then I always have something on hand when I need to tie up flowers and tomato plants that need some support.
  —**JANET LUSCH**, *Vandalia, Illinois*

- Recycled paper egg cartons work well for starting seeds. Simply fill the compartments with seed-starting mix and seeds. You can even plant the carton to reduce any possible transplanting shock.
  —**GAIL RUSSELL**, *Greendale, Wisconsin*

- Filling large flowerpots with soil is expensive. Instead, put empty aluminum cans in the bottom of the pot to save money and keep it lighter.
  —**VI CONCANNON**, *Fair Oaks, California*

- I recycle large coffee cans to use as flowerpots. I spray-paint them and sometimes add painted scenes or decals. —**ANN WARD**, *Naples, Florida*

- Instead of buying a garden tool wagon or bag, I purchased an old golf bag for $5 at a flea market. I use it to haul my tools around the yard. The pockets are perfect for twine, clippers and other small items.
  —**LINDA VIZZA**, *Peterborough, Ontario*

- Why buy a garden kneeling pad when a piece of old carpet will suffice? Just cut a handle at one end to carry it around. —**POLLY KELLY**, *Birmingham, Alabama*

- My yard was plagued with dandelions. I spent a fortune on weed killer until I found something in my kitchen that worked. Mix 1 part salt to 3 parts vinegar, heat until it's warm, then cool and pour into a spray bottle. This also kills other plants, so use with caution.
  —**DEBBIE HEATON**, *Toccoa, Georgia*

- If you live in an area with mild winters, it's easy to start new rosebushes from your existing ones. Whenever you prune them, use the cuttings to root new plants.
  —**JULIE SOILEAU**, *Marbury, Alabama*

- I had pavers left over from a project, so I stacked them and made a flowerpot stand.
  —**MACK ORDUBEGIAN**, *St. Catherines, Ontario*

- Old spatulas and spoons make great plant markers. Use a fine-tip permanent marker to write the plant name on the front of the utensil and the planting date on the back. —**LINDA RAMSEY**, *Chelsea, Oklahoma*

- I like to keep a bar of soap in my watering can. When I water my plants, they get a dose of antibug soap, too.
  —**SUSIE FISHER**, *Lewistown, Pennsylvania*

- I have found that if I plant two or three dill seeds in each squash hill, I won't have any squash bugs.
  —**DEE HANCOCK**, *Fremont, Nebraska*

- Before I plant onions, radishes or carrots, I sprinkle the row with leaves from a tea bag. I find this keeps the root maggots away.
  —**JOANNE HAMILTON**, *Randleman, North Carolina*

SEEDLINGS, MAILBOX: RDA-GID

for less

Save money with these easy birding and gardening ideas.

grow your own birdseed

Goldfinch on blazing star

Attract more birds to your garden by growing the flowers that will produce their favorite seeds. These plants produce so many seeds that there are always plenty for next year's garden.

Agastache. Blue-flowering varieties are most attractive to birds. Trumpet-shaped flowers attract hummingbirds, sphinx moths and butterflies, too. Seed heads provide food for birds.
Blazing star (Liatris). Spikes of rose, lavender or white flowers attract hummingbirds and butterflies. Goldfinches, tufted titmice and other seedeaters savor the seed heads.
Cosmos. Colorful, pinwheel-shaped blooms with feathery foliage are attractive to birds. It thrives in a variety of conditions and produces a plethora of seed heads.
Millet. This seed grass produces seeds that are an absolute favorite of birds.
Purple coneflower. Large, showy blooms attract birds, butterflies and bees. Needs little upkeep, is drought-tolerant and self-sows readily.
Safflower. In summer, safflower bears loose, thistlelike flower heads. Birds can't resist its seeds.
Sunflower. Give the birds a treat with a sunflower garden. The flowers offer plenty of seeds and are easy to grow.
Zinnia. With new varieties appearing all the time, this annual is heat-, drought- and disease-resistant. The blooms last until the first frost and supply birds with lots of seeds to eat.

Cosmos

SUNFLOWER SEEDS, MARCEL JANCOVIC / SHUTTERSTOCK.COM; GOLDFINCH, CAROL L. EDWARDS; COSMOS, RDA-GID; FRAME FREEDER, HEIDI HESS

feeder from a frame

If you have a picture frame lying around—maybe the glass broke or you found it at a thrift store—turn it into a delightful bird feeder.

— **BY ALISON W. AUTH,** *Richmond, Virginia*

Old picture frames make perfect feeders. With a few supplies and these instructions on this page, make an inexpensive tray feeder for winter birds.

WHAT YOU NEED:

- Old picture frame
- 4 screw eyes
- Chain or wire for hanging
- Shower curtain hanger or something similar for gathering the chain
- Window screen
- Paint
- Staple gun and staples
- Wire cutters (if using stiff chain)
- Snips or scissors for cutting screen
- Hammer and finish nail or drill for pilot holes

DIRECTIONS:

1. Paint your picture frame, if desired.
2. Cut your screen to fit your picture frame opening and staple it to the back. (My staples went through to the frame's front, so I used caulk as if it was cake icing to cover them up and make a fake filigree!)
3. Using either a hammer and finish nail or drill bit, make pilot holes in the four corners of the finished side of the frame for your screw eyes. Twist in the screw eyes.
4. Cut four equal lengths of chain or wire and attach one to each screw eye. Gather at the top and run your shower curtain hanger through the ends of the chain. Hang from the nearest branch!

homemade suet & fruit feeders

These colorful coil feeders are perfect for holding suet or fruit.

BY DAISY SISKIN, NESHOBA, TENNESSEE

These little cuties are a snap to make, cheaper by the dozen (teacher gifts, anyone?) and the perfect size for—get ready for glamour—homemade suet in a toilet paper tube.

WHAT YOU NEED:

- 14-gauge galvanized wire (sold in 100-ft. rolls in the picture-hanging supplies section of the hardware store)
- 2 pairs of pliers (one needs to have a wire-cutting surface)
- Glass spice jar or other 2-in.-diameter jar
- Duct tape
- Spray primer and paint approved for metal

DIRECTIONS:

1. Cut wire using the wire-cutting portion of the pliers into one 6-ft. section and one 14-in. section per feeder.

2. Tape one end of the long section of wire to the side of the jar with a piece of duct tape. It helps to gently bend it into a jar-sized curve before you start.

3. Holding the taped end of the wire securely with duct tape, begin to smoothly wind the wire around the jar. Keep winding until you have wound all the wire around the jar.

4. Remove the coil from the jar. Now, using both sets of pliers, curve one end of the wire into a smaller curlicue. This will be the bottom of the feeder; the smaller curve will keep the suet from falling out. Holding each end, carefully stretch the coil until it measures approximately 4½ in. long.

5. Take the shorter segment of wire, hold either end, and bend it in the middle to make a handle shape.

6. With the pliers, bend over about ¾ inch of wire toward the center. Hook these ends over the first two coils of wire on opposite sides of the top of the feeder, making sure one end of the handle is near the cut end of the wire. Crimp the ends securely using both pairs of pliers.

7. To prepare for the paint, wash your feeder in warm, soapy water, rinse and allow to dry completely. Prime and paint your feeders. Then fill with homemade suet (see recipe above right) or treat the birds and butterflies to juicy slices of fruit.

Wind the wire around the jar.

Curve one end of the wire into a curlicue.

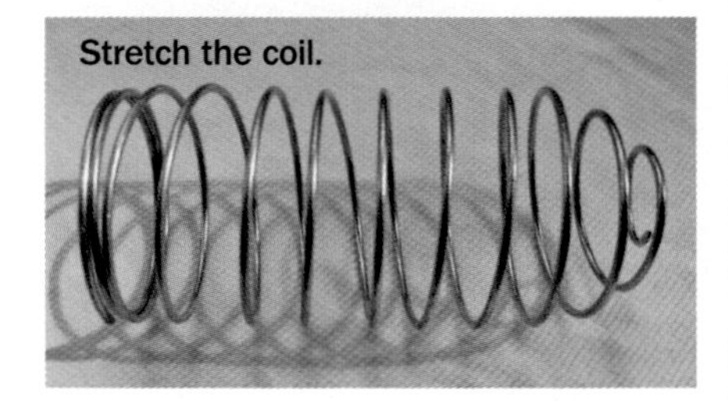

Stretch the coil.

homemade suet

- 1 lb. suet, cut up (ask at the butcher counter)
- 1 cup each wild birdseed mix, cornmeal, oatmeal and peanut butter

Melt the suet over medium heat. Remove from heat and stir in the remaining ingredients. Pack into toilet paper tubes, covering one end with foil secured with a rubber band. Store in the freezer until ready to use, then tear the paper mold away and pop into the feeder.

orange wreath for orioles

Simple and elegant, these little feeders are sure to attract oodles of orioles.

BY ALISON W. AUTH, RICHMOND VIRGINIA

I enjoy the bright silhouettes of orioles in my window, especially after a long winter. They love fresh oranges and are also attracted to the color orange, making these wreaths the perfect enticement. Hang one near a sturdy branch so an oriole has a perch from which to peck!

WHAT YOU NEED:

- Coat hanger with a cardboard tube (pictured below)
- Needle-nose pliers (or strong hands)
- Wire cutters
- Oranges
- Cutting board
- Good slicing kitchen knife
- Ribbon and berries (optional)

DIRECTIONS:

1. Remove the cardboard tube from your hanger and bend the two sides of the hanger toward each other until they are spaced about 1 inch apart.

2. Shape the outline of a bird, as shown. I found that using my hands was the easiest way to start. Then I used needle-nose pliers to shape and smooth any rough curves.

3. Use pliers or a wire cutter to snip the curled ends off the hanger.

4. Cut oranges into about ¼-inch slices. Cut little pieces of rind from the orange ends into roughly ½-inch triangles. These will serve as spacers between the slices and will help keep everything in place.

5. Thread an orange slice through both wires. Then thread a piece of rind next to it on one or both wires.

6. Repeat step 5, threading more oranges, until you run out of wire.

7. Tie a little bow around the bird's neck and add some berries at the end if you wish. Hang from a tree close to a window so you can see the orioles when they come for a snack!

mini greenhouse

Get growing earlier by building your own cold frame.

BY DAISY SISKIN, NESHOBA, TENNESSEE

A cold frame is nothing more than a mini greenhouse (or a monster cloche, depending on how you look at it). It's often used in spring to harden off seedlings started indoors or in fall to extend the growing season for cool-weather crops. I used scrap lumber for this project. Here's how I did it:

Ready for seedlings or plants!

1. I built a rectangular box, 4 ft. long and 2 ft. wide. Using glue and galvanized ring-shank nails, I hammered the first tier together provisionally.

2. With the table saw set to a 30° angle, I made a cut along the long edge of another 4-ft. board for the tall back side, where I would hinge the window for the cold frame.

3. I snapped a chalk line along the side of a 2-ft. length of board, following the 30° angle of the top edge of the backboard. Then I cut the two side pieces of equal size. I glued and nailed this second tier together and stacked it on top of the basic box.

4. To reinforce the box, I marked and cut pieces of two-by-two to fit in the corners, angling the cut on the top edge to follow the angle of the boards. Then I glued and screwed these "cleats" to the box corners.

5. The next step was to build the window frame. I used some old scrap pieces of molding for this, along with Plexiglas for safety and ease of cutting. It was most economical to buy two pieces of the plastic, each 28 by 30 in., and cut them to fit the opening with a utility knife and a straightedge. I built two frames for the plastic and used small screws to attach the plastic windows to the frames. (Don't screw them in too tight or they'll crack. I learned this the hard way.)

6. Next, I attached the windows with strap hinges. Then I insulated the interior with ¾-in. Styrofoam covered with whiteboard. Finally, I caulked all the joints, and I was ready to go!

Depending where you live, cold frames can extend your growing season by weeks and even months!

Frame to your desired size.

Reinforce corners with cleats.

design your own fairy garden

Invite a little magic into your backyard with a mini garden.
BY DAISY SISKIN, NESHOBA, TENNESSEE

12 Miniature Plants

Stonecrop sedum
Elfin thyme
White moss thyme
Corsican mint
Hens-and-chicks
Irish moss
Angel's tears
Ornamental strawberry
Creeping veronica
Green mound juniper
Satsuki azalea
Ginkgo

One of my favorite childhood memories is searching for acorn cups for the little creatures who inhabited the imaginary world in the woods by my house. Today, I'm still building habitats for the imagination. They're called fairy gardens. You can make your own fairy garden, too. Whether you choose to have one in a container or out in your garden, it will charm visitors of all ages (and sizes).

1. Decide on a theme. Do your fairies deserve a formal environment, or would they feel more at home down on the farm? Maybe you have something exotic in mind, like a Gothic manor with a couple of gargoyles or a tropical paradise with a beach.

2. Choose a location. Whether it's a sunny patio or a shady corner, this will be key when selecting your plants.

3. Design the garden. Sketch out your ideas on paper. Include places for your fairies to lounge, a fence or an arbor, and perhaps a water feature.

4. Pick a container. Just about anything you can plant in is suitable, but keep in mind you want enough depth to maintain soil moisture, particularly in a sunny spot, enough surface area to accommodate all the elements you envision, and drainage holes.

5. Select the plants. Once your design is roughed out, choose plants that look mature in miniature, borrowing from the art of bonsai. Don't aim for a patchwork of color; variations in height and texture give a more natural, cohesive look to your fairy garden.

6. Dig in! As with any container plant, ensure good drainage and use a quality container soil mix. For a true-to-life appearance, use full-size landscaping techniques such as flagstones (mini, of course!) set in sand or a dry creek bed beneath a bridge. Using your plan as a guideline, have fun installing your tiny garden.

7. Accessorize. It's tempting to go overboard with the trinkets, but use a light hand. Tuck something away that's noticeable only upon close examination. Your fairy garden will be guaranteed to inspire lots of smiles. For miniature supplies, try *twogreenthumbs.com* or the site *miniaturegardenshoppe.com*.

for less

lickety-split lanterns

Light up your outdoor world with this inexpensive idea.

BY DAISY SISKIN, NESHOBA, TENNESSEE

Whether you're planning a garden party or looking to brighten a dark night, garden lanterns add just the right twinkle of warmth and illumination to your outdoor space. When they're this easy to make, you may have trouble knowing when to stop!

WHAT YOU NEED:

- Glass jars
- Adhesive-backed shelf liner
- Assorted leaves
- Pen
- Scissors
- Frosted glass spray
- Sand
- Candles
- Wire (optional)

DIRECTIONS:

1. Trace the leaves onto the shelf liner and cut out with scissors.
2. Remove the paper backing from the leaf shapes.
3. Press leaves securely to the outside surface of the glass jars.
4. Spray the frosted glass spray, according to product instructions, all over the outside of the jars. Allow to dry.
5. Remove the adhesive shapes.
6. If you want to hang your lanterns, cut a piece of wire the length of the diameter of the jar mouth, plus extra for twisting and for your desired handle size. Twist wire around the mouth of the jars, below the threads. Bend the wire over the jar in a handle shape and twist onto the wire on the opposite side of the mouth.
7. Fill jars about a third full with sand and push a candle into the sand to secure.

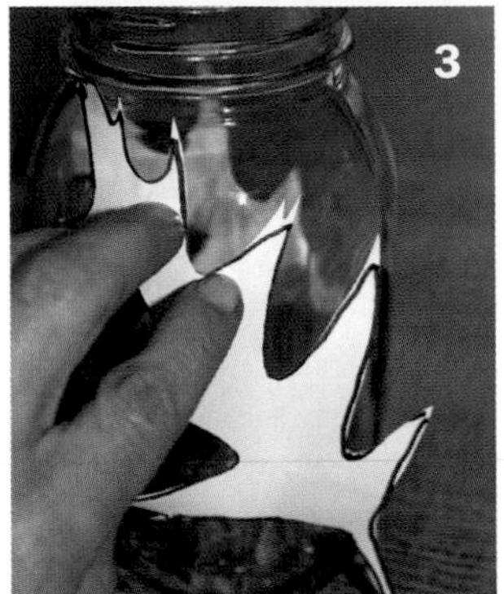

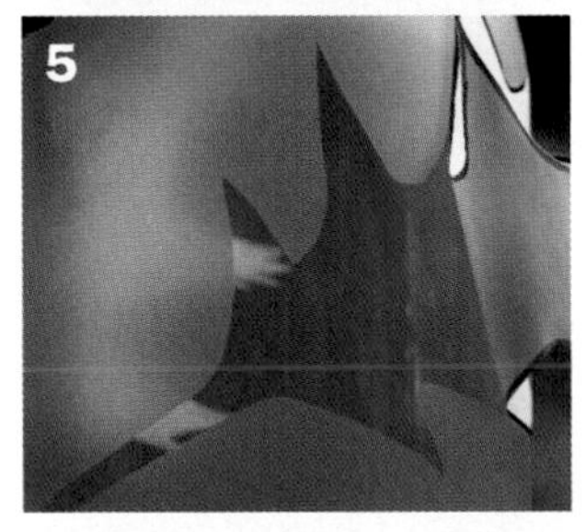

tips to perfect garden lanterns

- Wipe down the outside of the jars with rubbing alcohol to remove any oil from your hands that might hinder adhesion.
- Choose leaf shapes that are bold and graphic to make them easier to trace and cut out.
- If your leaves want to curl and twist, try pressing them with a warm iron under a piece of paper.
- If you prefer not to use sand, drop in chunky votives or tea lights. Light with a long candle lighter.
- Thinner-gauge wire is easier to twist. Use gloves and needle-nose pliers to work with heavier wire.
- Paper backing can be tricky to remove. Cut leaf stems extra long. With the paper side up, fold down the tip end of the stem and tear the paper back at the fold. Snip away the extra bit of stem at the end with scissors before sticking to jar.
- To hang lanterns from branches, use S-hooks or a length of wire.

instant garden bench

Create a seating area in your garden from an old bed frame.

BY DAISY SISKIN, NESHOBA, TENNESSEE

A place to sit is what turns your garden into a destination, a place to linger, a respite from the daily grind. Seating transforms your yard into an oasis where you can soak in the beauty of what you've labored to create.

The problem with garden seating, though, is the expense! Any step above plastic stackables and folding lawn chairs starts to get scary, especially if you want something with a little more character.

Enter the bed-into-bench. The beauty of this project is in its economy, its simplicity and its endless variety. No two are alike.

Start with an old bed's headboard and footboard, rails optional. Check garage sales and thrift stores. A full or twin bed works best. You're probably going to be painting it, so surface condition isn't important.

Because each bed is unique, the construction details will vary, but the basic principles are the same.

The headboard will form the back of the bench.

The footboard will become the sides of the bench.

You'll frame a box to support the seat. That's it!

HERE ARE SOME TIPS:

1. Place the footboard perpendicular to the headboard and eyeball it to help decide how deep you want the bench to be. Mark your cutting line accordingly, and saw the footboard into two equal pieces.

2. You may need to alter the height of either the headboard or the footboard pieces. For my bench, I cut down the legs of the headboard a few inches so the arms would intersect the back at a better place.

3. Predrill all holes to avoid splitting the wood. Use heavy-duty construction lag screws for stability. These have star drive holes in the heads so you can drive them in flush with the surface of the boards.

4. L-brackets may be useful to improve the strength of the joints.

5. Use heavy-duty exterior glue.

6. Take advantage of the bed rails if you have them. I used them to form part of the seat and the front apron of the bench. I used scrap lumber to form the seat supports and part of the seat.

7. Finish the bench to suit your style with exterior-grade paint if the bench will be exposed to the elements. Try bright colors, an antique finish, stenciling or whatever strikes your fancy.

8. Enjoy your one-of-a-kind creation!

CHAPTER 3

Photo *know-how*

Skilled nature and wildlife photographers share their first-class photos as well as topnotch tips and techniques to aim, point and shoot your way to fantastic snapshots.

DONNA KRISCHAN

365 days of *blooms*

Thanks to a yearlong photo challenge, this photographer celebrates the art in nature very day.

STORY AND PHOTOS BY MATT CLARK, TAMPA, FLORIDA

It all started last year. Four months of shivering—and watching my flower beds wilt and turn brown—ended, and one of the harshest winters on record was finally over.

As I looked into the crystal-blue Florida sky, I noticed a Spanish needle plant growing on the roof of my neighbor's lanai. It seemed to be blooming happily as it swayed in the cool breeze. What resilience, what triumph, what awesomeness, I thought. It was a true inspiration.

I've always enjoyed nature photography, but at that moment I was inspired to do something more. I wanted to celebrate the beauty and tenacity of nature and share it with others.

A few short weeks later—on March 20, 2010, the first day of spring—*bloomingdaily.com* was born. My goal for the site was to feature a new photo every day for a year of nature's most precious, delicate and irrepressible gifts—flowers!

I knew it would be a challenge to photograph 365 flowers in a single year, but I was ready. Since March, I've been traveling to find and shoot the most extraordinary flowers and scenes to wow my online viewers. I've stopped at botanical gardens, theme parks, muck ponds and roadside ditches. As a bonus, I've discovered not just flowers but deer, alligators, hedgehogs, butterflies, birds and more.

The year has held tough challenges and hours of hard work, but it's all been worth it. I like to think that Blooming Daily has inspired people to get out and explore the beauty of nature around them. After all, finding it isn't hard—it's right outside the door.

Matt successfully completed his personal goal. Go to his website, *bloomingdaily.com*, to see more of his work and to follow his journey.

"I knew it would be a challenge to photograph 365 flowers in a single year, but I was ready."

Firebush

Plumeria

Silk floss tree

Hibiscus

Matt's Flower Power Camera Secrets

Use point-and-shoot cameras. Know the minimum distance that your camera is capable of focusing. Closer isn't better if the result is out of focus. If your camera has a flower or macro setting, enable this feature.

Shoot white flowers. Too much light will ruin your pictures of white flowers. If your camera has an exposure compensation feature, set it to underexpose –2/3. This will protect your images from blowing out the highlights. If you don't have this feature, use a piece of cardboard or something similar to cast a shadow on the flower. And always try to shoot in the early morning or late afternoon.

Perfect the cookaloris effect. It's a cool word and an even cooler effect! This classic tool is generally used to give some character to a bland background in a studio, but I think it works equally well outdoors. When photographing flowers in bright sunlight, you can prune a small branch from a tree and hold it in such a way that it dapples light and shadow on your subject.

Create a misty look. Keep a spray bottle with your camera gear, so you can mist your flower and capture those lovely morning dew shots. If you have your tripod set up, try misting and shooting at the same time. If the sun is at the right angle, you'll even get a rainbow.

Fuchsia

bird

Grab your binoculars and digital camera to discover the photo technique called digiscoping.

STORY AND PHOTOS
BY SHARON STITELER
MINNEAPOLIS, MINNESOTA

ZOOM

photos MADE EASY

It was my very first morning in Panama City, and I was enjoying fresh papaya and sipping coffee. As I relaxed on the deck, I saw a rainbow of birds like tanagers and orioles flock to feeders filled with bananas.

I dashed back to my room, grabbed my spotting scope and camera, and returned to the deck to settle into a chair. Then I spent the morning digiscoping some souvenir shots of those truly amazing birds.

So what is digiscoping, anyway? It's really just a fancy word for using a digital camera with a pair of binoculars or spotting scope to take a photo of birds or wildlife.

Digiscoping started as a method for documenting unusual birds in a pinch, but now it's a big hobby for birdwatchers everywhere.

You don't have to be a hard-core birder to enjoy this photo technique. It's just another way to get to know the birds visiting your backyard or to capture photos when traveling.

The most basic method of digiscoping is simply to hold a point-and-shoot camera up to the eyepiece of a pair of binoculars or scope and take photos. However, it's virtually impossible to hold the camera steady. This is where special equipment can come in handy. Many manufacturers make adapters that slide over eyepieces to hold the camera firmly in place, minimizing the chance of blurry shots.

READY FOR MY CLOSEUP. Digiscoping helped Sharon get these shots. From top left: Bohemian waxwing, Lincoln's sparrow, eastern bluebird and blue-winged warbler.

Equipment Basics

You don't need a fancy camera to digiscope. A variety of cameras will work, from the basic point-and-shoot to the professional single-lens reflex types. Even BlackBerry phones and iPhones can be used.

The key is to buy the best scope you can afford. The current selection is a bit overwhelming, but I find that a large objective lens (meaning there's a large lens at one end of the scope) is best. To put it simply, the bigger the objective lens, the brighter the image will be through your scope.

Many scope manufacturers design camera adapters specifically for their scopes and keep a list of cameras that work best with each setup. So another method is to work backward: First choose a scope and then find out what camera options you have from there.

If your scope is older or if the company doesn't make an adapter, look for a universal adapter. These work with almost all scopes and cameras, though they tend to require last-minute adjustments to line up the camera with the eyepiece. Keep in mind that this can be frustrating when you're in the field; you might want to get a little more practice before you use a universal adapter.

Many people make their own adapters. I've seen homemade models that use everything from vitamin bottles and pesto jars to empty toilet paper tubes—recycling at its finest!

A Whole New World

The rule of thumb is that when you have a better-quality scope and camera, you're going to get better photos. But even with a midprice scope and cheap digital camera, you can get some memorable shots. Nowadays, most digital cameras you can buy even have a video option, so digiscoping can also come in handy for backyard bird movies.

Like anything else, digiscoping takes a little practice and patience until you master it. But it's a fun and easy hobby. Just take as many photos as you can. You'll get better every day, and you just might discover a few surprise visitors at your feeder, too!

DIGISCOPERS IN ACTION. Nature photographers can place a camera or video camera up to a scope to get exceptional photos or videos of birds at a distance.

enhance your bird studio

- Add colorful touches such as bittersweet branches on tray feeders to accent your photos.
- Attach a bare branch to your pole system. When birds perch on it before flying to the feeder, you'll get a natural-looking shot.
- Keep your feeders clean. Dirty feeders look tacky and spread disease to wild birds.
- Many species, especially bluebirds, find live mealworms irresistible. Try them as bait for insect-eating species.

The 3 P's of Digiscoping

PRACTICE
The main reason people abandon this technique is that they take 10 bad photos and give up. For every excellent photo you see, there are 250 bad ones that came before it on the camera.

PREDICTABLE PERCHES
Birds will perch on a hook or nearby branch before landing on a feeder. Aim your setup on the perch and tweak your focus. You will be ready for the shot when a bird lands.

PLACEMENT
Make sure you're in the best place for photos. Have the sun behind you to take advantage of the light. Try for a colorful background behind the bird, such as fall leaves.

Red-bellied woodpecker

PHOTOGRAPHERS, DAVID TIPLING / ALAMY

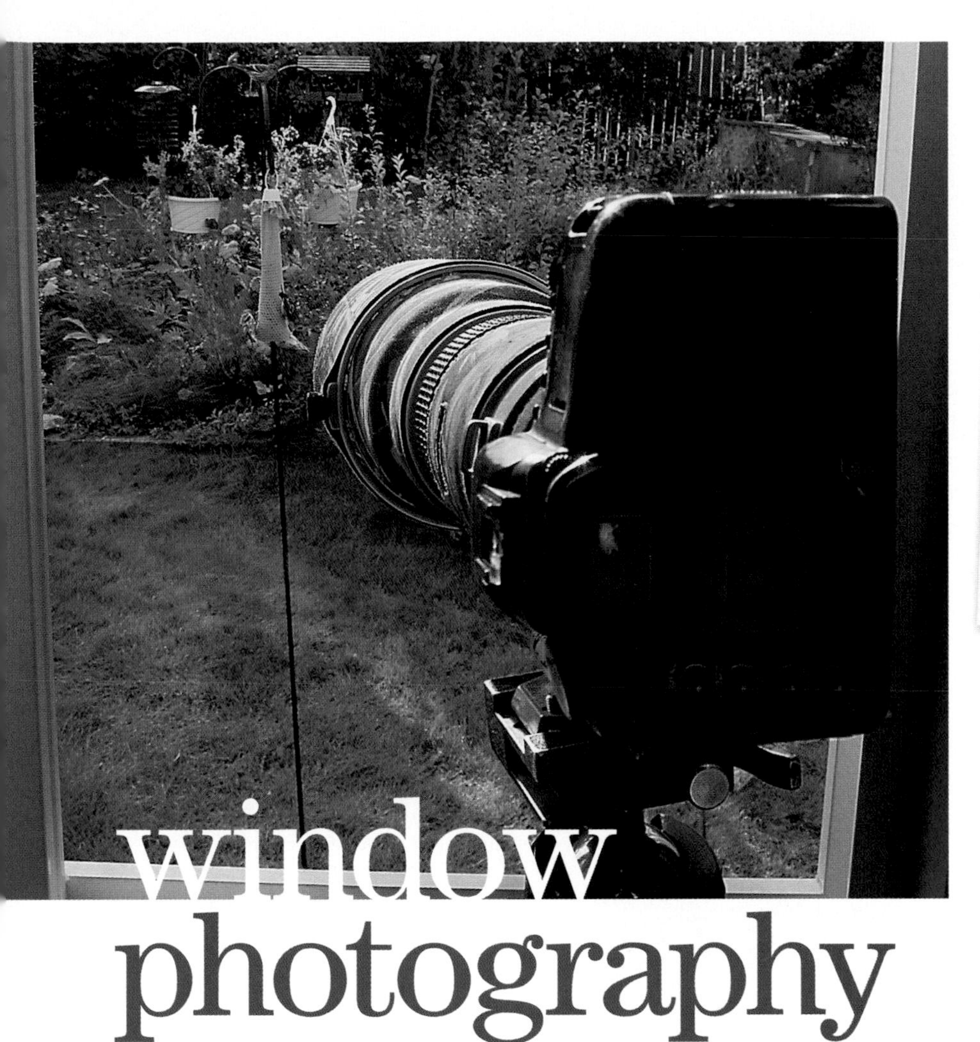

window photography

Get fantastic bird photos from the comfort of your home.

BY GEORGE HARRISON, CONTRIBUTING EDITOR

I have shot thousands of images of birds and other wildlife through my window, and they're just as good as the ones I took outdoors. Give it a try from the comfort and warmth of your home. Here are a few tips to help you along the way.

Put your camera against the window. To eliminate any distortion, hold the lens as close to the glass as you possibly can. If a flash is required, there should be no reflection if the camera is against the window. Likewise, if you hold the lens on or near the window, the autofocus capabilities of the camera won't be affected.

Check the quality of glass. Modern windows have high-quality glass. Even double-glazed windows should pose no problem. Just make sure the glass is as clean as possible, with no streaks.

Use a tripod. To eliminate camera motion, which is the photographer's worst enemy, use a tripod or some other kind of holder. Pretend your house is a blind. A wonderful thing about shooting indoors is that you're hidden from the wildlife. Birds get used to seeing movement inside the house, and eventually they'll pay no attention to a photographer on the other side of the glass.

Bring the subject up close. Not everyone has long telephoto lenses to reach out into the yard for pictures. That's no problem if your feeder, birdbath or birdhouse is close to the window. Think about where you place these objects, though. It is best to have good natural light on the subject, so first consider where the sunlight will fall.

Go natural. If you want photographs of your birds in a natural setting away from feeders or baths, place a twig, branch or flower to the side or above, where birds will land before having a bath or snack. Many superb images of wildlife by top professionals have been captured this way.

Think about your background. Before you begin shooting, take a thoughtful look through the camera. The simpler the background, the better the photo.

Have fun. Nature photography is usually hard work that demands enormous patience. But shooting wildlife from inside your house and on your own schedule can be lots of fun. And in the end, you'll have a visual record of your visitors you can keep forever.

FROM THE WINDOW. These pine siskins are the same birds as in the photo at left.

ROBIN, BILL JOHNSON / THE IMAGE FINDERS; CAMERA, PINE SISKINS: FRANCIS & JANICE BERGQUIST

focus on *education*

Want to take better pictures? Seek out tips from photo pros around you.

STORY AND PHOTOS BY DONNA KRISCHAN, BIG BEND, WISCONSIN

Unlike many nature photographers, I have not been taking pictures all my life. In fact, I started just before my 40th birthday. Around that time, I lost my job as an information systems manager, so I was faced with the challenge of finding a new career.

My husband, a botanist, asked me what I wanted to be when I grew up, and it immediately hit me. I wanted to be a nature photographer!

I had no experience, but it didn't matter. I was ready to be a student and soak up as much as I could from others in the business.

Learn From the Best

As my dream grew, I studied photo magazines for inspiration and information. The articles about wildlife and nature photography were always my favorites. They were a visual feast!

After studying the magazines and making a few visits to the photography section of my local bookstore, I zeroed in on the nature photographers whose work I admired. I called them my modern-day masters.

With a little digging, I started finding weeklong workshops with some of these masters. I became a workshop and seminar junkie, attending everything I could find within a day's drive.

The workshops proved to be the ultimate learning experience, totally immersing me in the subject. Every single class I took made me a significantly better photographer.

Turk's cap lily

Making Time for Class

I know not everyone is able to do weeklong workshops, what with family commitments, time constraints and tight budgets. But I encourage every budding photographer to try to make time. Even a weekend or a one-day event is worthwhile.

It also helps to get involved online. Online photo magazines such as *apogeephoto.com* are wonderful. Blogs are also terrific resources for tutorials and tips.

Talk to folks at your neighborhood camera store. They may offer classes to help you get started, and they probably know of local camera clubs that focus on education.

Always remember that the most important thing you need to do is get out there and take lots of pictures. Between that and a little help from modern masters, anyone can learn to be a photographer at any age!

Lady's slippers

Sunflower

Monarchs on goldenrod

Quick Photo Tips from Donna

- Study photographs in books and magazines, and try to mimic the ones you like. Eventually you will develop your own style.
- Learn to love your camera manual. Don't read it all at once. Just take it a section at a time until you really understand each concept.
- Practice makes perfect. Take many different pictures of the same subject using varied camera settings to learn their effects.
- Critique your photos. What worked and what didn't? Learn from your photos so you can take better ones next time.
- Enjoy your photos. I often make little art pieces using my photos to tell a story. This should be a fun hobby, so make sure you take time to savor it.

lens-worthy *location*

Despite a harsh climate, this photographer figured out how to entice birds into his backyard.

STORY AND PHOTOS BY ROWLAND K. WILLIS, RANCHO MIRAGE, CALIFORNIA

I am a retired chemical plant engineer and environmental manager from England who recently moved to America to pursue my favorite pastime, wildlife photography. Over the years, I have captured thousands of wildlife images and staged several exhibitions in England.

But when I moved to Rancho Mirage, California, in 2006, I found few subjects for photography. Wildlife was thinly spread across the high-desert area, which has a harsh climate, very low rainfall, hot summers, strong winds and penetrating winter frosts.

Without enough water to support a lush wildlife garden, I installed a variety of bird feeding and watering stations, which have attracted a wide range of colorful, interesting birds to our property.

The feeding station is built from two 5-foot-tall steel fence posts placed about 8 feet apart, with a steel cable stretched across like a tightrope.

I use thistle seed feeders, suet and nut cages, hummingbird feeders, flat trays and a wire cage feeder to hold unshelled peanuts. I set various fruits on trays, on the ground and pressed onto short branches in surrounding trees. Fresh pineapple is definitely the favorite among the orioles.

The water system is in semi-shade to prevent the water from getting too hot. It consists of an 18-inch-round by 2½-inch-deep flowerpot saucer set into the ground and decorated with local rocks so it looks natural and provides perching surfaces and variable water depth. The water is automatically fed twice a day using a 40-foot-long, ¼-inch feed from a battery-powered sprinkler valve.

I established a permanent viewing and photography blind near the bird station. It is situated away from the house to give timid birds more confidence and prevent buildings from showing up in my photos. The blind is a 60-inch-high, 30-inch-wide box, constructed from spare timber, that is just big enough for a camp chair, a tripod and a slot for a camera lens. The blind is southeast of the feeders to ensure good lighting in the mornings, which is the best time to photograph.

"My blind allows me to comfortably observe and photograph birds through every season."

Western scrub-jay

Western tanager

House finches courting

The blind allows me to comfortably observe and photograph birds through every season. Sitting inside, I have observed behaviors that I would not likely have witnessed if birds were aware of me. I have seen house finches courting, Scott's orioles dining at hummingbird feeders, and dozens of acrobatic pinyon jays feeding on the nuts of the pinyon pines. Both Anna's and Costa's hummingbirds come to visit, as do quail, hawks, tanagers and grosbeaks.

Once birds accept this kind of station, you'll be surprised how the traffic will increase. Maybe your neighbors, seeing the beautiful birds around your home, will even follow your example. Just imagine the potential benefit to the bird population!

Bullock's oriole

Get the Shot!

If you would like to photograph your feathered visitors in a similar manner, give it a go. Here are a few tips to get you started.

1. It's widely known that birds cannot count, so have someone escort you inside your blind and leave once you're settled. The birds will think the blind is empty. Employ this strategy for a few weeks, and birds will realize they have nothing to fear from the little house.
2. To keep from frightening birds away, introduce feeders and perches one at a time over a period of time.
3. Ensure that shots look natural by incorporating local plants and using branches to create perches within your landscape.
4. Try to avoid centering the bird in the image, and take the shot when the bird is looking across and not out of the frame.

Lesser goldfinch

captured up *close*

Macro photography experts share their best tips for taking fantastic close-up photos.

STORY AND PHOTOS BY ALAN DETRICK WITH LINDA DETRICK, GLEN ROCK, NEW JERSEY

For anyone who loves flowers, taking a photograph is one of the best ways to remember an especially beautiful blossom. Macro, or close-up, photography is very popular because it allows you to go in tight and fill the frame with a single bloom, magnifying all the tiny details.

I enjoy macro because it offers an opportunity to visit a whole new world, one that most people walk right by. While some people are intimidated by macro photography, I believe that with a little time and practice, anyone can learn to capture beautiful close-up images.

When I teach macro photography, the most frequent question I get is about equipment. What you need depends upon how you plan to use the pictures. If you're just looking to take some hobby photos to share with family and friends, many point-and-shoot cameras have a built-in macro capability that will do the job.

But if you're looking for higher-quality pictures, a DSLR camera with a dedicated macro lens, extension tubes and supplemental filters is the answer. You'll spend more, but you'll get better images and more flexibility.

Taking a close-up is different from taking a snapshot. It's important to slow down, think about what caught your eye and decide on the best way to approach it. Using a tripod automatically slows the process down and lets you make decisions about depth of field, focus and exposure. It also keeps the camera steady during the long shutter speeds common in this type of shooting.

If your favorite subjects are butterflies, bees and other insects, there are a few useful tips to try. Most insects are easier to photograph early in the morning when they're covered with dew and moving slowly or not at all. If you're shooting later in the day, take a moment to observe their behavior patterns. Many times they will repeatedly visit a favorite flower. Finally, don't wear bright clothing, which attracts their attention, and try to keep your movements low and slow.

With practice, your macro images will continue to improve. You'll become comfortable with the technique and find your photographic horizons expanding. So go ahead and give it a try. It's something of a challenge, but the results are well worth it.

A MATTER OF PERSPECTIVE. Below, a sunny day made it hard to shoot this peony bloom, so Alan decided to catch the light coming through the blossom instead. At left are Alan's shots of lily-of-the-valley blooms and a skipper butterfly.

MAKING IT WORK. Alan initially loved this shot but then realized the background could be a problem. He didn't want it to become too busy, so he framed this single rudbeckia blossom with ones behind it that were out of focus.

VISUAL INTEREST. The texture and arching fronds of this fern caught Alan's attention. He adjusted the composition to highlight the grace of the bending fronds as the light brushed their tips.

USE THE LIGHT. Alan loved the light coming through on this morning glory blossom. He placed the camera so he could catch some of the soft green background to make the bloom stand out. On the background photo, Alan found the lighting flat on this magnolia blossom, so he focused on a small leaf to give the image depth.

pocket camera magic

Learn just one tip, and you'll instantly have better photos with your compact camera.

STORY AND PHOTOS BY MARK TURNER, BELLINGHAM, WASHINGTON

Pocket cameras are wonderful. Sure, as a professional, I'm usually armed with several pounds of equipment, but smaller cameras still have their place. By following one simple tip—learning how to hold your camera—you can get amazing photos. Let me explain.

A Matter of Perspective

The position of your camera determines what is included in the frame, the perspective, and the way light and shadow play across the subject.

I could hold my small camera, or even my camera phone, out in front of me at arm's length, the way so many people do. But the result is often an uninspired photograph. With that in mind, you have to ask yourself a few questions.

Would the image be stronger if I walked closer to my subject and placed it on one side of the frame instead of in the middle? What if I bordered a distant landscape with some nearby bushes or trees for a stronger sense of depth?

Could I back up a few inches and put one blossom in the foreground, with a few dewy buds in the background? Instead of looking down at my cat, what if I crouched or lay down at her level and looked her in the eye with my camera?

Take a Little Time

Great photographs take time. Experienced photographers study their subject and explore its visual possibilities, shooting several variations. Using a single lens, I may start with an overview photo and then move in to play with the effects of different angles, focal lengths, composition or lighting. I look around and try to find a way to place my subject in a larger environment. I'll hold my camera high, then low, as well as at eye level, to vary my point of view.

As you're practicing, take your time and experiment. With digital cameras it doesn't cost anything extra to play. Back at your computer, look at your pictures and think about which ones you like best and why. Consider how you could make the inevitable clunkers better next time.

Repeat the process, and in time you'll see a significant improvement in your photographs—just by changing where you hold your camera when you press the shutter button. Oh, and one more thing: Remember to have fun along the way!

MARK TURNER PORTRAIT, DAVID E. PERRY

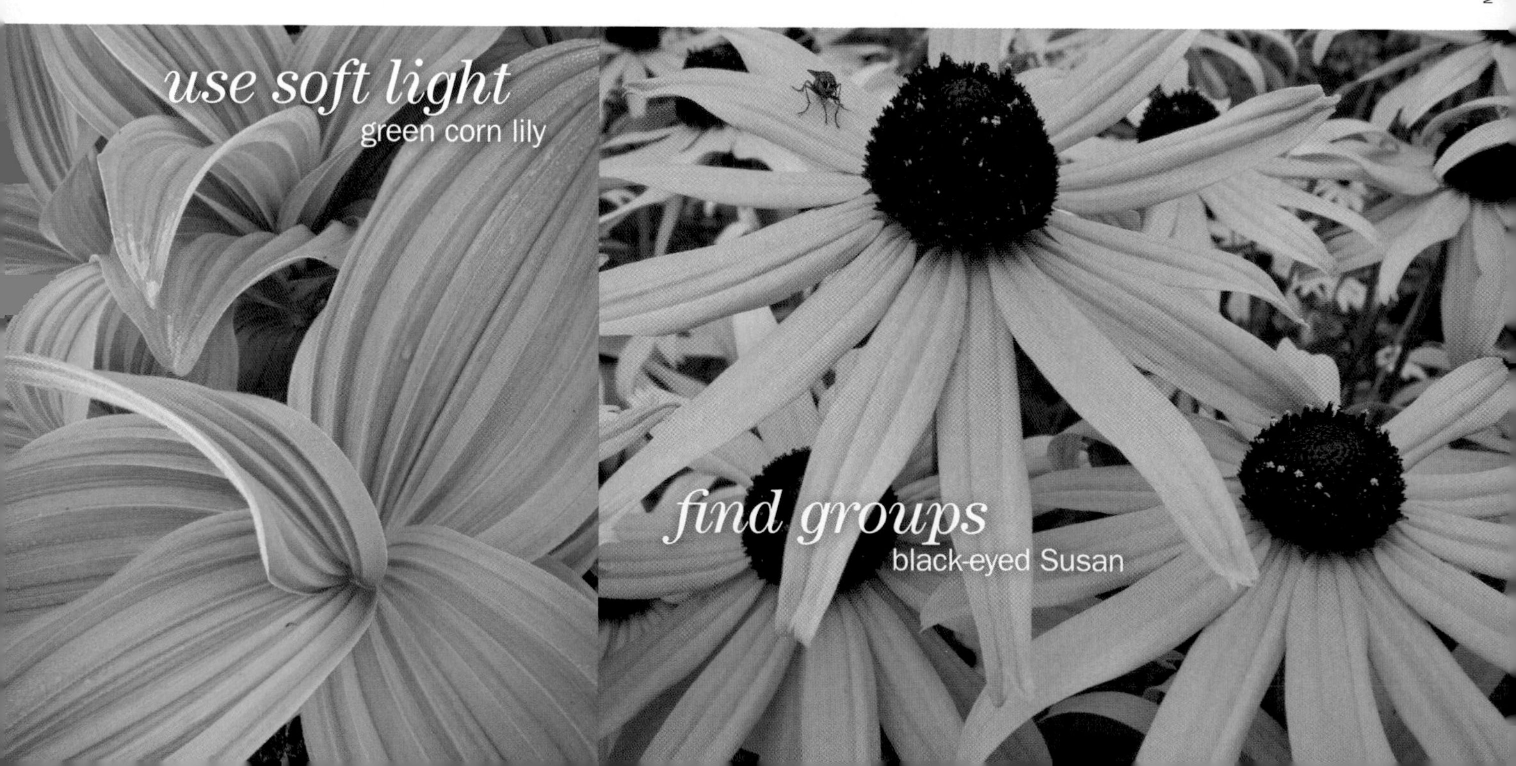

use soft light
green corn lily

find groups
black-eyed Susan

Mark's top tips

Put these tips to work for you the next time you're out photographing your garden, friends, kids or pets with your pocket camera.

1. FILL THE FRAME. Ask yourself, "What's the subject of this photo?" Then move in close so that's all you see in the frame. As a general rule, though, you don't want parts of your main subject touching the edge of the frame.

2. FIND GROUPS OF THREE. Odd-numbered assortments of flowers and other subjects are easier to arrange in pleasing compositions than even numbers. Look for triangles in the scene in front of you. They help your eyes move around the frame instead of being drawn away.

3. USE SOFT LIGHT. Flowers always look better under an overcast sky than in midday sun. Colors will be more saturated, and your camera will be able to capture detail in both bright blossoms and dark foliage. If it's a sunny day, shoot in the shade whenever you can.

4. CREATE DEPTH. Your main subject can be in the foreground, middle or background of your photo. It's important to have all three to give a three-dimensional feel to a two-dimensional photo. With garden photography, the main subject is in the foreground or middle. If It's in the middle, you might use some foliage in the foreground to lead the eye to the blossoms.

5. GET ON THE FLOWER'S LEVEL. Don't stand and shoot down at a flower or plant. Instead, get your camera down to the same level as your subject—or even below it, looking up. Getting eye to eye with your subject is almost always a good idea.

Prairie warbler
Photo by Bill Leaman

Tiger swallowtail on lilac
Photo by Rolanda Stone

Eastern bluebird
Finalist in our Backyard Photo Contest
Photo by Hazel Erikson

Ladybug on gazania
Finalist in our Backyard Photo Contest
Photo by Gina Kucharek

CHAPTER 4

Magnificent *hummingbirds*

These tiny winged treasures continue to capture readers' hearts. Read about their lives from hatching to first flight, discover the very best blooms to attract them, try photo secrets from a pro and create your own no-fuss sugar-water feeder.

TIM FITZHARRIS

TOP 10

hummingbird award winners

You're sure to lure lively hummers to your backyard with these picks from All-America Selections.

BY DANIELLE CALKINS, ASSISTANT EDITOR

Summer isn't quite complete without the cheerful buzz of hummers in your backyard. With so many plants to choose from, it can be overwhelming to pick the right ones. This is where our friends at All-America Selections can help. We looked at some of their best nectar-rich picks from past years to put together this list of award-winning annuals. Give them a try in your garden. Your hummingbirds will thank you!

1

2
3
4
5
6
7
8
9
10

1

Sparkler Blush cleome

(*Cleome hasslerana*, 2002 winner)

Not your typical cleome, this hybrid was a breeding breakthrough when it was introduced. Densely covered with pink flowers, it's more closely branched than other cleomes, giving it a denser appearance on a more compact plant.

Why we love it: The airy blush-pink florets attract not only hummingbirds, but butterflies and bees, too. It makes an excellent annual garden hedge.

2

Quartz Burgundy verbena

(*Verbena* x *hybrida*, 1999 winner)

The intense wine-colored florets will attract hummers first with their color, then with their nectar. Improved resistance to mildew means this annual will flower a lot longer than many other verbenas.

Why we love it: With a full season to blossom, this verbena will thrive in any container or hanging basket.

5

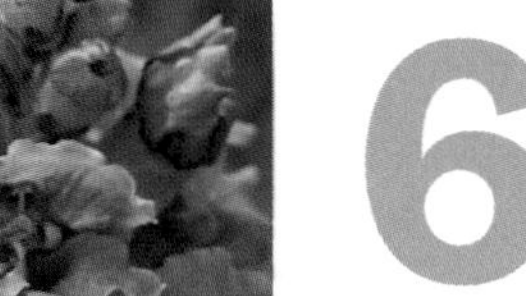

Twinny Peach snapdragon

(*Antirrhinum majus*, 2010 winner)

The shape of this variety's colorful florets makes it especially easy for hungry hummingbirds to reach the nectar. With their bewitching blend of peach, yellow and light-orange blooms, these snapdragons provide excellent coverage for both annual borders and containers.

Why we love it: These easy-care plants show exceptional tolerance to hot summer growing conditions.

6

Avalon Bright Pink nicotiana

(*Nicotiana* x *sandarae*, 2001 winner)

This dwarf variety of flowering tobacco is one of the smallest and earliest-blooming available. Plants are super-branched, providing a framework for masses of bright-pink flowers that blossom freely all summer long—a real treat for hummers!

Why we love it: The star-shaped blooms are visible from quite a distance, and the plant is virtually maintenance-free, making it perfect for both border and container planting.

9

Moonsong Deep Orange marigold

(*Tagetes erecta*, 2010 winner)

The flower color is fade-resistant and such a rich orange it makes others look pale by comparison. Easy to grow in 5- to 6-inch pots, plants will flower in about 70 to 84 days.

Why we love it: Over the summer, the old blooms will be covered with green foliage, which keeps the plants looking fresh throughout the growing season.

10

Magellan Coral zinnia

(*Zinnia elegans*, 2005 winner)

This garden zinnia produces masses of clear, bright-colored double coral blooms on bushy, well-branched plants. After the first bloom is over, it treats you to another flush of flowers, lasting all season long.

Why we love it: This is only one of six colors in the Magellan series, which performs beautifully outdoors in gardens and containers.

ALL PLANT PHOTOS COURTESY OF AAS

3

Pin Up Flame begonia

(*Begonia* x *tuberhybrida,* 1999 winner)

This stunning tuberous begonia variety produces loads of 4- to 5-inch single blossoms in a glowing combination of deep yellow with scarlet and orange edges. A prolific bloomer with good weather tolerance and durability, Pin Up Flame will give you fabulous color from summer through fall.

Why we love it: All by itself, this begonia will brighten up a shady garden. With minimal care, it's perfect for a patio container, even in your least sunny spots.

4

Supra Purple dianthus

(*Dianthus interspecific,* 2006 winner)

Exceptional, long-blooming garden performance, heat tolerance and attractive flower form and color make this winner worth considering for your garden. Hummers will be attracted to the color and to the plentiful supply of blossoms this annual produces throughout the season.

Why we love it: In addition to its grace in the garden, Supra Purple makes a lovely cut flower.

7

Evolution salvia

(*Salvia farinacea,* 2006 winner)

This variety expands the salvia color range with its lilac spikes. Hummingbirds, bees and butterflies are attracted to the well-branched, robust plants.

Why we love it: Pair it with a Lady in Red or Summer Jewel variety, and you have a hummingbird magnet!

8

Purple Wave petunia

(*Petunia* x *hybrida*, 1995 winner)

This highly popular variety has flower power to spare. The abundance of iridescent purple blossoms draws both hummingbirds and bees. Even better, it was recently improved for earlier bloom time and slightly larger flowers without sacrificing the eye-catching color.

Why we love it: This petunia has a vigorous spreading growth pattern that carpets gardens or delivers an astounding hanging basket.

How'd they get the vote?

These Top 10 plants, like all other AAS winners, are top of their class. How does it work, exactly? AAS is an organization made up of seed-industry professionals, and they conduct confidential and impartial trials of never-before-sold seed varieties throughout North America.

They grow established varieties next to the new entries for a comparison of growth habit, flower or fruit size and many other factors. Only the best performers—eight in 2011—are declared AAS Winners.

Sugar-Water feeder in a jar

Turn a recycled baby food jar into a pretty, practical hummingbird feeder.

BY KRIS DRAKE, SANTEE, CALIFORNIA

What You Will Need

- Shallow jar with lid
- Polymer clay (including red)
- Flower-shaped cookie cutters
- 16-gauge galvanized wire
- Drill
- Needle-nose pliers
- Rolling pin
- Glass beads

Hummingbirds are easy to please. They don't require a fancy feeder or a special mixture. This sugar-water feeder cost me just pennies to make. I used an empty baby food jar and some craft supplies I already had lying around. This is a fun project you can finish in just a few hours, and it's ideal for kids, too. Good luck attracting hummingbirds!

1. First, be sure to clean out your jar thoroughly. I used a baby food jar, but you can recycle anything you have around the kitchen. Shallow jars are the easiest to keep clean and filled.

2. Next, use a rolling pin to flatten the clay. I like to use three different colors. Take whatever color you want to be the base of your flower and press the top of the jar lid into it to remove any air pockets. Then trim any excess clay away and smooth clay down the sides of the lid.

3. Using the other clay colors, design the flower to go on top of this base. Have fun rolling out the colors and playing with different shapes and designs. You can use cookie cutters if you'd like, or just freestyle it. Just remember that hummingbirds are attracted to the color red, so be sure that's part of your palette.

4. After you've cut out the clay, experiment with layering. This helps give the illusion of a real flower, which will bring in the hummingbirds!

5. Gently press the layers of clay onto the lid base. You don't want to push too hard because it will smudge your design, but you do want the layers of clay to fuse when you bake them.

6. Bake according to the directions on the clay you are using. A pretty good approximation is to bake at 275° for 15 minutes.

7. Allow the clay to cool, and then drill a small hole through the top of the clay flower lid. This will give the hummingbirds access to the nectar.

8. Cut about 32 in. of wire, and then fold in half, leaving a loop at the top.

9. Make a larger loop with each end of the wire, then bring them together and twist about eight times. Play with the shape of the loops until you have a design you like. Wrap each end of the wire around the jar, bringing them together and twisting three times, making a tight loop to hold the feeder. Trim away the excess wire, leaving about ¼ in. for a loop to add beads. Fill with nectar and enjoy the show!

RDA-MKE

WAITING *for hummingbirds*

This wildlife photographer is living proof that good things come to those who wait.

STORY AND PHOTOS BY STEVE BYLAND, SOMERSET, NEW JERSEY

Hummingbirds are some of the most entertaining, enjoyable and easy birds to photograph. Yes, I really did say "easy." Even though they're tiny and move at lightning-fast speed, all it takes is a little planning to capture memorable hummingbird photos.

Now, this hasn't always been my mantra. I've been a wildlife photographer for years, and I used to have a horrible time trying to attract hummingbirds. In fact, I probably spent more than 10 years trying all the textbook advice, with no success.

I planted bee balm, cardinal flowers and every other red bloom at my garden center, but the only action at my sugar-water feeders was from ants and bees. Like many people, I just assumed there weren't hummingbirds in my area. I was ready to give up altogether, but then I finally had a breakthrough.

Trying Something Different

In all my studying, I learned that the most important part of attracting hummingbirds is providing them with a reliable source of food. I had tried this before, offering a combination of flowers and feeders, but it never worked. So what was I doing wrong? With a little more research, I discovered that ruby-throated hummingbirds migrate through my area from around mid-April through mid-May. Then it occurred to me—I have almost no flowers in April! And the few that I do have aren't on the list of hummingbird favorites.

As it turns out, many hummingbirds migrate to their breeding grounds before most flowers are in bloom, so the birds rely on insects, sap and other food sources. I decided it was time to try something different.

RUBY VISITORS. Since Steve lives in the East, he has only ruby-throated hummingbirds in his yard (like the male above and female at left). He said that it took him more than 10 years to attract them, but that they definitely were worth the wait.

Steve's **flower advice**

What flowers work for me? Almost any trumpet-shaped bloom seems to keep them coming back. And for some reason, they just love lantana, especially the red ones, like those at right. Other plants that work well for me are butterfly bush, because it blooms all summer, as well as cardinal flowers and trumpet vines.

KNOW YOUR CAMERA. Once you have the right elements in place, it's easy to get memorable hummingbird photos (like these below). Get to know your camera and play around with shutter speeds to find out what works.

feeder *with a view*

When hummingbirds do find a feeder, they often linger for a day or two before moving on. Try placing a feeder on a pole right in the middle of the yard so that they can see it from far away.

The following April, I went to my garden center and bought two hanging baskets—one with small red and yellow petunias and the other with lantana, which I had to take in at night if frost was expected. At the same time, I also put out two feeders filled with sugar water.

Within just a few short days, a male hummingbird claimed the feeders and the flowers as his own. A week or two later, I saw his mate. It was an instant success—as long as you don't count my previous 10 years without a single hummer!

Now, years later, I've been enticing hummingbirds each spring using this same method. In addition to setting out feeders, I plant or pot a variety of flowers to ensure that something bright will be blooming from April through September.

A Window of Opportunity

If you, too, want visits from these tiny charmers, remember that planning and patience are key. Birds in spring tend to be in a hurry to get to their breeding grounds, so unless you're lucky, they might not stay long.

The southbound migration that begins in early August and ends in mid-September is a much more leisurely journey. Even on the East Coast, where there are fewer hummers than out West, I often see a dozen or more ruby-throated hummingbirds on an August day, and I may take more than a thousand photos in a single afternoon.

Now it's time to get to work! With a few of my secrets, you can take your own hummingbird photos that will impress your family and make your friends envious. When they ask how you got such terrific photos, just smile and tell them that you planned months in advance, because you did!

GLASS FEEDER: SOUTH12THPHOTOGRAPHY / SHUTTERSTOCK.COM; ALL OTHER PHOTOS: STEVE BYLAND

great photo secrets

Hummingbirds are fearless and are creatures of habits, which makes them easy subjects to photograph. Here are some of my best tips for capturing photos you'll prize.

Remove perches for hovering shots.

SET UP YOUR CAMERA WITHIN 10 FEET OF A FEEDER THAT IS GETTING ACTIVITY. Once the birds have found the feeder, you can move it to a location with good light and a pleasing background.

STUDY THE HABITS OF EACH BIRD THAT VISITS. Does it drink steadily at the feeder? Does it drink for a second, then pull back to swallow? Take your photos when birds are hovering in one spot—they can hold surprisingly still when they hover. Hummingbirds can be very predictable in their feeding habits. I can almost set my watch by some of my birds.

SIT QUIETLY IN A CHAIR. Hummingbirds aren't much afraid of people. If you minimize your movement, they should get used to you very quickly. I like to use a blind, which keeps me out of the sun. Hanging a sheet between you and the feeder works, too.

Place tape over all but one of the ports on the feeder to **BRING THE BIRDS TO THE EXACT SPOT THAT YOU WANT THEM.**

If you want shots of hummingbirds in flight, **REMOVE THE PERCHES** from the feeder.

If you want photos of the birds drinking from flowers, **PLACE A SINGLE CUT FLOWER IN WATER NEAR THE FEEDER.** Chances are, they'll investigate it.

PAY ATTENTION TO YOUR BACKGROUNDS. Green grass in the distance makes for a nice backdrop. Hanging baskets or flats of flowers placed far enough away to be out of focus can make for colorful photos.

Unless you really need one, **DON'T WORRY ABOUT USING A FLASH.** There is generally enough natural light to get fine shots. No flash also allows for rapid-fire shooting with many of today's cameras.

Cut flowers and place them where you want the shot to happen.

the lure of columbines

Learn why this hardy perennial is the perfect choice for hummingbirds.

BY SALLY ROTH, CONTRIBUTING EDITOR

I'm often a few days late when it comes to putting up my hummingbird feeder in spring. First I have to remember where I stored it at the end of the season, then I have to round up the little yellow bee guards that rolled way back in the corner, then I have to find a new piece of wire to replace the hanger I forgot to fix before packing it away last season.

But I don't feel too guilty about not having the feeder out when the first birds arrive, because my columbines fill the gap with splashes of alluring red.

Native red columbines are simple to grow, they bloom for months and they flourish in sun or shade. Start with red species, but don't stop there. Columbines come in just about any color you can dream up, and hummers visit them all.

HUMMINGBIRDS AND COLUMBINE. Whether you plant purple, white, pink or red columbines, hummingbirds love them all (as you can see from this juvenile ruby-throat, left). The plants are a reliable nectar source all season.

Cultivating Columbines

Buy potted plants, or start them from seed. I simply scatter the seeds in an open spot in my garden in fall, then let the weather work the seeds into the soil.

Columbines need no coddling to bloom their hearts out. They'll even sow themselves into crevices in a rock wall or paving. When your columbines start to look tired after a season of bloom, cut off the entire plant about 3 inches above soil level, and fresh leaves will soon grow.

When you take a closer look at different kinds of columbines, you'll see variations in the length, width and angle of those "spurs" that the petals form. The position of the blossoms varies, too. Some hang straight down, others dangle at an angle and some face outward or upward instead.

Think of the columbine clan as a buffet laid out for pollinators. Each insect that visits this assortment of flowers gets to choose the dish that suits it best. White Sierra columbine, for instance, holds its flowers facing up. At night, those ghostly blossoms

HUMMINGBIRD, BARBARA MAGNUSON / LARRY KIMBALL; BLUE COLUMBINE, ISTOCKPHOTO.COM / KIPP SCHOEN; RED COLUMBINE, LINDA FRESHWATER ARNDT

beckon to long-tongued sphinx moths, which hover above them.

Rich blue columbines call to bumblebees with their irresistible hue, then follow through on that invitation with shorter, wider spurs that accommodate their hungry visitors. Hummers head for red ones first but will dip their bills into any columbine in hopes of finding nectar, so any variety is a good one for your garden.

Taken by Surprise

I love columbines of any kind, but my sentimental favorite is the cottage garden variety (*Aquilegia vulgaris*) that I first fell in love with in my mother's garden more than a half-century ago. Each year's crop of self-sown seedlings brought the possibility of new shapes and colors, because columbines crossbreed willy-nilly.

Columbine seedlings might look like their parent, but don't count on it. Waiting for self-sown columbines to come into bloom the following year is like watching kittens being born. Maybe you'll get a pure-white flower among a patch of blue companions, or a deep purple-black, or a frilly pink. It's all part of the joy of growing columbines.

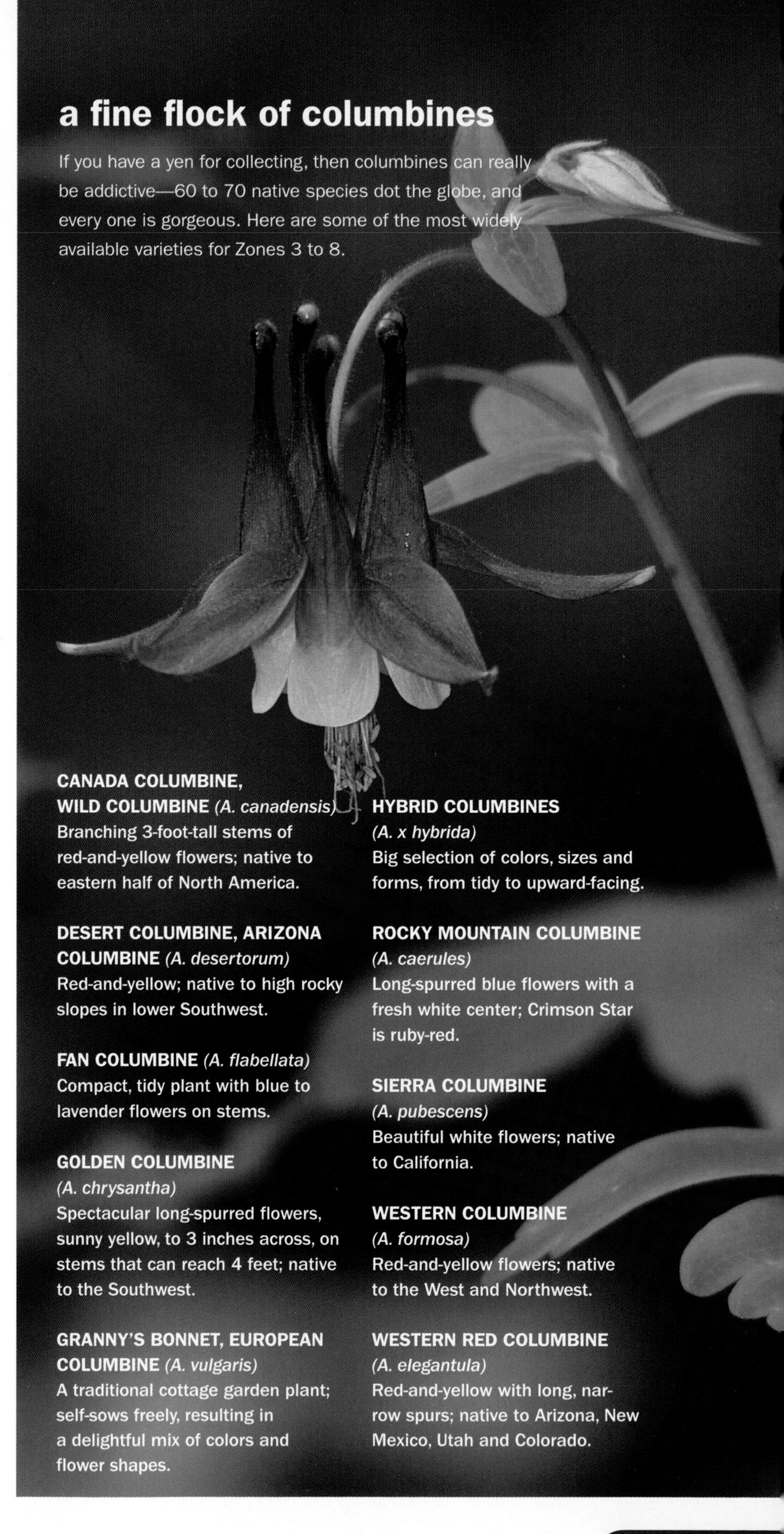

a fine flock of columbines

If you have a yen for collecting, then columbines can really be addictive—60 to 70 native species dot the globe, and every one is gorgeous. Here are some of the most widely available varieties for Zones 3 to 8.

CANADA COLUMBINE, WILD COLUMBINE *(A. canadensis)*
Branching 3-foot-tall stems of red-and-yellow flowers; native to eastern half of North America.

DESERT COLUMBINE, ARIZONA COLUMBINE *(A. desertorum)*
Red-and-yellow; native to high rocky slopes in lower Southwest.

FAN COLUMBINE *(A. flabellata)*
Compact, tidy plant with blue to lavender flowers on stems.

GOLDEN COLUMBINE *(A. chrysantha)*
Spectacular long-spurred flowers, sunny yellow, to 3 inches across, on stems that can reach 4 feet; native to the Southwest.

GRANNY'S BONNET, EUROPEAN COLUMBINE *(A. vulgaris)*
A traditional cottage garden plant; self-sows freely, resulting in a delightful mix of colors and flower shapes.

HYBRID COLUMBINES *(A. x hybrida)*
Big selection of colors, sizes and forms, from tidy to upward-facing.

ROCKY MOUNTAIN COLUMBINE *(A. caerules)*
Long-spurred blue flowers with a fresh white center; Crimson Star is ruby-red.

SIERRA COLUMBINE *(A. pubescens)*
Beautiful white flowers; native to California.

WESTERN COLUMBINE *(A. formosa)*
Red-and-yellow flowers; native to the West and Northwest.

WESTERN RED COLUMBINE *(A. elegantula)*
Red-and-yellow with long, narrow spurs; native to Arizona, New Mexico, Utah and Colorado.

Discover the making of this award-winning hummingbird book and movie.

STORY AND PHOTOS BY
NORIKO AND DON CARROLL
LAS VEGAS, NEVADA

a humming

When we first encountered Honey, a female black-chinned hummingbird, it was April 2002 and the fragrant star jasmine was in bloom. It was the day we moved from our photo studio in New York City to our house in Las Vegas. We noticed a handwritten sign on the back porch, with an arrow pointing up: "Be Careful! Hummingbird's Nest Above!"

As we looked up, Honey flew in. Her tiny nest, about the size of a walnut, was built on a clothesline, with an old clothespin as a stabilizer. Excited, we grabbed our photo equipment and started setting it up. Honey curiously hovered over us to inspect each new item popping up around her nest.

Not long after that, we saw her gripping the edges of the nest. Soon one pearly white egg, then a day later a second, emerged from her tiny body and slipped into the softness of the nest. Each was the size of a coffee bean.

Our strategically mounted cameras captured the many wonders that followed: two minute baby hummingbirds kicking through their paper-thin eggshells, Honey feeding them the nectar and pollen she energetically gathered, and finally the fledglings' first flight

CAPTURING A MOMENT. When Noriko and Don noticed Honey's nest on a clothesline in their Las Vegas backyard, they knew they had to capture the moment. They chronicled the journey over the course of several years, capturing every moment from Honey building her nest to the egg hatching. Below, you can see this series through their photography.

bird story

and their own forays into gathering nectar and insects.

But because no wild creature takes direction, it took us three spring nesting cycles to document the complete process to our satisfaction. The result was our 2006 book, *First Flight: A Mother Hummingbird's Story* (Andrews McMeel Publishing, $14.95).

We thought that was the end of the story—but Honey came back on the nest and gave us another opportunity. This time we decided to shoot a high-definition video. On the first morning we set up a video camera, Honey flew into the nest as the sun rose slowly, painting her in a pastel glow. It was the most beautiful light a photographer could wish for.

In the process of shooting both the book and the video, and after consultations with ornithologists and birders, we learned more about hummingbirds than we ever dreamed we'd know. The former owner of the house told us that the nest was first built in 2000. It became taller each year as Honey added more reinforcing material, mostly soft plant fibers bound with sticky bits of spiderweb she collected from our porch and yard. When we observed Honey in close-ups, her dedication to her nest and her chicks became even more obvious.

Through the book and the DVD, also called *First Flight*, Honey's charm and that of her chicks have captured hearts worldwide. The film has won awards at international wildlife and nature film festivals, and we are currently working on Spanish, French, German and Japanese versions. Though we came to Las Vegas to continue our careers as advertising photographers, the making and marketing of the book and video have put everything else on the back burner.

We finished editing the video in early 2009, and that was the last year we saw Honey on the nest. We'd noticed that, in the last season or two, she seemed to have a bit less energy when she returned from her winter migrations to Mexico, so we knew her visits were numbered.

But we continue to see hummingbirds flittering through our patio and yard. And we have no doubt that among them are Honey's offspring.

You can see a trailer of the Carrolls' DVD, First Flight: A Mother Hummingbird's Story, *including the hatching sequence, at* hummingbirdstory.com. *The site also includes ordering information for the book and the DVD.*

GROWING UP. Once the young hummingbirds hatched in Honey's nest, the entertainment really began. Below, Honey feeds insects to her young. At right, the two nestlings have outgrown their nest and are just about to fledge. Far right, one of the juveniles tries out its wings. The series of photos and the story are available in both book and DVD. Learn more at *hummingbirdstory.com*.

captivating & colorful

Attract hummingbirds with a few containers filled with their favorite plants.

Even small spaces can burst with plants that hummingbirds love. Try placing a few containers filled with nectar-rich or brightly colored plants near your nectar feeders for an instant hummingbird haven that will boost bird traffic!

Purple Pleaser

Hummingbirds go gaga over the Superbells® line of calibrachoa from Proven Winners. This delightful plum color blends nicely with the sweet potato vine and the purple of the petunias. Plant this combination in a 12-inch container and hummingbirds will be frequent guests.

A. Superbells® Plum calibrachoa (1)
B. Sweet Caroline Sweetheart Red sweet potato vine (1)
C. Supertunia® Priscilla® petunia (1)

Tropical Twist

Add a hint of the tropics to your backyard with a container filled with elephant ear, coleus and calibrachoa. Substitute any coleus for the ones listed. A red petunia-like flower—use any you have on hand—helps make this 24-inch container one that hummingbirds will love.

A. Upright elephant ear (1)
B. Jurassic Dark™ elephant ear (1)
C. Dappled Apple™ coleus (1)
D. Superbells® Red calibrachoa (1)
E. Religious Radish coleus (1)
F. Splash coleus (1)
G. Goldilocks creeping Jenny (1)

economical **ant deterrents**

Get rid of ants at your sugar-water feeder once and for all with these clever reader ideas.

As I peel oranges, I save the peels and place them in a small yellow bowl near the hummingbird feeder. Not only do ants appear to dislike the color yellow, but it seems to keep them from climbing up the tree and eating the sugar water. —**ANNA VICTORIA REICH** *Stafford, Virginia*

I found a way that seems to work for keeping ants out of my hummingbird feeders. I put a small shepherd's hook in a flowerpot, and then I hang the feeders from the hook. If I put the bottom of the hook directly into the ground, I still get ants. But when I put the hook in a flowerpot and then set it on my deck, I don't get any!
—**DAMIEN WISSOLIK** *Gibsonia, Pennsylvania*

If ants have found your feeder, don't despair. I've found they will not cross a line of chalk! I use sidewalk chalk, and it really works. Simply refresh it after it rains to keep the pesky ants away. —**JANE DUNKIN**, *Manzanita, Oregon*

I use Avon's Skin So Soft to keep ants away from my feeder. Of course, after a good rain, you'll need to reapply. Similar oils should work, too.
—**VIRGINIA HARMON**, *Antioch, Illinois*

My sugar-water feeders kept dripping, causing ants to congregate beneath them. I kept buying new feeders, thinking there was a crack in the plastic, when I suddenly realized that the plastic must be expanding in the heat and allowing air to seep in the neck of the bottle.

To fix this, I used a roll of Teflon pipe tape of the type plumbers use for a waterproof seal. I wrapped the neck of the bottle with a layer before screwing the plastic base on, and it worked! I now have no more wasted sugar water and no ants! —**PAT BENNETT** *Warwick, New York*

I tried everything to keep the ants away from my hummingbird feeder, but nothing seemed to work. Finally, I found a solution by taking a cotton ball, spraying it with insect repellant and securing it to the top of the line with a plastic bag tie. This worked. I haven't had problems with ants since.
—**ANNIE JANE FOLSOM** *Hahira, Georgia*

We made this hummingbird feeding station (above) from an old light fixture we had in the attic, along with some leftover red paint. Then we hung four feeders from it and placed it in the center of our garden arbor.

Of course, we didn't forget about the pesky ants that always seem to invade sugar-water feeders. To avoid this, we caulked the bowl-shaped part of the fixture at the top of the chain to make an ant moat. Now we just fill the top with water and the ants can't get down to take over the feeder. The birds love this, and we get a show every day. —**ARCHIE HAZEL** *Jonesboro, Illinois*

CHALK, ROBYN MACKENZIE / SHUTTERSTOCK.COM; ANT, EVGENIY AYUPOV / SHUTTERSTOCK.COM

hummer happenings

Enjoy the best hummingbird stories and photos from readers.

Bottle Bound

This hummer flew directly behind the glass bottle of our feeder just as my husband, Alfred, snapped a picture. Except for the tip of the bill, it looks as if the bird is inside the bottle, almost like a fish in a fishbowl!

—**NONA KELLEY CARVER,** *Mesa, Colorado*

Sticky Situation

We put jelly out for the orioles, and last summer we were shocked to find a juvenile hummingbird stuck bottom-first in the jelly. At first we didn't think it was alive, but when I touched its head, it immediately opened its mouth.

I carefully washed it off, and when I tried feeding it sugar water, it immediately put its little bill in the eyedropper and started drinking like crazy. My two granddaughters watched and occasionally petted its little head.

The young hummer worked its wings but couldn't seem to get into the air. My husband brought a dish of warm water, and I very gently removed the bird from my finger.

After it had splashed around for a few minutes, I put it back on my finger. This time it flapped its wings faster, making a buzzing sound. It rose up a little, then landed back on my finger. Then it flew straight up and into the trees. I was elated to see it all!

—**VICKIE ROMSKA,** *Lake, Michigan*

Insect Invader

One morning a hummingbird kept fussing, flying from me to the feeder. I told the bird that the feeder was full, but it kept whizzing back and forth. I wondered if there might be a bee or wasp on the feeder, so I investigated. There, sitting on the top, was a praying mantis! I removed it with a stick, and the hummer zipped to the feeder, free to feast without fear.

—**MARIE VALDEZ,** *Seguin, Texas*

▲ What an Act!

My sister sent me this photo of her husband, Ralph, and his little friends. She amazed me with tales of these hummers landing and sitting on him! Both retired, they like telling people they're going to Vegas with their show to subsidize their income!

—**MARY TIPTON**, *Teaneck, New Jersey*

Star Attraction ▶

A different-looking hummingbird appeared in my backyard in September 2004, and for months she drew in bird-watchers aplenty. Though ruby-throated hummingbirds began migrating, this unusual hummer that we named Hannah stayed.

September gave way to October, and as flowers faded I hung out more sugar-water feeders, and this ever-curious flier visited every single one. By mid-November, with the help of licensed bird bander Allen Chartier, we determined that Hannah was a first-year rufous hummingbird, likely hatched in Alaska or British Columbia. Hannah had taken a wrong turn and ended up in my backyard!

Birders from all over Ontario and New York state and as far away as Ohio came to view our celebrity flier. Nature clubs and field-tripping ornithologists arrived en masse; more than 500 people signed Hannah's guestbook.

Unfortunately, even though we supplied winter shelter and placed a heater by Hannah's feeder, she died on Dec. 18. Ornithologists from the University of Guelph carried her remains to the Royal Ontario Museum, where she is being kept as a specimen to be studied by researchers. Though I miss Hannah, I will always remember the joy she brought and the wonderful people who came to visit this star of our gardens!

—**JANICE HAINES**, *Niagara Falls, Ontario*

Seeing Red

My hummingbird feeder and regular bird feeder hang side by side outside my kitchen window. Last summer, while I watched a male cardinal eat seed from his feeder, a hummingbird flew in and landed on the cardinal's back! I guess it's true that hummers are attracted to *anything* red.

—**THELMA SCOTT**, *Meadows of Dan, Virginia*

◀ Hummer Heaven

We live in southeastern Arizona, seven miles from the Mexican border, in the foothills of the Huachuca Mountains. If you love hummingbirds, plan to visit our area, which we like to call the Hummingbird Capital of the U.S. We regularly see 14 species, plus occasional "accidentals" from Mexico. Our rarest sighting was a bee hummingbird; too bad we didn't have the camera handy. But other species provide excellent snapshot opportunities, like these photos of a rufous and of a magnificent with a black-chinned.

—**LINDA GRANT**, *Patagonia, Arizona*

hummer happenings

◀ Hold It!

After years of attempting to photograph hummingbirds hovering over the window feeder, I decided to try something new. I cut some fresh flowers short, with 3-inch stems, and put one in each feeding port. I was surprised how well it worked! Unable to fit their bills in the ports, the birds jockeyed around, above, below and sideways, hovering for moments in between. One male Anna's slammed into a flower, perhaps trying to shove it out of the way! I snapped a few quick photos, then ran to remove the flowers so my little friends could refresh themselves.

—**DESIREE SKATVOLD**, *Livermore, California*

God's Creatures

I'd never seen a hummingbird nest, although they are my favorite birds. Then one fall, while on holiday in Los Cabos, Mexico, I saw one—in a church! During Sunday Mass, I noticed movement in the chandelier directly above our heads. A female hummingbird briefly left her nest and returned. What a perfect experience!

—**LUCY BEAUCHAMP**, *Barrie, Ontario*

Faint Little Friend ▶

One late afternoon, I heard a faint cry coming from my hummingbird feeder. A young hummingbird was trying to reach the holes but couldn't. When it saw me, it flew across the yard and landed on a rose.

The bird tried unsuccessfully to feed from the rose, then made several more attempts to find food, even investigating a red leaf on the ground.

Early the next morning, I went outside and heard a faint squeak coming from a hanging basket, where the bird was huddled, eyes closed. I tried feeding it with a dropper bottle of sugar water, but it didn't have the strength to drink droplets. Then I inserted its bill into the dropper spout, and it finally responded.

After 45 minutes I had to leave, but on my return I saw that it had left the hanging basket. I like to believe I helped it grow into one of the healthy hummers that flutter around my head when I fill their feeder.

—**GINGER ENGLISH**, *Bauxite, Arkansas*

Shot of a Lifetime I've taken plenty of hummingbird pictures in my 70 years, but I always hoped for one extra-special shot. One day, as I watched this male ruby-throat feeding through my camera lens, a female approached and the male flipped backward. I can't tell you how excited I am to have caught this moment. —**JOYCE TRUMBO**, *Blanchard, Oklahoma*

Helpless Little Hummer

Several years ago we had a cold, wet spell in spring. Looking out my window, I saw a female rufous sitting motionless on the feeder perch. At first I thought she was just cold and sitting there to rest.

After some time she was still there, and I became concerned. Looking more closely, I noticed she had something stuck halfway up her bill. I figured she'd be able to get it off herself, but after more minutes passed, I saw that her eyes were closed, and my heart began to sink, thinking she was in real trouble.

When my husband, Ray, and I went out to inspect her, I saw she was in a predicament! A small berry was impaled on her bill. It had dried into a hard little vise that prevented her from opening her bill. By then my tears were flowing—I needed to help!

I gently broke apart the berry, peeling it off her bill. Then I put some sugar water in a shallow jar lid and brought it to her. In doing so, I noticed the hummingbird's dried-up little tongue. Not knowing what else to do, I wet my finger and used it to moisten her tongue. After a few minutes, her tongue became soft and flexible, and she was able to eat.

By the time the operation was over, the sun was out. I set our little patient on the warm car hood. Still not knowing if she had recovered, we were thrilled to see her fly off through the tree branches at full speed, happy to be alive. What a joy and privilege it was to help out one of God's precious creatures! —**JANET HERRIOTT**
Kalispell, Montana

▲ Long-Awaited Photo

For years I have watched the ruby-throated hummingbird antics at my feeders and have taken pictures of them when I get a chance. I've never seen a hummingbird with its bill open before, so one day I decided to catch some feeding in front of my window, and I got a real treat. Finally, a hummer with its bill open! And a picture to prove it.

—**ALLEN BARLOW**, *Midland, Michigan*

Broad-tailed hummingbird
Photo by Barbara Magnuson / Larry Kimball

Rufous hummingbird
Photo by Tim Fitzharris

Ruby-throated hummingbird
Photo by Jerry Acton

Broad-tailed hummingbird
Photo by Barbara Magnuson / Larry Kimball

Ruby-throated hummingbird
Photo by Bud Hensley

CHAPTER 5

FAB *flowers & foliage*

Find the top plant picks to add color and interest to your backyard throughout the year, uncover the most fragrant blooms, grow eye-catching perennial grasses and create a colorful winter garden.

PROVEN WINNERS, PROVENWINNERS.COM

TOP 10

absolute ALL-STARS

We asked Birds & Blooms *readers what their favorite plants are, and this is the result: our ultimate Top 10 list!*

BY CRYSTAL RENNICKE, SENIOR EDITOR

It's hard to pick your favorite anything, let alone your favorite flower or plant from the thousands available for your garden. We asked our readers to choose their favorites in each of the following categories. With everything they've got going for them, it's easy to see why these winners rose to the top.

1

LUKIYANOVA NATALIA / FRENTA / SHUTTERSTOCK.COM

2
3
4
5
6
7
8
9
10

1 favorite annual

Sunflower

(*Helianthus annuus,* annual)

The cheerful petals and abundant seeds of sunflowers are as popular with birds and wildlife as they are with gardeners. This summer bloomer grows 2 to 15 feet tall and comes in an array of yellows, whites, reds and golds. Sow seeds directly outdoors after your last frost date; some of these beauties grow to 15 feet tall in one season!

Why we love it: Charming, easygoing sunflowers are great fun for kids to grow. They give you some height in the garden, and they provide a feast for birds!

2 favorite hummingbird flower

Bee balm

(*Monarda didyma,* Zones 4 to 9)

It's no wonder readers picked bee balm as their favorite hummingbird flower. This showy plant has red, violet, purple, pink or white tubular blossoms that teem with nectar. It grows 3 to 4 feet high in full sun and quickly spreads to fill in garden space. Many cultivars are resistant to powdery mildew.

Why we love it: Bee balm's glorious colors and nectar-rich blooms are a guaranteed lure for hummingbirds.

5 favorite butterfly flower

Butterfly bush

(*Buddleja davidii,* Zones 5 to 9)

When you see a butterfly bush, chances are you'll see a butterfly or hummingbird nearby. The sweetly scented purple, white, pink or yellow tubular blooms are filled with nectar for these flying jewels. Growing 3 to 15 feet high, butterfly bush will bloom from midsummer through the first frost. Take note, this beauty is invasive in some areas.

Why we love it: It's the perfect plant for attracting birds, butterflies and bees—and it's beautiful, too.

6 favorite perennial

Daylily

(*Hemerocallis,* Zones 3 to 10)

There are few flowers as dependable in the summer garden as the daylily. These carefree perennials grow 1 to 4 feet tall and wide and are highly adaptable, although they do best in rich, well-draining soil. With colorful trumpet-shaped blooms and grassy leaves, daylilies are a sure way to brighten perennial beds and borders.

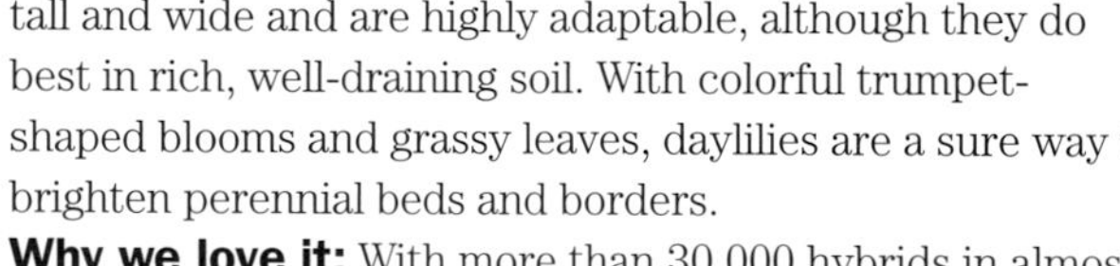

Why we love it: With more than 30,000 hybrids in almost every shade but blue, many of which are rebloomers, it's easy to find a daylily that suits your style.

2, 4, 5, 6, 7, 9, 10: PERENNIALRESOURCE.COM; 1, 3: RDA-GID; 8, HILDA SMITH; SUNFLOWERS: WOLGIN / SHUTTERSTOCK

effortless feeding

We have a bird feeder on the far end of our backyard, so getting to it during our snowy winters is a challenge. Our solution was to grow sunflowers in the summer using black oil sunflower seeds. Once the sunflowers were full of seeds, we harvested them and stored the heads in a large, dry container.

During the winter, instead of plowing a path to the feeder, we toss the entire sunflower head into the yard. This eliminates the cost of purchasing seed at the store, and I don't get snow in my boots when I want to feed the birds!

—DONNA ADCOCK, RIGBY, IDAHO

3 favorite bulb

Daffodil

(*Narcissus,* Zones 2 to 9)
In many backyards, daffodils are the first to show their pretty yellow or white heads in spring. Growing 6 to 20 inches high, they're planted in early fall in the North and late fall in the South. Bury the bulbs at a depth two to three times their diameter and 4 to 8 inches apart.

Why we love it: Easy to grow no matter what soil you have, daffodil bulbs are also toxic, so deer, squirrels and rabbits tend to leave them alone.

4 favorite shade plant

Bleeding heart

(*Dicentra spectabilis,* Zones 2 to 9)
It's easy to fall in love with this perennial's delicate heart-shaped flowers. Long-lasting pink, white or bicolor blooms open in late spring. These 2- to 3-foot-tall plants do best in shaded areas but will tolerate a little sun if the soil is moist.

Why we love it: The delightful blooms burst forth even in full shade and readily self-seed, ensuring a heartwarming display each spring.

7 favorite drought-tolerant plant

Black-eyed Susan

(*Rudbeckia,* varies—most are Zones 3 to 9)
A fuss-free flower that thrives even when water is at a minimum, black-eyed Susans are a delight in the perennial garden. Yellow, orange and russet petals surround black-brown or green centers on 1- to 6-foot-high stems. Grow them in full sun by sowing seeds directly into the soil in early spring or fall.

Why we love it: Once established, these bright beauties require nearly no additional work. Some grow up to 6 feet tall in full sun!

8 favorite tree or shrub with berries

Dogwood

(*Cornus florida,* Zones 5 to 8)
One of spring's loveliest sights is a flowering dogwood in bloom. While its true flowers are small and green, the colorful pink, white or rosy-red bracts put on a gorgeous display. In fall, the foliage turns pink, deep red or purple. Not overwhelming in size, it grows up to 20 feet high and 25 feet wide.

Why we love it: In summer, the bright-red berries are a magnet for birds and wildlife.

9 favorite foliage plant

Hosta

(*Hosta,* Zones 3 to 8)
Hostas have it all: They're low-maintenance and shade-loving and can be budget-friendly. The fabulous foliage comes in endless colors, textures, sizes and shapes, growing 4 inches to 3 feet high and 6 inches to 6 feet wide. It can easily be divided and requires minimal care.

Why we love it: Don't have much time to fuss in the garden? Hostas are survivors. With new varieties introduced regularly, you're sure to find one you love.

10 favorite vine

Clematis

(*Clematis,* Zones 4 to 9)
This versatile vine grows 4 to 30 feet high and 3 feet wide. Available in dozens of colors, including whites, pinks, reds, purples, blues and yellows, clematis vines are perfect for a spot in the yard that needs a little vertical interest.

Why we love it: Need something to cover or decorate your mailbox, lamppost, arbor or trellis? Clematis is simple to train and bears a lot of blossoms on one vine.

backyard color guide

Learn which hues will attract wildlife to your garden. BY SALLY ROTH, CONTRIBUTING EDITOR

It seems as if I'm always fiddling with my flowers, prying out the flaming-red azalea that's always been in the wrong spot, or moving wild columbines across the yard.

Rearranging is half the fun of gardening for me, but hummers don't give a whit about the beauty of our gardens. To them, flowers are nothing but food.

When I shift their favorites, such as that azalea and those columbines, I'm moving their dinner plate. Come spring, they'll be hovering at the old location of the plants, just as they do when I'm a little late getting their feeder back into its place.

Luckily, no matter how often we rearrange our plants, there's a major clue that shows hummingbirds and other nectar-seeking garden visitors where the food is—color.

Birds and the Bees

We all know that hummingbirds can't resist investigating the color red. Whether it's a plastic feeder, a tall stem of a canna or a dab of bright lipstick, the tiny birds zoom to the hue.

Almost all flowers that depend on hummers for pollination are red or orange-red. Their nectar is held deep inside a long tube, where it's inaccessible to other pollinators. No wonder hummers hone in on red—a sweet payoff is practically guaranteed.

Not so for bees. Bumblebees, mason bees and our other buzzy friends see the ultraviolet spectrum. To their eyes, vivid red hummingbird flowers simply blend into the background. It's blue that inspires a beeline—especially deep blue and blue-purple.

Butterflies and Other Insects

While bees get the blues, butterflies wing their way to purple and yellow.

HUMMINGBIRD, BUTTERFLY: KELLY S. ANDREWS; MOONFLOWER, BILL JOHNSON; BLACK-EYED SUSAN, ISTOCKPHOTO.COM / WENDY HOLDEN; PETUNIA, HYACINTH: RDA-GID; COLUMBINE, BALL HORTICULTURE; WILD GINGER, MARK TURNER

A CLUE FROM THE HUES. Red will always attract hummingbirds, as shown by the bee balm and ruby-throated hummingbird at left. Above, a gulf fritillary is drawn to this yellow lantana bloom.

Countless flowers in those colors offer a secure perch where butterflies can sit and sip to their hearts' content.

Maybe you'd rather have flies instead? Dull-red or red-brown blossoms will do the trick. They mimic rotting flesh to lure their pollinators. *Mmmm,* say flies as they zero in on the "dead meat."

Pollination doesn't stop when the sun sets. White or pale blooms angle for the attention of moths (and, in the desert Southwest, bats), long after red and blue flowers have disappeared in the dark. Sit under an arbor of moonflower vines (*Ipomoea alba*), and you're likely to spot a hummingbirdlike sphinx moth hovering at the snowy blossoms.

Color is just one part of the pollination puzzle—fragrance and form count, too—but it's the element most of us gardeners notice first. Even if our purple flowers aren't planted in quite the right place.

understanding color

Boost your butterflies, tempt more hummers or bring in the bees by planting more of their favorite colors.

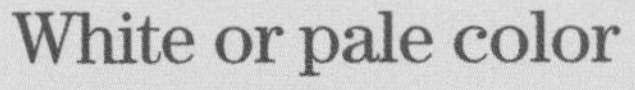

White or pale color

Attracts: Night-flying moths; bats, in some areas.

Try these flowers: Moonflower, angel's trumpet (*Datura* or *Brugmansia*), white or pale petunias, evening primrose.

Yellow

Attracts: Butterflies.

Try these flowers: Sunflowers, **black-eyed Susans**, gaillardia, marigolds, golden alyssum.

Purple

Attracts: Butterflies.

Try these flowers: Butterfly bush, purple coneflower, verbenas, perovskia, **petunias**, lavender, anise hyssop, asters, rhododendrons, azaleas.

Red or orange

Attracts: Hummingbirds.

Try these flowers: Scarlet honeysuckle, bee balm, **columbines**, canna, gladiolus, lilies, salvias, trumpet vine, ocotillo, azaleas.

Blue to blue-purple

Attracts: Bees.

Try these flowers: Crocus, **hyacinth**, grape hyacinth, salvias, anise hyssop, blue spirea (*Caryopteris*), campanulas.

Dull red or red-brown

Attracts: Flies.

Try these flowers: Wild ginger, Dutchman's pipe vine, trilliums, pawpaw trees and certain arums, including skunk cabbage. Another flower in this color category is the notorious *Rafflesia arnoldii*, the largest flower in the world, which boosts its fly appeal with a fetid aroma that you probably don't want in your yard!

fragrant flowers

Treat yourself to a garden filled with heavenly scents.

BY CRYSTAL RENNICKE, SENIOR EDITOR

There's nothing sweeter than a garden that smells as good as it looks. But flower fragrance isn't just for our enjoyment; it plays an important role in pollination. Insects are attracted to a flower by its smell, color or shape, or a combination of these.

Gardeners often argue that modern-day flowers don't smell like they used to. Since flowers are often bred or chosen based on their appearance, size, color, disease resistance and bloom duration, fragrance sometimes is lost when newer varieties are developed. These 10 classic, aromatic plants will make your garden worthy of taking long, appreciative breaths—without sacrificing any beauty.

2
3
4
5
6
7
8
9
10

1
Gardenia

(*Gardenia*, Zones 8 to 10)

Known for its fragrant white flowers and glossy green foliage, the gardenia is synonymous with gardening in the Southeast. Growing from 2 to 8 feet tall and wide, gardenias have glossy, dark green leaves and brilliant white flowers that appear from mid-spring into summer.

Why we love it: This long-blooming, sweetly scented shrub can also be grown as a houseplant in colder climates. Newer varieties hardy to Zone 7 are also now available.

2
Wisteria

(*Wisteria floribunda*, Zones 5 to 9)

Wisteria is known for the intoxicating scent of its pea-like flowers and its vigorous growth. It can climb to 25 feet or more, with an abundance of fragrant violet-blue blooms, but requires a gardener committed to keeping it in bounds. Multijuga (pictured) bears lilac-blue flowers; Honko Fuji has pink flowers.

Why we love it: If you have space and time, it is worth the effort. Try American or Kentucky wisteria; they're more restrained and flower reliably in Zones 4 to 9.

5
Jasmine

(*Jasminum polyanthum*, Zones 9 to 10)

Known for its sweetly scented flowers and glossy leaves, jasmine bears small white blooms in warm climates. This climbing variety grows to 10 feet or more, with pink buds that open into aromatic white flowers.

Why we love it: Its shiny leaves and unique scent make it a popular choice in the South. For cold-climate gardeners, it makes a wonderful indoor or patio plant.

6
Nicotiana

(*Nicotiana*, Annual)

This is a perfect plant for night gardens. Nicotiana blooms day and night, but its jasminelike scent emerges after the sun sets. It's available with white, red, pink, lavender, yellow and green flowers, depending on the variety. For small, fragrant, red flowers, try Nicki Red. Lime Green (pictured) has fragrant, bright-green flowers.

Why we love it: Low-maintenance nicotiana is best enjoyed when planted near your patio or windows. It's also a great hummingbird and butterfly plant.

9
Rose

(*Rosa* species, Zones 3 to 9)

Fragrance has always been a primary reason for growing roses, but newer varieties bred for disease resistance and bloom time have lost some of their scent. Floribunda, shrub and grandiflora roses are the most heavily scented. Handel (pictured), a climbing rose, has lightly scented flowers. Mister Lincoln, a very fragrant hybrid tea, has velvety, dark red flowers.

Why we love it: There's no denying the beauty and sweet smell of a rose. It's just a matter of finding your favorite scent.

10
Lilac

(*Syringa vulgaris*, Zones 3 to 8)

Blooming lilacs are among the most welcome sights and scents of spring. A deciduous shrub growing 8 to 15 feet tall and 6 to 12 feet wide, it's best used in small groupings or as specimen plants. Sensation (pictured) has single purple flowers with distinct white edges.

Why we love it: Lilacs produce one of the most nostalgic scents around, and they're easy to maintain once established.

1, NIC NEISH / SHUTTERSTOCK.COM; 2-10 & CHIVES: RDA-GID

3 Daphne

(*Daphne* **species**, Zones 4 to 8)
Also grown for its foliage, evergreen or deciduous Daphne shrubs feature fragrant flowers in early spring. Although the plant is somewhat finicky, some cultivars, such as Carol Mackie, are relatively carefree. For beautiful, light purple, scented flowers, grow deciduous Gurkha (*Daphne bholua* 'Gurkha', pictured).
Why we love it: Daphne shrubs are versatile in land scapes, with low-growing varieties as well as taller, 6-foot shrubs.

4 Lavender

(*Lavandula angustifolia,* Zones 5 to 9)
A perennial favorite, gardeners love lavender for its attractive flowers and foliage, compact habit and calming scent. In mid- to late summer, pale to deep purple flowers emerge on 12- to 24-inch stalks with silvery green foliage. Hidcote is hardier—often surviving Zone 4—with dark purple flowers. Twickel Purple (pictured) has gray foliage.
Why we love it: Lavender attracts bees and butterflies, is drought-tolerant when established, and is prized for its oil's calming properties. What's not to love?

7 Mock orange

(*Philadelphus*, Zones 4 to 8)
For a scented late-spring deciduous shrub, try mock orange. The citrusy fragrance varies among varieties; choose your plants while they're in bloom if possible. Since the size also varies, pick one that suits your landscape needs. Belle Etoile (pictured) grows 6 feet tall and has very fragrant white flowers.
Why we love it: An old-fashioned favorite, this fragrant plant will bring back memories of Grandma's garden.

8 Heliotrope

(*Heliotropium arborescens*, Annual)
Also aptly called cherry pie, heliotrope has an intense, vanillalike fragrance. Its compact growth, dense foliage and profuse blooms make it a good choice for containers and flower beds alike. Plants grow 12 to 24 inches tall and 12 to 15 inches wide. Try the compact Princess Marina (pictured), with deep violet-blue, heavily scented flowers, or White Lady, with pink-tinged white flowers.
Why we love it: The sweetly fragrant, tiny violet flower clusters are also attractive to butterflies.

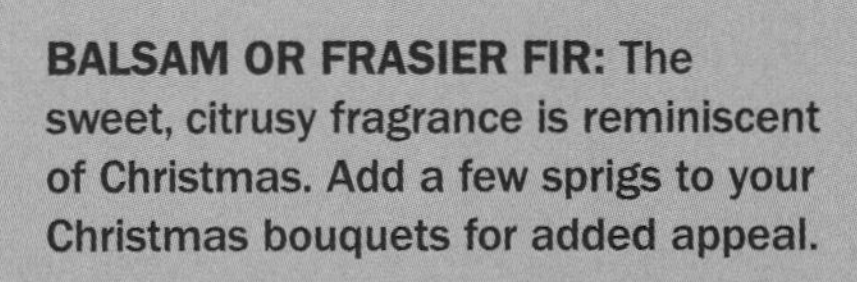

Nose-Worthy

Scent can originate from several parts of the plant, most noticeably the flowers. However, some plants release their fragrance when "petted," or brushed; when the leaves are crushed; or on a warm, breezy day.

BALSAM OR FRASIER FIR: The sweet, citrusy fragrance is reminiscent of Christmas. Add a few sprigs to your Christmas bouquets for added appeal.

HERBS: Rosemary, thyme and other herbs produce delightful aromas when their leaves are crushed.

SCENTED GERANIUM: Pet the leaves—this plant boasts a variety of fragrances, from pungent mint and lemon to the more subtle scents of roses and sweet fruit.

ALLIUM SPECIES: The foliage and flowers of this species have a strong oniony scent, like the chives pictured at left.

TOP 10

1

ornamental GRASSES

No perennial garden is complete without a few of these top picks.

BY STACY TORNIO, EDITOR AND ELLIE MARTIN CLIFFE, ASSOCIATE EDITOR

We love grass. No, we're not talking about the luscious green stuff that grows like crazy in spring and then turns to a crusty brown by the end of summer. We're talking about ornamental grasses—the unsung heroes of gardens across North America.

They are some of the easiest, most resilient and longest-lasting perennials you can grow. Take a look at some of our favorite ornamentals and get tips for growing them in your backyard. Once you try a few of these top picks, we're sure you're going to have a whole new outlook on grass, too.

FOUNTAIN GRASS, O.DIGOIT / ALAMY

2
3
4
5
6
7
8
9
10

1

Fountain grass

(*Pennisetum alopecuroides*, Zones 5 to 9)
With full tufts of fuzzy flower spikes, this ethereal grass seems to be heaven-sent. One or more of its many varieties will add charm to your backyard paradise. This grass reaches 2 to 5 feet.
Why we love it: A backyard staple, it is easy to care for and has distinctive foliage. If you add only one grass to your yard, this might be it.

2

Miscanthus

(*Miscanthus sinensis*, Zones 4 to 9)
You'll be on cloud nine with the fluffy tops of this ornamental. The big, showy flower heads and height of up to 12 feet give it a graceful profile. In autumn, its silky gray panicles turn maroon or purplish-brown. Plant miscanthus in a sun-drenched area.
Why we love it: You definitely get your money's worth with this plant. With heights of up to 12 feet, it's a natural for the back of borders.

5

Pampas grass

(*Cortaderia selloana*, Zones 7 to 11)
Add some drama to your yard with these fast-growing, eye-catching plumes. Feathery pampas grass grows up to 10 feet high and 5 feet wide, but some of the more compact cultivars, including Pumila and Compacta, produce plants up to 6 feet. Note: Invasive in some areas.
Why we love it: You can find pampas grass plumes in many shades, including white, yellow and pink, like the Pink Pampas pictured here, available from Burpee.

6

Blue fescue

(*Festuca glauca*, Zones 4 to 8)
Lovers of this grass don't mind having the blues at all. You'll warm up to blue fescue, too, for its compact, container-friendly tufts and bright hue. It grows about 6 to 12 inches tall.
Why we love it: It's one of the few true blue foliage plants around. Plus, there are many cultivars to pick from.

Indian grass

(*Sorghastrum nutans*, Zones 4 to 8)
Indian grass will add stunning greens, glowing bronzes and cool blues to your garden throughout the year with just a little work on your part. It grows up to 4 feet high and 2 feet wide. For a grass with bluish leaves, try the cultivar Sioux Blue.
Why we love it: It's a sturdy, upright grass with a spectacular columnar look.

10

Japanese blood grass

(*Imperata cylindrical*, Zones 5 to 9)
Get ready for color when you plant Japanese blood grass. Its showy apple-green blades turn blood-red from middle to top in the summer and stay lovely through autumn. This grass stands erect, topping out at 2 feet, and tolerates a variety of soils. It can become invasive, so plant with care.
Why we love it: It's a smaller grass, but it packs a big punch. As far as fall color goes, it takes top honors.

1, 8, 10: RDA-GID; 2, 4, 7, 9: PERENNIALRESOURCE.COM; 3, STEFFEN HAUSER / BOTANIKFOTO/ ALAMY; 5, W. ATLEE BURPEE & CO.; 6, THE GARDEN PICTURE LIBRARY / ALAMY

3

Japanese forest grass

(*Hakonechloa macra*, Zones 5 to 9)
This slow-growing plant has dense masses of arching golden stems that take on a reddish-pink tinge in fall. To enliven a shady area, plant it as a specimen, ground cover or border.
Why we love it: The color it provides is phenomenal and often lasts into winter.

4

Feather reed grass

(*Calamagrostis* x *acutiflora*, Zones 4 to 9)
This plant's tall, upright habit gives it plenty of winter appeal. In fact, this drought-tolerant grass is handsome almost year-round: Starting in summer, its green foliage is topped by plush, silvery-bronze to purple flowers that turn to wheat-colored seed heads that last into snowy weather.
Why we love it: The popular, easy-to-grow Karl Foerster grass is one of the cultivars of feather reed grass.

7

Blue oat grass

(*Helictotrichon sempervirens*, Zones 4 to 8)
Planted in a border or container, or used as a stand-alone accent, blue oat grass commands attention. This ornamental attains greater height and stronger blades than blue fescue. For best foliage color, give it full sun in cool regions and light shade in warm areas.
Why we love it: It tolerates poor soil and adapts well to a variety of conditions.

8

Switchgrass

(*Panicum virgatum*, Zones 4 to 9)
This versatile grass is a good choice for wet conditions, drought or partial shade. Growing narrow and upright, with a cloud of seed heads in fall, switchgrass can reach more than 5 feet tall. This grass is native to North America and reseeds readily. Select a variety for more contained growth.
Why we love it: The light-brown leaves make an interesting winter accent.

Drought-Tolerant Grass Picks

Many grasses are naturally drought-tolerant, but what are some of the best picks overall? In *Designing with Grasses,* published by Timber Press, author Neil Lucas gives smart ornamental grass recommendations for specific growing conditions. Here are some of his top picks for drought areas (listed by botanical name). For more ideas, look for Neil's book at *timberpress.com*. Editor's Note: Make sure these are suited to your region before planting.

Achnatherum
Ammophila
Aristida
Austrostipa
Bothriochloa
Bouteloua
Calamagrostis
Elymus
Eragrostis
Festuca
Helictotrichon
Jarava
Leymus
Muhlenbergia
Nassella
Panicum
Pennisetum
Poa
Sesleria
Sporobolus
Stipa

ultimate fall

1. VAL THOERMER / SHUTTERSTOCK.COM; 2, 3: PERENNIALRESOURCE.COM

favorites

BY ELLIE MARTIN CLIFFE, ASSOCIATE EDITOR
AND STACY TORNIO, EDITOR

With 50 top picks to choose from, you'll have the best autumn color in the neighborhood.

Great gardening doesn't happen just in summer. With the right plant picks, you can enjoy gorgeous blooms, foliage and color throughout autumn. And as a bonus, temps are cooler—perfect for sitting around your backyard, strolling through local parks and visiting botanical gardens. So consider adding a few of these fall favorites to your collection. You won't be disappointed!

Ultimate Fall Flowers

Find out why these picks peak when it's cooler out.

1. Aster

(Aster species, Zones 3 to 9*)*

Popular as cut flowers, asters bring an explosion of color to the end of the growing season. From miniature alpine plants to giants up to 6 feet tall, they'll brighten up fall in your backyard. Hundreds of varieties give gardeners plenty of hues to choose from.

2. Black-eyed Susan

(Rudbeckia species, Zones 3 to 11*)*

Lovely as a background planting or in a wildflower garden, black-eyed Susan also shines when grouped with other daisy-shaped flowers. Plants range from 1 to 6 feet in height, making a big impact in any backyard.

3. Chrysanthemum

(Chrysanthemum and Dendranthema, Zones 4 to 8*)*

Mum's the word for many gardeners in autumn, and with good reason. The chrysanthemum is prized for painting landscapes with vivid color. Its excellent frost tolerance ensures a long and lovely show. Mums that are able to set their bloom earlier in fall when days are still a bit long are called "hardy mums." Increase hardiness by planting mums in spring. Mums planted in fall are often treated as annuals. Flowers are long-lasting, both outdoors and in bouquets.

2

3

4. Common bugleweed

(Ajuga reptans, Zones 3 to 9*)*
Masses of green, bronze, burgundy or variegated foliage make this evergreen perennial a perfect ground cover. Purple-blue flowers appear mostly in spring, but some varieties also bloom sporadically through summer and fall. Bugleweed is an aggressive grower and may invade lawns, so plant it within a barrier.

5. Coral bells

(Heuchera, Zones 3 to 9*)*
If you want texture, look no further than coral bells. Though the name comes from this mounding plant's spires of small bell-shaped blossoms, many varieties have stunning foliage that intensifies in fall. Grow it in afternoon shade for the most vibrant shades. In milder climates, coral bells is evergreen (or ever-purple, -black, -bronze, -silver, etc.).

6. Dahlia

(Dahlia, Zones 8 to 11*)*
It's no wonder the dahlia is the darling of many gardeners. With thousands of cultivars to choose from, there's a color, shape and size for everyone. Some varieties will tower over the rest of your garden, easily surpassing 5 feet. Gardeners in cooler climates should dig up the tubers once the plants have died back.

7. False aster

(Boltonia asteroides, Zones 4 to 8*)*
Add a natural look to your yard by planting false aster, a North American native often seen growing in sunny wetlands and along riverbanks. An eye-catching border backdrop, this perennial's flowers have narrow pink, purple or white petals; the plants grow up to 6 feet high and 3 feet wide. Give false aster a haircut each spring to help keep it in shape.

8. Goldenrod

(Solidago species, Zones 3 to 9*)*
Light up your autumn garden with goldenrod's wispy yellow blooms, which also make long-lasting cut flowers. Deadhead to ensure continued blooming and limit self-sowing. Be sure to plant goldenrod near other assertive plants to maintain balance.

9. Japanese anemone

(Anemone x hybrida, Zones 4 to 8*)*
Well suited to sun or partial shade, the Japanese anemone produces saucer-shaped white or pink flowers throughout the season. Be sure the spot you choose for it has moist, humus-rich soil and receives some sun during the day. A natural choice for fall, Japanese anemone thrives in cool, damp conditions.

ultimate fall flowers

4, PERENNIALRESOURCE.COM; 5, 17: TERRANOVANURSERIES.COM; 6, 7, 13, 16, 19: PROVEN WINNERS, PROVENWINNERS.COM; 8, 9, 11, 12, 14, 15: RDA-GID; 10, ZANOZARU / SHUTTERSTOCK.COM; 18, JULIE DANSEREAU / GAP PHOTO: LEAF, FOTOSAV / SHUTTERSTOCK.COM

10. Knotweed

(Persicaria affinis, Zones 3 to 8*)*
Spreading knotweed's spiky pink or red flower clusters are sure signs that autumn is near. As temperatures drop, green foliage changes to shades of red, bronze and even chocolate brown, enlivening an otherwise drab landscape. Wear gloves when working with this plant, and keep little ones from ingesting it.

11. Monkshood

(Aconitum, Zones 3 to 8*)*
Distinguished by the unusual hooded shape of its flowers, monkshood contributes bursts of blue, yellow, pink or violet to the fall garden. It grows best in partial shade but will tolerate sun. Because this plant is toxic, it's important that children and pets keep their distance.

12. Ornamental cabbage

(Brassica oleracea cultivars, annual*)*
While it's not technically a bloom, the foliage of ornamental cabbage is wonderful in shades of green, lavender-blue, purple, red, pink or white. The colors get richer as the season goes on into early winter. Growing 10 to 18 inches tall and wide, they prefer full sun to partial shade. Your local nursery should have plenty to choose from—or consider challenging yourself and starting them from seed in late summer.

13. Osteospermum

(Osteospermum, annual*)*
This bloomer adds pop to any sunny space from planting until hard frost. With varieties ranging from 4 to 20 inches, it makes an outstanding filler plant or a taller focal point. The rich color palette includes orange, lavender and white. Be sure to plant osteospermum in a spot with good drainage.

14. Purpletop vervain

(Verbena bonariensis, annual to Zone 7*)*
Attract fall-migrating butterflies with these delicate purple flowers. The plants can reach up to 5 feet tall. Check with your local extension office before planting; this prolific reseeder in milder climates is being evaluated in some areas for invasiveness.

15. Sedum

(Sedum species, Zones 3 to 10*)*
Many cultivars of this late-season favorite, including the popular Autumn Joy, have broccoli-shaped light-green flower heads that slowly change to pink and deepen to burgundy. Other types boast bold-hued foliage, ranging from red to gold. Most sedums are succulent and hardy in all but the coldest climates.

16. Strawflower

(Bracteantha bracteata, annual*)*
These papery, daisy-shaped flowers will grace your autumn garden with a rainbow of color, from red and yellow to pink and white. Plants come in a wide variety of sizes, so there's a type for every space. Bring the cut flowers indoors for a dried bouquet.

17. Toad lily

(Tricyrtis, Zones 4 to 9*)*
Orchidlike blooms in white, mauve and yellow earn toad lily a closer look. Better yet, this easy-to-grow plant's distinctive speckled blossoms emerge just as many other plants are winding down for fall. Perfect for a small woodland shade garden, this plant grows 1 to 2 feet wide and up to 3 feet tall.

18. Willow blue-star

(Amsonia tabernaemontana,
Zones 3 to 9*)*
In spring and early summer, this bushy green perennial is dotted with small blue flowers, but when autumn arrives, willow blue-star's foliage takes the spotlight. The gold to garnet plants, which typically reach just 2 to 3 feet tall, make a lovely addition to any fall landscape.

19. Wood spurge

(Euphorbia amygdaloides,
Zone 6 to 9, annual elsewhere*)*
Spring flowers and reddish cool-season foliage give wood spurge valuable multiseason appeal. Once flowers have faded, pinch them off to encourage branching. Heights range from 1 to 2½ feet. Grow wood spurge in light shade and moist, rich soil for optimal results.

9 10 11 17 18 19

Ultimate Fall Shrubs

Make a big impact in a small space with these top shrubs.

20. Burning bush

(Euonymus alatus, Zones 4 to 9*)*
An autumn landscaping classic, burning bush adds a burst of scarlet to any yard. Because of its popularity, varieties of this mounding shrub are available in a range of heights, from 7 to around 20 feet. Select dwarf cultivars or prune in early spring. Invasive in some areas. Plant in full sun for the best fall show.

21. Camellia

(Camellia, Zones 6 to 11*)*
If you live in Zone 6 or up, camellia is a must-have for your garden. It has beautiful roselike blooms that start in fall, winter or early spring. Growing 3 to 20 feet tall, it sports flowers in red, pink or white. It does best in partial shade.

22. Crape myrtle

(Lagerstroemia indica, Zones 7 to 9*)*
Southern gardeners, rejoice: You can grow crape myrtle! This flowering tree blossoms in endless shades of pink, red, white or purple. Then fall foliage takes over, bringing a kaleidoscope of red, orange and yellow, often mingling on the same tree. In winter, the smooth, peeling bark adds a subtle charm to the landscape.

23. Doublefile viburnum

(Viburnum plicatum f. tomentosum, Zones 5 to 8*)*
Distinctive flat white or pink flower heads and a wide-reaching silhouette make this viburnum a winner from spring till fall, when its deeply veined foliage turns a bold maroon. Varieties of this shrub can reach up to 15 feet, and most thrive in full sun.

24. Fothergilla

(Fothergilla species, Zones 4 to 8*)*
With foliage that turns gold, purple and orange in fall, this shrub is a garden standout long after its spiky spring flowers have finished blooming. Larger varieties of fothergilla reach 8 feet tall, while dwarf cultivars are less than half that size. Plant it in a sunny spot with acidic soil.

25. Japanese barberry

(Berberis thunbergii, Zones 4 to 9*)*
This shrub's foliage isn't just attractive in fall, when it's aflame in red or orange: Its round little leaves are chartreuse or burgundy for the entire growing season. Barberry's dense, compact growing habit makes it a natural choice for foundation plantings and hedges. Select a noninvasive variety for your garden.

26. Oakleaf hydrangea

(Hydrangea quercifolia, Zones 5 to 9)

The white blooms on this 4- to 6-foot shrub change to a purplish-pink in late summer. Then the leaves take over and put on a spectacular fall show in shades of red, orange, brown and purple.

27. Smoke bush

(Cotinus coggygria, Zones 4 to 9)

Mounding smoke bushes have red-violet or bluish leaves in the warmer months, which change to purplish-gold in autumn. Because of their open growth habit, smoke bushes look best when planted in groups, or can be used as a specimen plant.

28. Staghorn sumac

(Rhus typhina, Zones 3 to 8*)*

For a glowing orangey-red display in fall, turn to staghorn sumac. When female and male plants grow near each other, the females produce long, upright clusters of deep-red fruit that last into winter. This broad shrub reaches around 15 feet tall and 20 feet wide if left to itself. Grow this aggressive plant in a contained area. Prune and dig out suckers in early spring.

29. Virginia sweetspire

(Itea virginica, Zones 5 to 9*)*

This native shrub bursts with fragrant summer flowers and vibrant fall color, generally growing 4 to 5 feet high. And since it doesn't have many disease or insect problems, it works in any landscape. The bright-red autumn leaves often last well into the season.

30. Witch hazel

(Hamamelis virginiana, Zones 3 to 8*)*

If the name doesn't win you over, the fall color will. You'll get rich, glorious leaf color and fragrant yellow blooms with this tree. It grows 12 to 25 feet tall and thrives in moist, well-drained soil in full sun to partial shade.

Ultimate Fall Vines

These climbers take center stage in autumn.

31. Boston ivy

(Parthenocissus tricuspidata, Zones 4 to 8*)*

A close cousin to Virginia creeper (they even share part of a botanical name), Boston ivy is a very aggressive grower and can reach up to 70 feet. It's a good choice for colder climates, surviving in Zones 4 and up. For purple-red blooms, look for cultivars Beverly Brooks and Purpurea. The Fenway cultivar has golden leaves.

32. Grape

(Vitis species, Zones 5 to 10*)*

You don't have to harvest grapes to enjoy the benefits of growing grapevine. It's one of the easiest vines to grow and will benefit from regular pruning. Your birds will love it, likely stealing the grapes before you get your chance. *Vitis vinifera* 'Pupurea' is a purple-leafed grape, while *Vitis coignetiae* has crimson coloring.

33. Morning glory

(Ipomoea purpurea, annual*)*

This beauty is invasive in some areas, and all parts are toxic if ingested, but if you can get past that, it's a dependable vine that looks stunning until first frost. Beyond the traditional blue blossoms, you can find plants that bloom in white, purple, pink or red. Grow in full sun; it will reach up to 20 feet tall.

34. Sweet autumn clematis

(Clematis terniflora, Zones 4 to 9*)*

This beautiful vine teems with fragrant white flowers in late fall. Prune sweet autumn clematis in early spring to maximize its growth potential for the remainder of the season.

35. Virginia creeper

(Parthenocissus quinquefolia, Zones 3 to 9*)*

This aggressive vine needs taming, but the brilliant red color may make it worth a little extra effort on your part to enjoy this fall beauty. *Parthenocissus henryana* has blue-green foliage all season that also turns a brilliant red in fall.

ultimate fall vines

33

34

35

20, 23, 24, 25, 26, 28, 31: BAILEY NURSERIES; 21, 27, 30, 32, 33, 35: RDA-GID; 22, GARDEN SPLENDOR; 29, PROVEN WINNERS, PROVENWINNERS.COM; 34, PERENNIALRESOURCE.COM

Ultimate Fall Trees

You'll want to find the space for some of these mighty picks.

36. American persimmon

(Diospyros virginiana, Zones 4 to 9*)*
Often grown for its round yellow-orange fruit, the persimmon prefers loamy soil and full sun. A medium-size tree, it has a wide canopy of glossy green leaves that turn to red, yellow, orange and purple late in the season.

37. Bald cypress

(Taxodium distichum, Zones 5 to 11*)*
Though this tree resembles many other conifers during the warmer months, it's called bald for a reason: Each year, it drops its flat, feathery needles, which turn golden-brown in fall. This columnar tree, which can reach 120 feet, does best in moist, acidic soil. Dwarf bald cypress varieties are also gaining in popularity.

38. Bigleaf maple

(Acer macrophyllum, Zones 5 to 9*)*
Even if you don't think bigger is always better, check out this tree, which boasts the largest leaves of all maples—up to a foot long! In fall, bigleaf maple's foliage turns bright-yellow or orange—quite a sight on this tree, which can reach 70 feet tall and wide.

39. Copper beech

(Fagus sylvatica f. purpurea, Zones 4 to 7*)*
With season-long purple-green leaves, this tree certainly has a place in North American landscapes. In spring, the copper beech unfurls rich purple leaves, which take on a greenish cast in summer. When fall arrives, the foliage turns a golden bronze and some leaves persist over winter.

40. Freeman red maple

(Acer x freemanii, Zones 4 to 8*)*
More tolerant of alkaline soil than its classic cousin, the Freeman red maple contributes a powerful presence, especially in autumn, when the leaves turn a glowing garnet. It reaches heights of 40 to 70 feet and grows best in sunny spots.

41. Ginkgo

(Ginkgo biloba, Zones 4 to 8*)*
Though the gingko is a conifer, it doesn't have needlelike leaves: Its scalloped, fan-shaped leaves change to golden-yellow and carpet the ground each autumn. The ginkgo does best in sunny, well-draining spots and is not susceptible to disease.

42. Honeylocust

(Gleditsia triacanthos, Zones 3 to 9*)*
Reaching 70 feet tall and 40 feet wide, honeylocust makes an excellent border tree. Its small green leaflets give it an airy appearance; they turn a brilliant yellow as the temperatures cool in autumn.

ultimate fall trees

43. Japanese maple

(Acer palmatum, Zones 5 to 8*)*
This delicately sculpted tree has a weeping silhouette and colorful foliage combinations. In sizes ranging from cascading dwarf shrubs to 25-foot trees, it's among the most enchanting of all the maples, with more than 1,000 cultivars to choose from.

44. Japanese zelkova

(Zelkova serrata, Zones 5 to 8*)*
Although often confused with the elm, Japanese zelkova is in a league of its own. This often vase-shaped tree produces elliptical dark-green leaves in the spring, which turn yellow, orange or red in fall. Mature gray bark exfoliates to reveal vibrant orange wood. This tree thrives in many areas because it tolerates both drought and a variety of soil conditions.

45. Katsura

(Cercidiphyllum japonicum,
Zones 4 to 8*)*
Anything but ordinary, the katsura unfurls spiky red blooms in springtime, followed by dangling heart-shaped leaves. In fall, the green foliage turns shades of apricot and yellow. While you're outside raking, take a whiff: The fallen leaves smell a bit like burnt sugar. Plant it in an area protected from harsh winter winds.

46. Pin oak

(Quercus palustris, Zones 4 to 8*)*
Lure squirrels away from your bird feeder with acorns! This fast-growing oak starts out with a pyramidal shape but becomes more oval as it matures. Eventually reaching 60 to 70 feet tall, the pin oak enjoys full sun or partial shade. The glossy green leaves turn scarlet or copper in autumn.

47. Shagbark hickory

(Carya ovata, Zones 4 to 8*)*
As you might guess, this tree gets its name from its peeling exterior, a trait that creates year-round interest in mature trees. It's extra stunning in fall, when its oblong leaves turn a brilliant gold. Bonus: The nuts are delicious!

48. Sweet gum

(Liquidambar styraciflua,
Zones 5 to 9*)*
Sweet gum is a conical shade tree with glossy green lobed foliage. In fall, leaves turn to stunning yellows, purples and reds. Yellow-green spring flowers are inconspicuous, but watch for the abundance of spiky, spherical fruit clusters that follows.

49. Tall stewartia

(Stewartia monadelpha,
Zones 6 to 9*)*
An unsung hero of the fall landscape, tall stewartia is a must for gardens in milder climates. This columnar or conical tree boasts multiseason interest, with delicate white flowers in summer, blazing foliage in fall and peeling cinnamon-hued bark in winter. Tall stewartia grows in sun or dappled shade and prefers moist, well-draining soil.

50. Thornless cockspur hawthorn

(Crataegus crus-galli var. inermis,
Zones 4 to 7*)*
Lovely white blossoms in early summer, red-orange fall foliage and long-lasting red fruit make this hawthorn both pretty and productive. The drought-resistant tree reaches just 25 feet tall and around 30 feet wide. Plant a row for an eye-catching hedge or privacy screen.

36, RICHARD SHIELL / DEMBINSKY PHOTO ASSOC.; 37, FLORAPIX / ALAMY; 38, RICK WETHERBEE; 39, KEITH LEIGHTON / ALAMY; 40, 42, 43, 45, 46, 50: BAILEY NURSERIES; 41, 48: RDA-GID; 44, JAMES BARRETT / ALAMY; 47, ANNE GILBERT / ALAMY; 49, SARAH CUTTLE / GAP PHOTOS; 50, SCIENCE PHOTO LIBRARY / ALAMY

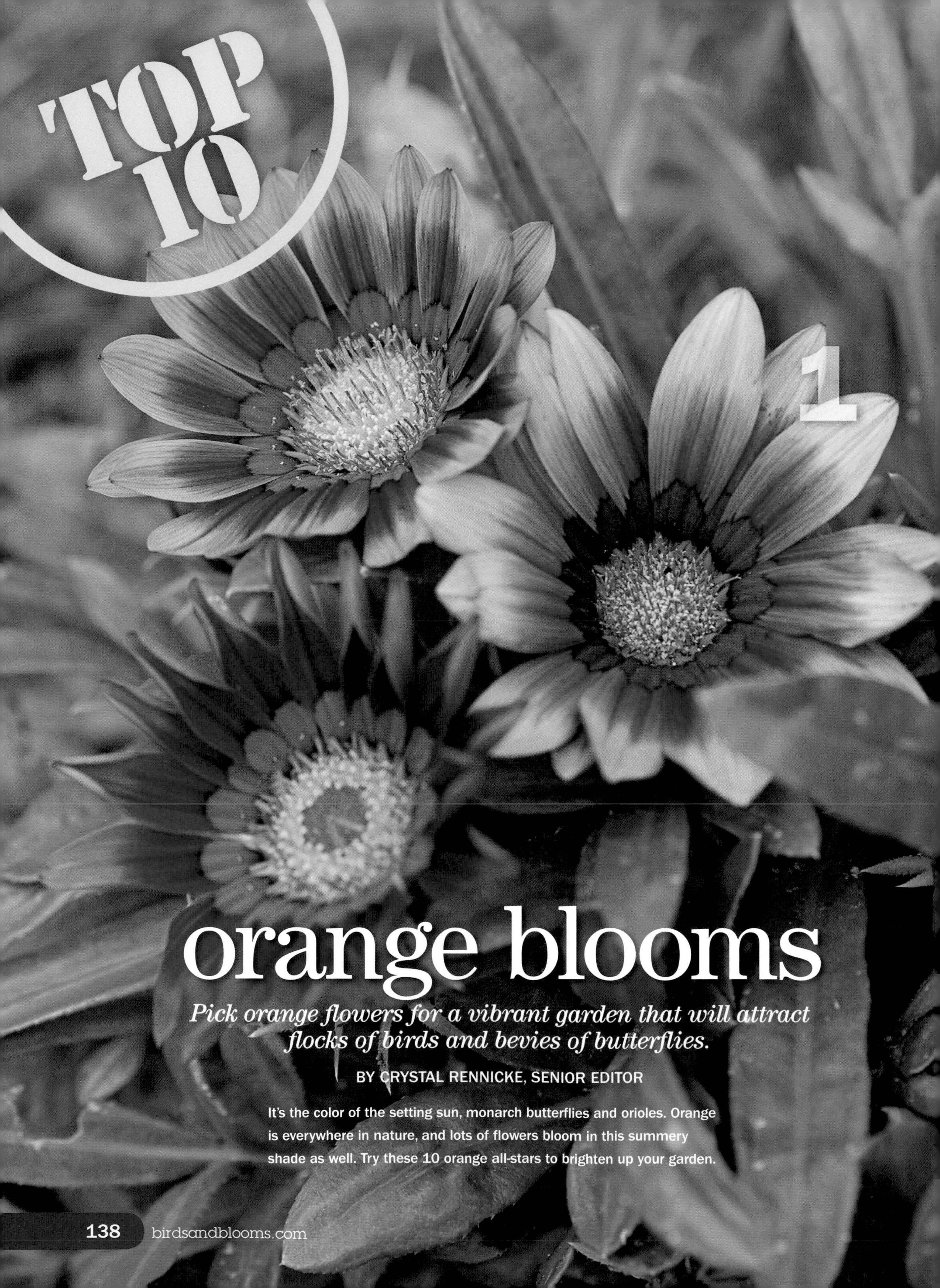

TOP 10

1

orange blooms

Pick orange flowers for a vibrant garden that will attract flocks of birds and bevies of butterflies.

BY CRYSTAL RENNICKE, SENIOR EDITOR

It's the color of the setting sun, monarch butterflies and orioles. Orange is everywhere in nature, and lots of flowers bloom in this summery shade as well. Try these 10 orange all-stars to brighten up your garden.

2
3
4
5
6
7
8
9
10

1

Gazania

(*Gazania*, annual except in Zones 8-10)

This popular daisy produces a stunning array of colors in less-than-ideal conditions. Gazania is drought-tolerant, but it does need sun; the flower heads close up every day, similar to moss roses. Tiger Stripes (pictured) is a bold variety that grows to just a foot tall.

Why we love it: Often planted as a ground cover, gazania also has gorgeous variegated foliage that spreads.

2

Mexican sunflower

(*Tithonia rotundifolia*, annual)

This fast-growing annual, which blooms in late summer and autumn, reaches 6 feet in height. Its hardy orange and red flowers glow in full sun. Try All-America Selections winner Torch, or for smaller spaces, Fiesta Del Sol, a dwarf variety that grows to just 3 feet tall.

Why we love it: A top choice for luring butterflies with its nectar and finches with its seed, Mexican sunflowers are also drought-tolerant.

5

Crown imperial

(*Fritillaria imperialis*, Zones 5 to 8)

These bell-shaped blooms at the end of 3- to 4-foot stems make a big, colorful statement in spring. The downward-facing flowers are topped by a crown of small leaves, which is probably where the plant got its name. For orange blossoms, look to Aurora and Garland Star cultivars.

Why we love it: Truly an unusual, versatile bulb, crown imperial will look elegant in containers, spring bulb beds and other garden spots.

6

Zinnia

(*Zinnia*, annual)

A wide variety of zinnias—ranging from 8 inches to 3 feet tall—boast blazing blooms that persist until the first frost. You'll love the Profusion Orange hybrid variety and Double Zahara Fire (pictured), both All-America Selections winners.

Why we love it: While their bright colors attract butterflies, zinnias are long-blooming, too, and many varieties are heat- and drought-resistant.

9

Red-hot poker

(*Kniphofia*, Zones 5 to 9)

Also called torch lily for its rocket-shaped orange plumes, this dramatic flower grows up to 4 feet tall. Bird-watchers love it for its looks and the abundant nectar produced in the orange, yellow and red blooms for hummingbirds to sip. For best results, well-draining soil is important; red-hot poker will rot in boggy or moist ground.

Why we love it: Attractive to bees, butterflies and hummingbirds while resistant to deer, this plant welcomes wildlife with its distinctive color and shape.

10

Oriental poppy

(*Papaver orientale*, Zones 2 to 9)

There's something romantic about Oriental poppies. Maybe it's their giant, crepe-petaled blooms, or the fact that they last only a week or two in May or June in the garden. These plants grow up to 4 feet and come in gorgeous pinks, reds and whites, but orange is a favorite.

Why we love it: In addition to their elegance in the garden, Oriental poppies make glorious cut flowers.

1,7: PROVEN WINNERS, PROVENWINNERS.COM; 2,5: RDA-GID; 3, BLUESTONE PERENNIALS; 4, ALICIA WYATT; 6, BALL HORTICULTURE; 8,HIGHCOUNTRYGARDENS.COM; 9,10: WALTER'S GARDENS; BALLOON FLOWER, PERENNIALRESOURCE.COM

3

Terra Cotta yarrow

(*Achillea millefolium* 'Terra Cotta', Zones 3 to 9)
Entice butterflies with this lovely salmon-colored yarrow that turns to a burnt orange in late summer. It grows 1 to 3 feet tall and wide but can quickly outgrow its space if not divided regularly. Try it in your cottage or rock gardens; once established, it's very drought-tolerant.
Why we love it: A pretty plant through the seasons, it has especially attractive seed heads and makes a good cut or dried flower.

4

Tiger lily

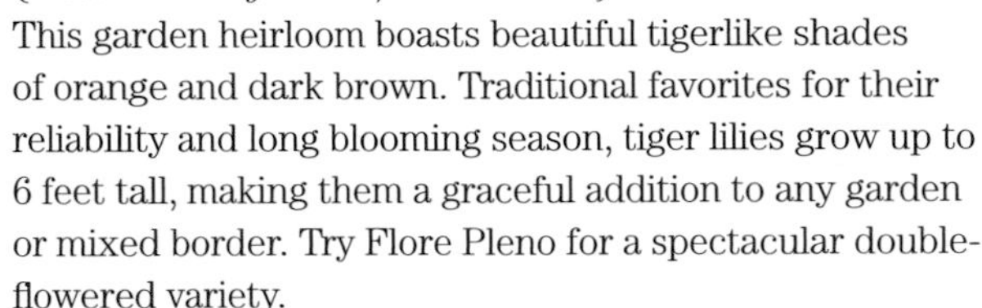

(*Lilium lancifolium*, Zones 3 to 9)
This garden heirloom boasts beautiful tigerlike shades of orange and dark brown. Traditional favorites for their reliability and long blooming season, tiger lilies grow up to 6 feet tall, making them a graceful addition to any garden or mixed border. Try Flore Pleno for a spectacular double-flowered variety.
Why we love it: It's not just beautiful. This backyard favorite also beckons butterflies and bees.

7

Calibrachoa

(*Calibrachoa*, annual except in Zones 9-11)
Calibrachoa comes in almost every color under the sun, but its orange varieties deserve special notice. The small flowers will steal the show all season, making fast-growing calibrachoa a hot choice for containers. Try Superbells Tangerine Punch® (pictured) for a low-maintenance plant.
Why we love it: Easygoing calibrachoa, especially the red and orange varieties, is a hummingbird magnet.

8

Tiki Torch coneflower

(*Echinacea* 'Tiki Torch', Zones 4 to 9)
A showy orange flower hybrid with long petals, Tiki Torch is a growing favorite among coneflower fans. Plant this 3-foot-tall plant in moist, compost-enriched soil with wind protection. A bit of afternoon shade will prolong the vivid color.
Why we love it: Big, long-lasting blooms make coneflowers a hit; this one adds fabulous color to the mix.

feeling blue?

Blue is the complementary color to orange, so azure, sapphire and indigo flowers coexist with orange ones splendidly. For a look that wows, try these lovely blue blooms near your orange favorites.

DELPHINIUM (*Delphinium*, Zones 3 to 8). Add punch to the back of borders with this towering blue beauty.

BALLOON FLOWER (*Platycodon grandiflorus*, Zones 3 to 9). A mid-sized grower at 2 to 3 feet tall, balloon flower (right) is a pretty choice in the front or middle of flower beds.

MORNING GLORY (*Ipomoea* spp., annual). This popular vine grows up to 12 feet high. It's invasive in some areas, so do a little research first.

PERENNIAL FLAX (*Linum perenne*, Zones 4 to 9). With flowers to match the summer sky, flax is an easy-care perennial that grows in a slow-spreading clump.

the wonders of WINTER

Make your garden come alive with just a few clever plant picks.

BY STEPHANIE COHEN AND JENNIFER BENNER, AUTHORS OF *THE NONSTOP GARDEN*

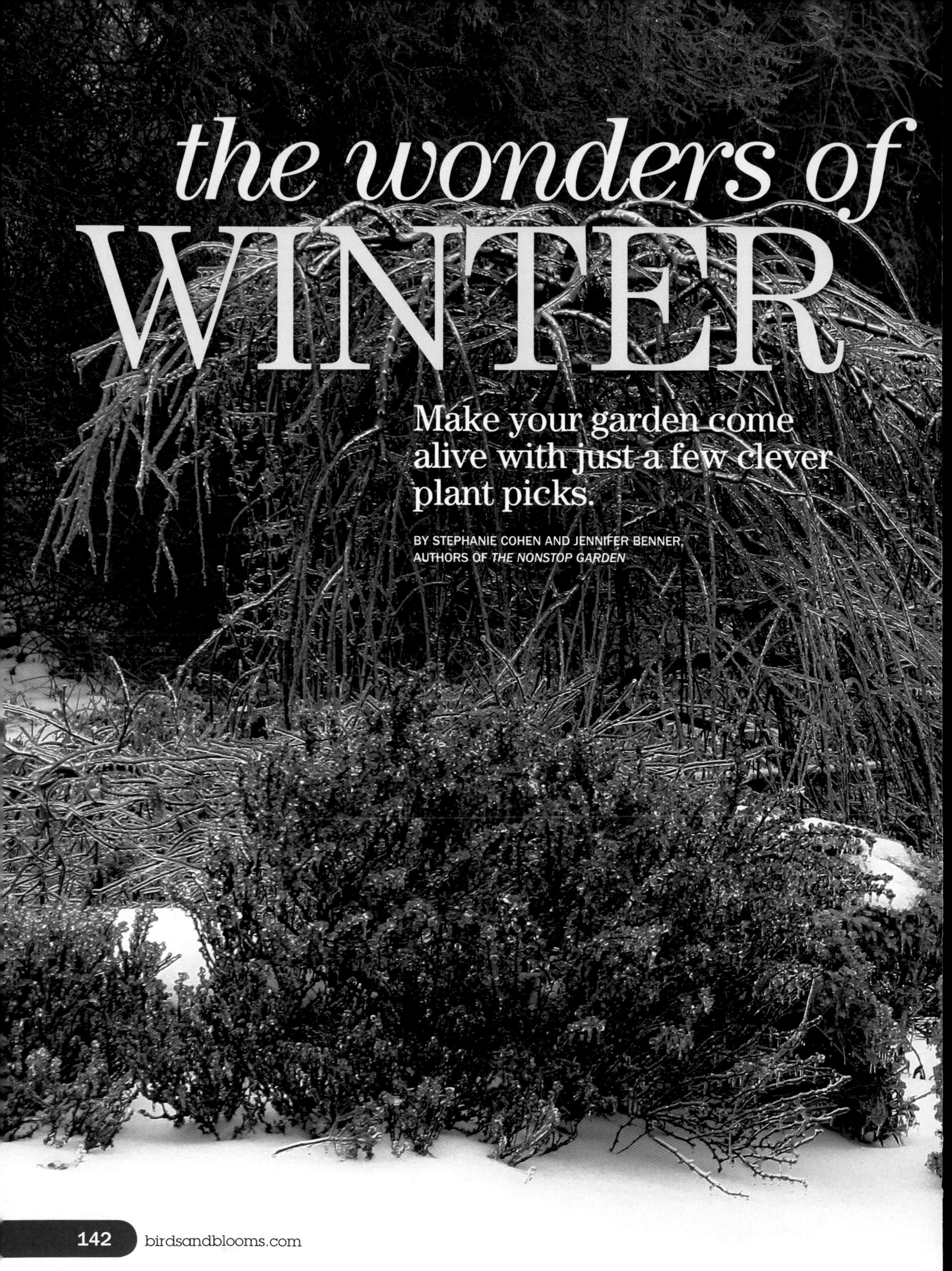

Winter is the time for a much-needed rest for both plants and gardeners. Many plants drift off into a seasonal dormant slumber, while we catch our breath and get ready for the next round of planting and weed pulling.

But just because this is the quiet time of year for many landscapes in the Northern Hemisphere doesn't mean our gardens are down and out. Structures and ornaments can still be enjoyed, and many plants offer the subtle beauty of bark, form and evergreen foliage in winter. A few even surprise us with flowers and fruit.

Winter is a time to appreciate the not-so-in-your-face gifts of nature. Even the remains of the day in the form of lingering seedheads and herbaceous stems supply us with memories of seasons past and a promise of what is to come. Without winter, we would not appreciate the other seasons nearly as much.

Anchor the borders.

Flowering herbaceous plants may steal the spotlight during the warmer times of the year, but structural woody plants carry a garden through the cool dormant months. Evergreen conifers like dwarf spruce (*Picea* species and cultivars, Zones 2 to 9) take center stage with their wonderful pyramidal green forms, while the cascading habits of deciduous trees like weeping cherries (*Prunus* species and cultivars, Zones 3 to 9) and Japanese maples (*Acer palmatum* and cultivars, Zones 5 to 8) add a dramatic arching contrast.

The mounding stems of shrubs like Japanese barberry (*Berberis thunbergii* and cultivars, Zones 4 to 8) and upright remains of ornamental grasses like maiden grass (*Miscanthus sinensis* and cultivars, Zones 5 to 9) offer additional winter interest. While barberries and maiden grasses can be invasive in some parts of the United States, plenty of less aggressive substitutes, such as spireas (*Spiraea* species and cultivars, Zones 3 to 9) and switchgrass (*Panicum virgatum* and cultivars, Zones 4 to 9), can provide the same effect in a sunny location with average soil and moisture.

Take advantage of herbaceous evergreens.

Depending on where you live, you will find long-lasting herbaceous plant options with leaves that can be enjoyed through the winter months. Gardeners who live in warmer zones than 5 and receive little snow cover are among the many who benefit from evergreen and semievergreen perennials.

To create eye-catching winter vignettes, choose a mix of plants in a range of sizes, shapes and leaf textures. For example, the thin, swordlike leaves of hardy yucca (*Yucca filamentosa* and cultivars, Zones 4 to 10) stand out against the oval, ground-hugging foliage of vigorous bugleweed (*Ajuga reptans* and cultivars, Zones 3 to 9), while the delicate lacy green of wood fern (*Dryopteris* species and cultivars, Zones 3 to 9) provides a softer touch when added to the scene. A trio like this not only makes the winter landscape a little less bleak but also looks good the rest of the year when given partial sun and somewhat rich, moist soil.

Gardeners in dry, temperate regions have the option of enjoying hardy succu-

HIDDEN VISIONS. You never know where you'll find winter beauties. At right, from top: yucca, evergreen boughs in a container, and purple coneflowers. Opposite page, an ice-coated garden structure.

Stephanie Cohen has taught herbaceous plants and perennial design at Temple University for more than 20 years. Jennifer Benner has spent many years working in nursery production, garden design installation and management. This excerpt on winter gardening was taken from their book, The Nonstop Garden *(Timber Press, 2010). For more four-season plant recommendations, look for* The Nonstop Garden *at a store near you.*

WINTER STRUCTURE. A little structure goes a long way in creating winter interest. Opposite page: icy, elegant fountain grass. At right, from top: crabapple, witch hazel and colorful winterberries.

lents such as agaves (*Agave* species and cultivars, Zones 5 to 11), aloes (*Aloe* species and cultivars, Zones 8 to 11) and cacti (*Echinocactus* species and cultivars, Zones 4 to 11) during the winter. These plants provide wonderful geometric forms in sunny locations.

Put blossoms, buds, berries and bark into play.

Scattering plants with interesting winter attributes throughout your beds and borders will keep your garden lively during the seasonal intermission. Some plants save their best show for winter. Witch hazels (*Hamamelis* species and cultivars, Zones 3 to 8) in the North and Japanese camellias (*Camellia japonica* and cultivars, Zones 7 to 9) in the South burst with spectacular blossoms, sometimes lasting for weeks on end right in the middle of the coldest months of the year.

The brightly colored fruit of shrubs like firethorns (*Pyracantha* species and cultivars, Zones 5 to 10) and winterberries (*Ilex verticillata* and cultivars, Zones 3 to 9) will begin wowing audiences in autumn and will keep the display going into early winter, sometimes longer. The plump, fuzzy buds of magnolias (*Magnolia* species and cultivars, Zones 3 to 9) and pussy willows (*Salix* species and cultivars, Zones 4 to 8) make an appearance toward the end of the season, while the beautiful, shaggy, cinnamon to creamy-white bark of birches (*Betula* species and cultivars, Zones 2 to 9) impresses throughout the year.

Leave garden cleanup for the spring.

Old habits die hard, but try to hold off on reaching for your pruners and rake until spring. Leaving dried seedheads and stems in the garden through winter can add another level of interest, as well as food and shelter for wildlife. Ornamental grasses such as fountain grass (*Pennisetum* species and cultivars, Zones 5 to 11) look stunning in the winter landscape blanketed with a fresh layer of snow or ice.

Many plants produce intriguing seedheads that linger for months. Allium (*Allium* species and cultivars, Zones 2 to 11) seedheads sometimes break off from their dried stems and are blown about the garden, creating serendipitous scenes with their starburst forms, while coneflowers (*Echinacea* species and cultivars, Zones 3 to 9) offer up attractive prickly spheres in beds located in full sun and average, moderately moist soil.

Rely on embellishments and structure.

Even in winter, garden ornaments and structures shine with their own sense of flair. When plants are dormant, unique supports, trellises and arbors provide something interesting to look at. Empty ornate containers and architectural embellishments continue to hold their charm despite harsh weather conditions. And while pots may not be oozing with summertime blooms, you can create pleasing container combinations by filling them with evergreen boughs or other stems and seedheads still lingering in the garden.

Finally, take advantage of the stunning silhouettes many trees and shrubs exhibit in the winter landscape. Whether it be their natural form or one created by a gardener's hand, these dramatic profiles stand out against a fresh blanket of snow or when placed near a solid backdrop such as a house, outbuilding or fence. Choose plants that also have attractive flowers, fruit or foliage, such as apples and crabapples (*Malus* species and cultivars, Zones 3 to 9), since these will provide interest at other times of the year, when winter is all but a distant memory.

WINTERBERRIES, JENNIFER BENNER; ALL OTHERS COURTESY OF TIMBER PRESS

Sunflower
Photo by Mary Jo Bell

Ostrich fern
Photo by Mark Turner

Hawthorn berries
Photo by Terry Wild Stock

Himalayan blue poppy
Photo by Mark Turner

Lily-of-the-valley
Photo by Getty Images, Garden Picture Library

CHAPTER 6

Spectacular *travel spots*

These fascinating destinations are best bets for bird-watchers and gardeners across the country. Take the ultimate birding challenge, tour amazing urban gardens, visit a magical butterfly sanctuary, find a few new birding friends or simply relax at blooming B&B retreats.

DORLING KINDERSLEY / GETTY IMAGES

EXTREME birding

BY CRYSTAL RENNICKE, SENIOR EDITOR

Birders will stop at nothing for a chance to compete in the ultimate birding challenge.

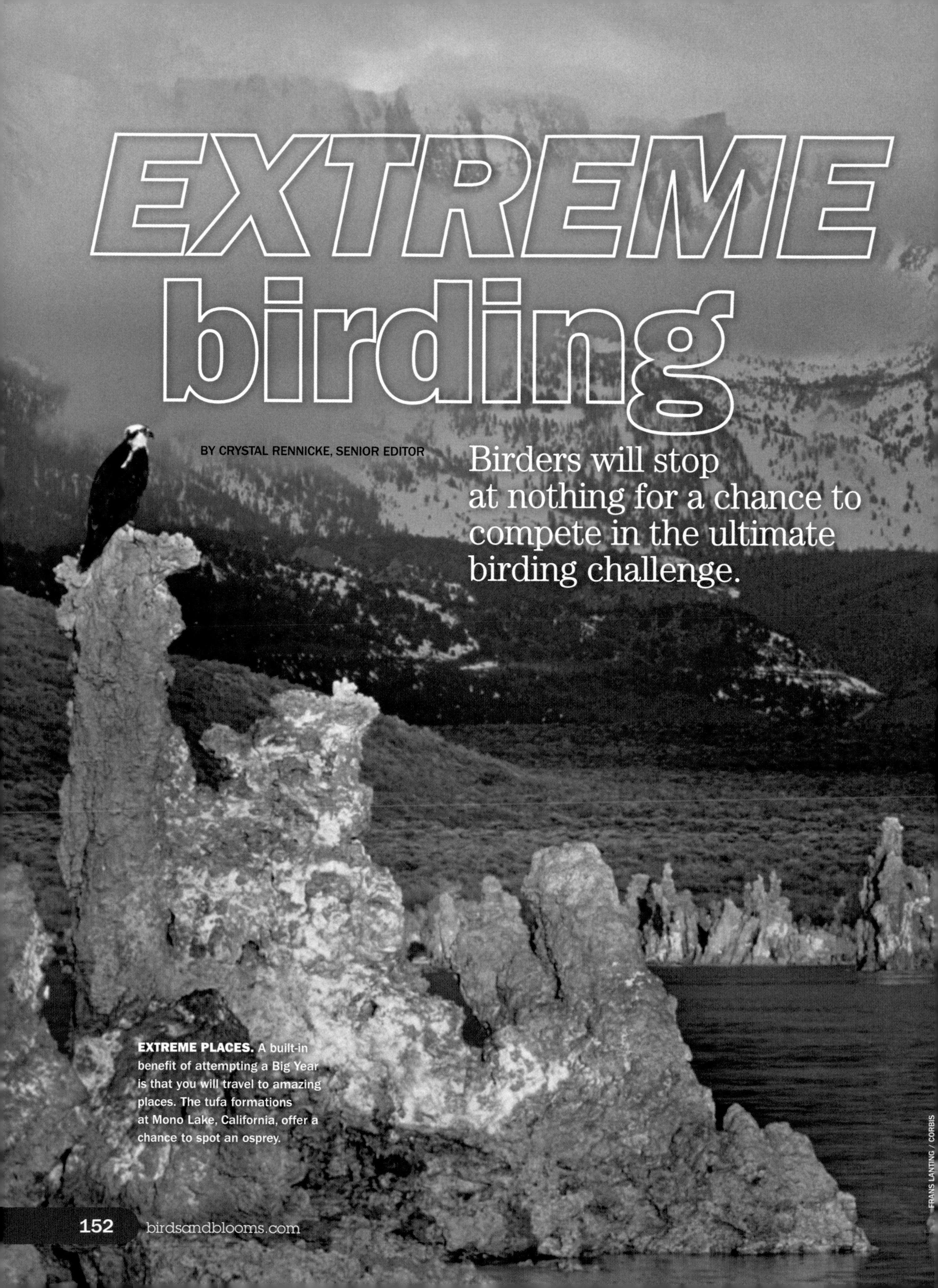

EXTREME PLACES. A built-in benefit of attempting a Big Year is that you will travel to amazing places. The tufa formations at Mono Lake, California, offer a chance to spot an osprey.

FRANS LANTING / CORBIS

Greg Miller has boldly gone where few birders have gone before. In the birding world, it's called a Big Year, with participants abandoning their ordinary lives and traveling across the continent to see as many different species as possible. Now, with a little help from Hollywood, the term—and the adventure—is no longer the exclusive property of self-proclaimed bird nerds.

The Big Year features A-list stars Owen Wilson, Jack Black and Steve Martin. They play three die-hard birders profiled in Mark Obmascik's book of the same name, which tells the true story of the legendary 1998 Big Year competition.

One of those featured birders is Greg, played by Jack Black. Though (spoiler alert!) he's not the winner of the Big Year, he turns out to be the unlikely hero, since he keeps his day job during the entire competition and has to travel on a limited budget.

To really appreciate Greg's story, the movie and extreme birding in general, you have to know a few fundamentals. How does a Big Year work? What's the point? And who's crazy enough to try it? You might be surprised at the answers.

Big Year Basics

Birders have been embarking on these yearlong quests since the 1930s. While there's much cooperation, there's also more than a little competition.

A ready reserve of cash is a bonus, especially if you need to take time off from work, but even more important is communication with the birding community. If a Xantus's hummingbird is spotted above the Mexican border, Big Year birders know about it in minutes. A Nutting's flycatcher in Patagonia Lake State Park? They've already booked their flights to Arizona.

How do birders get this insider information? The Internet has made it easy to get rare bird alerts in seconds. From birding Listservs and websites to the North American Rare Bird Alert (*narba.org*), once the news gets out, it spreads fast. Then competitive birders will do whatever it takes to make it to the right place at the right time.

But how do we know birders are telling the truth about their sightings? There aren't any formal rules, documentation or referees to verify sightings. Essentially, Big Year birders are on the honor system. But with reputations at stake and other birders all around, it seems to work.

A GREAT YEAR FOR BIRDS. Greg Miller is one of the three birders profiled in the movie *The Big Year*. He's pictured at right with actor Jack Black, who plays him in the movie. During Greg's adventure in 1998, some of the more unique birds he saw included (clockwise from top left) red-billed tropicbird, spotted redshank, hawfinches and bluethroat. Greg saw a total of 715 bird species that year, earning him second place overall.

Ultimately, a Big Year is a numbers game. About 675 species of birds show up faithfully every year in North America or its offshore waters, though many of these occur only in limited areas. If you want to beat the record, you'll need to see all of them, plus the unpredictable vagrants, as they're called, that visit the continent in any given year.

The Biggest Year

No Big Year has ever been as competitive or as talked about as the one Greg competed in. The 1998 event was no ordinary one. Powerful El Niño storms blew many vagrants and rare birds to the U.S. as Greg and two other power birders, Sandy Komito and Al Levantin, fought for top honors.

From January to December, these three paid close attention to migration and weather patterns. Then they visited birding hot spots all over the continent, hoping to be at the right place at the right time.

In an interview, Greg said that the relationship among the three birders was "cordial, respectful (but) always competitive."

Like any extreme birder, this trio has some memorable stories to share. There was the time Al got so close to a mountain lion in the Texas desert that he could count its whiskers. Or the time Greg got his canoe stuck in the mud of the Everglades. Or when Sandy's car got stranded on a snowdrift in Colorado and he had to walk into town for help, meeting a Vietnamese potbellied pig along the way.

By the time the year was over, the three men had had the time of their lives chasing birds. Sandy was the ultimate winner, beating his own previous record with an unbelievable 745 birds total.

Birders on the Red Carpet

It's rare for the world of bird-watching to capture the attention of Hollywood. And who knows? Maybe some moviegoers, seeing and hearing the magic of birding for the first time, will be inspired to take it up—or even embark on their own Big Year.

How does Greg feel about being portrayed by a movie star?

"I am quite blown away," he admitted. "It's rather surreal. I could never have imagined this happening."

He added: "I hope that in all this, the real stars are not forgotten—the birds. After all, there would be no Big Years, no stories or books without the wonderful creatures that motivate us."

TROPICBIRD, TUI DE ROY / MINDEN PICTURES; REDSHANK, MARKUS VARESVUO / npl / MINDEN PICTURES; HAWFINCHES, DUNCAN USHER / FOTO NATURA / MINDEN PICTURES; BLUETHROAT, DIETMAR NILL / FOTO NATURA / MINDEN PICTURES; JACK & GREG, CAM SHAW

notable BIG years

1939 Guy Emerson, a traveling businessman who timed his work trips to coincide with migrations, reported seeing 497 species.

1953 Roger Tory Peterson and James Fisher toured the continent to write *Wild America* while bird-watching at the same time. With side trips, Roger ended the year with 572 species.

1971 Ted Parker, an 18-year-old student, set a new record with 626 species. He started his Big Year while still in high school in Pennsylvania and finished it during college in Arizona.

1973 Kenn Kaufman hitchhiked 69,200 miles and saw 666 birds on a $1,000 budget, while Floyd Murdoch reported 669 in the same year. (Read Kenn's book *Kingbird Highway* for a fascinating look at a Big Year on a budget.)

1979 James Vardaman, a businessman from Mississippi, hired professionals to help him along his Big Year route. He was also the first to come up with a hotline to find more birds. He ended his year with 699 species and spent more than $44,000.

1983 Benton Basham focused on the rarest birds and tallied 711 species.

1988 Sandy Komito's first attempt at a Big Year scored him 721 birds.

1998 Sandy shattered his own record with 745 birds. He spent $100,000 and traveled 270,000 miles. His story was one of three featured in *The Big Year*.

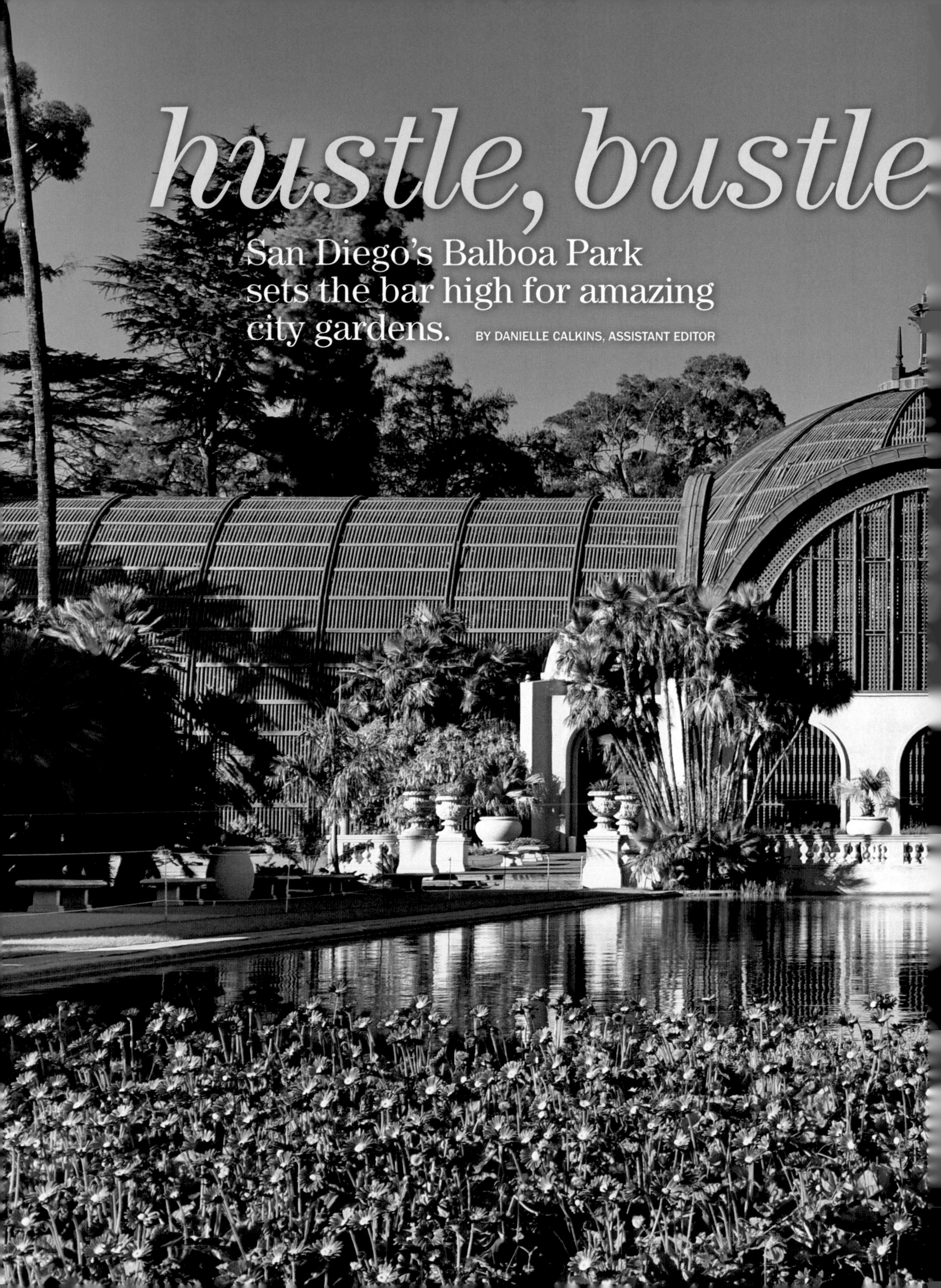

hustle, bustle

San Diego's Balboa Park sets the bar high for amazing city gardens.

BY DANIELLE CALKINS, ASSISTANT EDITOR

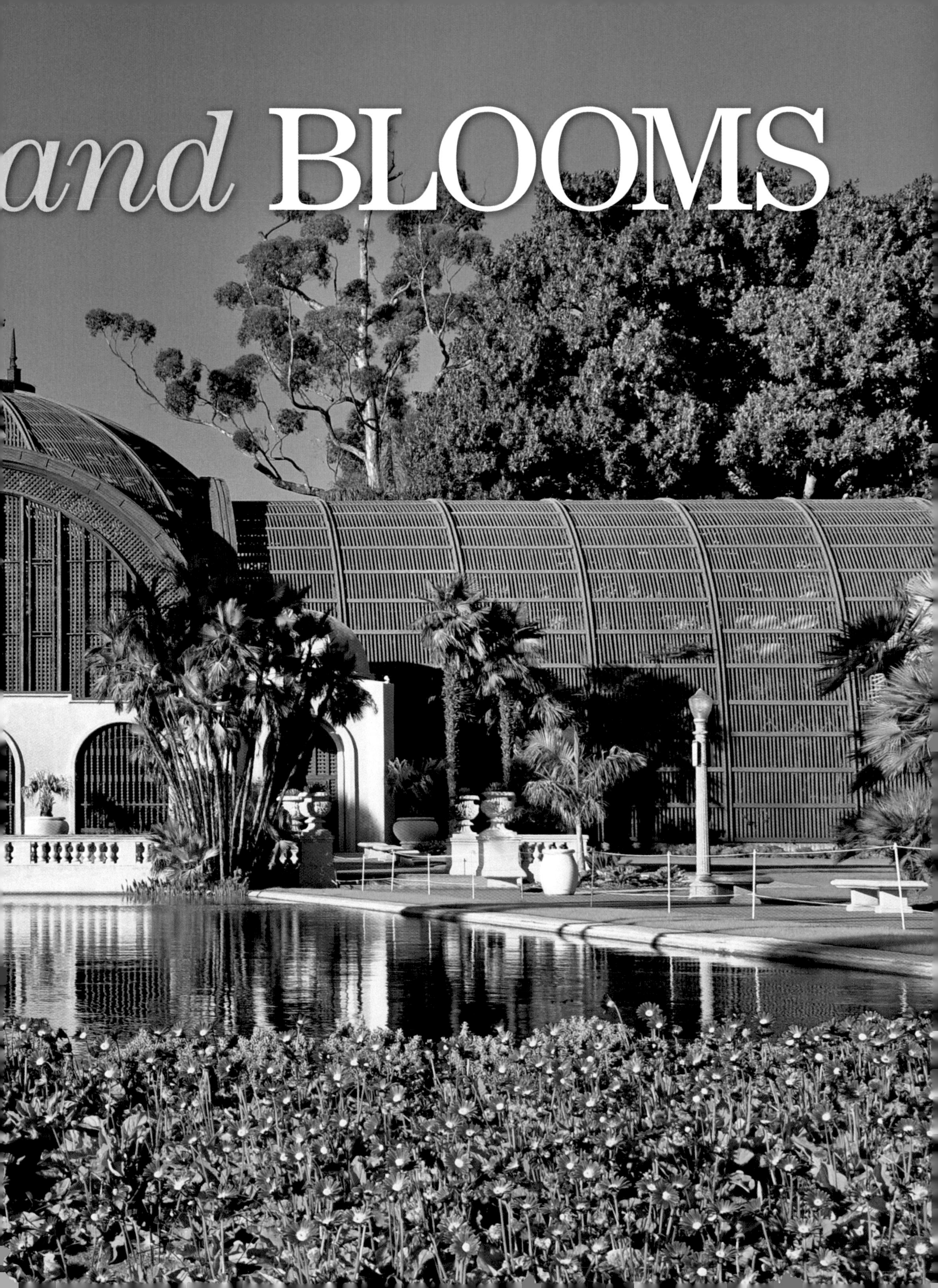
and BLOOMS

I consider myself a country girl. For starters, I attended a high school smack dab in the center of a cornfield. And, until recently, the closest shopping center to my house worth visiting was a half-day trip away.

Now I'm all grown up and have moved to the city. Although I'm on the outskirts and am still able to enjoy my small backyard, I can't help but notice the snippets of gardens all around me. Sure, they're often smaller than I'm used to, but that doesn't make them any less beautiful.

Gardens in a City of Millions

Truth be told, it's possible to find spectacular gardens in bustling urban areas. In a city with a population over a million, Balboa Park is a San Diego gem. With 19 gardens spread across 1,200 acres, including the San Diego Zoo, the park delights travelers and natives alike.

If you visit, you'll find that the gardens are designed with diversity in mind. The trees alone represent more than 1,200 species.

"We're lucky to have a park set within a Mediterranean climate, where almost anything can grow," says San Diego Park Ranger Kim Duclo. "Our gardens have native plants, but the bulk of them come from other regions with similar climates."

Kim promises guests will see delicate orchids, cacti and other plants from areas such as Australia, the Canary Islands and Chile.

"We've created an exotic natural landscape by bringing in over 2 million plants," Kim says. "One of the park's highlights is the combination of the Inez Grant Parker Memorial Rose Garden and the adjacent Desert Garden. With the variety of the two gardens, guests have fun contrasting and comparing them while both are in bloom."

According to Nursery Supervisor Mike Rasmussen, the focal point of Balboa Park, and the home of perhaps the most popular garden, is the Botanical Building. Built for the 1915-16 Panama-California Exposition, it is one of the largest lath structures in the entire world.

OF SPANISH DESCENT. The Alcazar Garden at Balboa Park mimics the design of the Alcazar Castle in Seville, Spain. You'll find ornate fountains and 7,000 annuals bordered by boxwood hedges. Admission to all the Balboa Park gardens is free 365 days a year.

"The Botanical Building is always kept in perfect condition," Mike says. "We rotate the orchids every week, creating a museum atmosphere. Guests know they can always find new plant material."

Along with the Botanical Building and the Rose Garden, the Japanese Friendship Garden is counted among Balboa's most cherished assets. It's a big part of why *Forbes* magazine ranked Balboa among the best city parks in the U.S. in 2009.

Top City Garden Contenders

Although beautiful, San Diego has some impressive competition. In New York City, for instance, the New York Botanical Garden (*nybg.org*) boasts more than 1 million plants. The garden's 3,500 roses represent so many different varieties that there's something blooming for six months out of the year.

What about extreme climates? With average summer highs reaching over 100 degrees, Phoenix, Arizona might be the last place you'd think to find lush gardens. Luckily, the Desert Botanical Garden (*dbg.org*) has you covered with more than 145 acres of plant displays, including an herb garden and a wildflower trail.

While smaller than the others, the Texas Discovery Gardens (*texas discoverygardens.org*) in Dallas feature both native plants and species from around the world. They're also the state's first public gardens to be certified 100 percent organic by the Texas Organic Research Center.

For a collection of 17 award-winning themed gardens, check out the Toronto Botanical Garden (*torontobotanicalgarden.ca*), where the emphasis is on education and hands-on learning. The compact gardens mirror the scale of typical urban landscapes, giving visitors plenty of ideas to try in their own backyards.

Cities can overwhelm the senses, but they can also surprise you with islands of calm and beauty. The next time you're craving an urban retreat, whether you're visiting or call the city home, find out whether there's a public garden nearby. You never know what you'll discover.

PREVIOUS PAGE: BOTANICAL BUILDING, STEVE MINKLER / SHUTTERSTOCK.COM; ALCAZAR GARDEN, LYNN WATSON / SHUTTERSTOCK.COM; TRELLIS, PATRICIA J. BRUNO / POSITIVE IMAGES

tips from some city folks

Gardening in your own small space? We asked other city gardeners how they deal with the challenge. Here are their best tips:

PLAY UP YOUR CONTAINERS.
Pretty self-explanatory, isn't it? Kick your containers up a notch by mixing your flowers with edibles. Chard makes a great ornamental—and it's tasty, too! When planting in a small space, opt for dwarf varieties of veggies. You won't lose out on taste, and you'll have more space to work with.

DECORATE WITH A TRELLIS.
Train vines such as peas and cucumbers to grow up a trellis, which will maximize space even more while adding an attractive accent to your yard. For vines with attractive blooms, try clematis and honeysuckle. (Just make sure the honeysuckle is not an invasive variety.)

KNOW YOUR YARD.
If it's mostly shade you're working with, a flower garden is your best bet. Herbs, vegetables and fruits need at least six hours of direct sunlight a day. When planting, pick a spot to build raised beds. That way your footsteps won't compact your garden, and you can focus your watering, fertilizing and weeding on a smaller area.

seven

Fascinating migration tales, record-breaking numbers and survival stories make these some of the most notable spring birding wonders in North America.

wonders
of the birding world

BY CRYSTAL RENNICKE, SENIOR EDITOR

Springtime is an exciting season in nature, but these places and birds have something extra special to celebrate each spring. They are North America's most intriguing bird tales. If you're near one of these wonders, stop by and check it out!

1 Whooping cranes at Wood Buffalo National Park.

Because of habitat loss and unregulated hunting in the '30s and '40s, only 15 whooping cranes were left in the U.S. by 1949. Extinction seemed certain.

Today, a lone migratory flock—still fragile, but bigger in number—is the only natural, self-sustaining group of whooping cranes in the U.S. The flock spends the winters on the Gulf Coast of Texas at the Aransas National Wildlife Refuge and breeds 2,500 miles north, in northwest Canada's Wood Buffalo National Park. Studying their migration patterns has helped conservationists save whooping cranes from extinction. Currently the flock has about 40 nesting pairs.

Thanks to conservation efforts, another flock now winters in central Florida and breeds in Necedah National Wildlife Refuge in Wisconsin. After a successful test with sandhill cranes, an ultralight aircraft led the whooping cranes to their wintering grounds the first year, and now they've mastered the flight. The long-term goal is to establish a self-sustaining population of a minimum of 1,000 whooping cranes by 2035. These amazing birds have come a long way in the past 60 years.

2 Red knot pit stop at Delaware Bay.

The red knot migration is fascinating: The sandpipers travel from their wintering areas as far down as the tip of South America to breeding grounds in the Canadian Arctic, a 20,000-mile round trip!

An extremely important pit stop, Delaware Bay, which lies between Delaware and New Jersey, is a sight to see in spring. Millions of red knots gather to fuel up for the rest of their trip. The menu? Horseshoe crab eggs. High in fat, the eggs help the birds double their body weight in preparation for the flight. This particular spot is so important because it has the largest concentration of mating horsehoe crabs in the U.S. To see multitudes of red knots feasting on these eggs is remarkable.

WHOOPING CRANES, JEFF FOOTT / DISCOVERY CHANNEL IMAGES / GETTY IMAGES; RED KNOTS, ROLF NUSSBAUMER

SPRING BREAK. During spring migration, millions of red knots (below) stop at Delaware Bay to fuel up on horseshoe crab eggs for their journey. The lone migratory flock of whooping cranes (left) heads to Canada to breed each spring.

Arctic tern

3 The arctic tern: world traveler.

As soon as an arctic tern chick can fly, it joins its parents on the world's longest migration.

These remarkable birds fly approximately 22,000 miles each year. In fact, most of an arctic tern's life is spent in the air. They rarely spend time on land except to breed.

The usual spring migratory path of the arctic tern starts in Antarctica. From there it flies up the African coast, over southern Europe, across the Atlantic Ocean and past North America, where it breeds as far north as the Arctic. Imagine all the sights it sees on this astonishing journey!

4 The American golden plover flight to Alaska.

American golden plovers are among the longest nonstop migrants in the world. They make the 3,000-mile trip from Hawaii to Alaska in about 50 hours, all at one go.

They breed on the Alaskan tundra, then abandon their chicks for the golf courses and lawns of Hawaii. (Wouldn't most parents like to do this from time to time?)

Meanwhile, the young birds are fattening up in preparation for their first migration without their parents. And while their parenting is questionable, the golden plovers' nonstop flight is nothing short of incredible.

5 Turkey vultures in Hinckley, Ohio.

If you live in Hinckley, Ohio, you likely consider the turkey vulture an icon. This bird is the local harbinger of spring. Every March 15, the town gathers to welcome the first turkey vulture of the season and to hold a festival in its honor.

While not exactly beautiful, it's quite a helpful creature. One of the few birds with a sense of smell, the turkey vulture sniffs out dead animals,

American golden plover

CONGREGATING CRANES. To see the largest flock of sandhill cranes in the world, visit the Platte River Valley in south central Nebraska in March. About 80 percent of the nation's population of sandhill cranes can be seen in one visit!

its primary food source. The bird's digestive system kills any virus and bacteria in the food it eats, so its droppings don't carry disease. Each member of the species is like a walking sanitation station. And for that, everyone should celebrate the turkey vulture's return.

Turkey vulture

6 Sandhill cranes, Platte River Valley, Nebraska.

To see tens of thousands of sandhill cranes in one spot, visit the Platte River Valley in south central Nebraska. Here, at dawn from mid- to late March, nearly 80 percent of the sandhill crane population of the world can be found.

Why here? The environment is ideal for cranes. Lush with cornfields and native grasslands, the valley offers abundant food for them. Shallow river channels, wet meadows, shallow lakes and uplands are perfect for roosting, protecting the cranes from predators and other disturbances. And the area gives birders a chance to get a closer look at these usually wary birds.

7 Cliff swallows return to Capistrano.

When the cliff swallows return to San Juan Capistrano, California, on March 19, a similar celebration occurs. Thousands of these orange-rumped migrants fly in to reclaim their old nests in the arches and walls of the ancient mission, which bears the same name as the city.

Historically, Capistrano has been an ideal spot for cliff swallows because billions of insects thrive in its open fields and wetlands.

But today Capistrano is a growing city. The swallows have found more eaves to nest under, but their food supply is dwindling. The swallows are nesting farther from the center of things, but they are still the city's most famous citizens. The birds are not only well known, they're also well loved and protected. The city is by law a bird sanctuary.

Cliff swallow

ARCTIC TERN, PAUL THOMPSON IMAGES / ALAMY; GOLDEN PLOVER, NIGEL PYE / ALAMY; CRANES, TOM & PAT LEESON; SANDHILL CRANE WITH TWO YOUNG, MARIE READ; TURKEY VULTURE, DAVID KLEYN / ALAMY; CLIFF SWALLOWS FLYING, ANTHONY MERCIECA; CLIFF SWALLOW, GREG LASLEY / KAC PRODUCTIONS

the *magic* of

Every year in late summer, monarchs fly into the spotlight as they undertake a lengthy migration from as far north as Canada to escape winter's chill in Mexico.

BY JULIE WARNER, MINNEAPOLIS, MINNESOTA

monarchs

MONARCH, MIGRATION: MASLOWSKI WILDLIFE; GIRL: WENDY PERRY / SHUTTERSTOCK.COM

You don't have to travel south of the border to witness the wonder of overwintering monarchs. California's central coast provides the sole U.S. winter habitat for the majestic migrants, attracting much of the population west of the Rockies. One city in particular has a special connection with monarchs.

Pacific Grove—nicknamed Butterfly Town, USA—attracts one of the largest overwintering populations in the area. Residents cherish the phenomenon. In 1990, they voted for public funding to create the Monarch Grove Sanctuary, protecting the habitat for the thousands of monarchs that make it their home from roughly October to February.

The celebration of the monarchs' arrival begins in early October, when costumed kindergartners lead schoolchildren through downtown in the Butterfly Parade, a decades-old tradition.

On the Saturday after Thanksgiving, the community's Museum of Natural History, located less than a mile from the sanctuary, hosts Monarch Magic. The one-day celebration features discussions led by experts, activities for kids and extended monarch-viewing hours.

Visiting the Sanctuary

The 2.6-acre sanctuary is just blocks from downtown, tucked into a residential neighborhood. Visitors may park for free next to the sanctuary's sign and advance down a long, narrow path next to the Butterfly Grove Inn. The path spreads out into a lovely wooded park filled with tall eucalyptus trees, Monterey pines and Monterey cypress, which shield the delicate butterflies from wind and storms.

During colder weather, the monarchs huddle on tree branches, mimicking dead leaves. Temperatures below 55 degrees ground the butterflies—their wings simply can't weather the cold. Rain will also shut down their flight.

Those who visit the sanctuary on a warm day, though, might see hundreds of flying butterflies. The warmth of the sun coaxes them to play in the air and alight on flowers to feed on nectar.

When the monarchs are in residence, volunteers staff the sanctuary from noon to 3 p.m. daily, greeting visitors and helping them view the monarchs through five scopes fixed on spots where the butterflies tend to cluster. Museum Director Lori Mannel describes this experience as magical.

"At the moment when visitors understand they're not looking at a cluster of leaves," she says, "there's a moment of enlightenment"—followed by gasps of delight.

Admission to the sanctuary is free. Visitors are welcome to drop in anytime from dawn to dusk. Those who come during unstaffed hours should bring binoculars and look toward the trees in the sanctuary's southeast corner, about 15 to 20 feet up, to spot the orange beauties.

Monarch numbers and activity peak from late November to early December. And if their timing is just right, visitors may be able to observe a bit of the mating season, which begins in early February, just before the monarchs depart.

The females lay eggs as they migrate back north in the spring. Each generation lives only four to five weeks, until the shorter days and cooler temperatures tell the current generation it's time to make the trek back to a warmer climate.

birding with friends

Learn why bird-watching is better when you share it.

BY KIMBERLY KAUFMAN, CONTRIBUTING EDITOR

My obsession with birds began as a solo flight. As I was waiting for a doctor's appointment one summer morning, something outside caught my eye. Perched on a feeder just inches from the window, looking utterly smashing, were eight tiny birds. Dressed in brilliant golden plumage, they were like lemon drops wearing black-and-white capes. It would be several days before I discovered that they were American goldfinches, but even without a name, they had me completely captivated.

STRUCK BY GOLD. Several American goldfinches (like these) get the credit for making Kimberly Kaufman a lifetime birder.

Discovering Birds

Before long I began searching for birds everywhere I could. Each exploration brought a kaleidoscope of discovery, and birds with names like indigo bunting, Baltimore oriole and rose-breasted grosbeak wove a colorful thread through my life. It was a joyous time for me, but I was still flying solo. Standing in the woods one spring morning, marveling over my first wood thrush and rejoicing in its ethereal song, I found myself longing for someone to share the experience with.

Ultimate Birding Companion

What I was experiencing is common. Most humans have an intrinsic desire to share. Even the most timid children feel the exhilaration of show-and-tell day when they get to reveal some special treasure. We call upon our friends to share good news and bad, reducing the impact of the bad things by dividing the sadness, and making the good things more splendid by celebrating them with friends.

Birding is no exception. While we all enjoy moments of solitude in the woods or in our own backyard or garden, there's nothing more rewarding than sharing birding experiences with a friend.

When I first became enchanted by birds, I was literally the only bird-watcher I knew. At that point I didn't own a computer, so finding birding friends wasn't quite as simple as it can be today.

While I struggled in the beginning to find someone to go birding with, I eventually found the ultimate birding companion when I met Kenn Kaufman, who is now my husband. He also happens to be one of the country's leading bird experts and author of the *Kaufman Field Guide to Birds of North America*. Spending time in the field with Kenn is like birding with a living, breathing field guide. I learn something new every time we go exploring together.

Flocking Together

Now, I know not everyone has a Kenn Kaufman at his or her fingertips, but you'll frequently find that local experts are willing to take you under their wings. While learning on your own is important, it's also nice to have someone who can help advance your bird identification skills and teach you something about songs and calls.

An extra set of eyes never hurts, either. While some birds are bright and colorful, others are subtle and camouflaged. Often foraging high in the canopy, in dense brush and thickets or soaring overhead, wild birds can be difficult to spot. Venturing out with a friend can improve your ability to detect birds—and if you encounter a rarity, it's also great to have someone who can corroborate your sighting.

Another practical reason for birding in pairs or groups is the gear. It's possible to enjoy birds sans the equipment, but having binoculars and a spotting scope can really enhance the experience. Combine those with drinking water, field guides and other supplies, and soon a birding partner who can share the load is pretty appealing. Kenn and I have hiked several miles to see a single bird, and taking turns carrying the scope and tripod meant we still had enough energy to enjoy looking at the star attraction when we finally got there!

Safety is a factor, too. Serious birding can require hikes over rough terrain, so it's good to have a buddy.

Finally, the best part of birding with someone else goes back to the simple joy of sharing. The aerial ballet of a ruby-throated hummingbird, the antics of a blue jay, the way your heart feels when a robin sings: All these become more memorable when you have a friend to share the experience with.

BIRD-WATCHERS, STEVE COLE / GETTY IMAGES; GOLDFINCHES, RICHARD DAY / DAYBREAK IMAGERY

a gardener's

Discover bed-and-breakfast getaways all over the country that boast stunning gardens and homegrown veggies.

BY DANIELLE CALKINS, ASSISTANT EDITOR

escape

There's something about a bed-and-breakfast retreat. Whether it's the smell of fresh coffee brewing, the attention to detail in each room or the friendly faces you'll meet, a welcoming B&B makes for a supremely enjoyable experience.

Now imagine this. In addition to the regular amenities, your destination also offers outstanding flower gardens for your enjoyment. Or how about breakfast prepared from the vegetable garden out back? We searched high and low to find great B&Bs around the country that cater to garden lovers. Take a look at some of our top picks.

Linden Plantation • Vicksburg, Mississippi

Prepare to be awed by the 750 azaleas that greet guests as they drive up to Linden Plantation. Soon the azaleas give way to a group of magnolias that have stood here for more than 150 years.

The gardens, which cover 8 acres and include 75 varieties of roses, offer stunning variety. They include a cottage garden, a butterfly garden, a parterre garden, and a ruins garden created from the rubble of the original pre-Civil War plantation home. A wild garden contains over 100 varieties of native plants nestled around five ancient red cedar trees. Find out more at *linden plantationgardens.com.*

Anna V's • Lanesboro, Minnesota

The innkeepers of this 1908 Victorian home, pictured at left, pride themselves on fresh garden produce, including raspberries, rhubarb and tomatoes.

Guests are encouraged to pick their own raspberries, as well as apples straight from Anna V's two trees. The apples are also used in an old-fashioned press to make sweet, fresh cider for guests. For eye appeal, there are hydrangeas and hostas. In fact, more than 300 species of hostas can be found at local farms. For more information, visit *annavbb.com.*

SWEET CIDER. Apples from Anna V's apple trees are used in an old-fashioned press to make cider for guests. Here, neighbor Frank Wright uses the press.

ANNA V'S, SWEET CIDER, DAYLILY: STEVE HARRIS; LINDEN PLANTATION, MAGNOLIA: JOY BRABSTON; IRIS: GINA, ABELLA GARDEN INN

BERRIES FOR BREAKFAST. A breakfast plate of fresh berries cupped within the petals of a colorful daylily is a feast for the eyes and the palate at Hillcrest.

Hillcrest Hide-Away • **Lanesboro, Minnesota**

Since Lanesboro calls itself the bed-and-breakfast capital of Minnesota, it's not surprising to discover Hillcrest Hide-Away just down the road from Anna V's. While breakfast is important at any B&B, the owners of the Hillcrest Hide-Away kick it up a notch. First, the savory breakfasts are prepared with a variety of fresh herbs found in the planters and gardens surrounding the property. And the wow factor? As often as possible, dishes are garnished with edible flowers, including daylilies, pansies, nasturtiums, scented geraniums, hibiscus and honeysuckle. The landscape includes a walking labyrinth bordered by 300 feet of flower beds. The gardens are designed to attract hummingbirds, which guests often spot on the honeysuckle vine in the late afternoon. Learn more at *hillcresthideaway.com*.

Blue Stone Cottage • **High Falls, New York**

With 18 cottage gardens to stroll through, this B&B is a gardener's delight. Guests use the gardens for meditation, yoga, inspiration, respite and renewal. They're also encouraged to cut their own bouquets to adorn their rooms, and then take them home after their stay is complete.

Furnished with antiques and bejeweled with flowerpots from the 1930s, Blue Stone Cottage is a find. Learn more at *bluestonecottagebandb.com*.

Steamboat Inn • **Idleyld Park, Oregon**

Perched on a river bluff in the Umpqua National Forest, the inn is known for colorful wildflowers and edible mushrooms. Bird and butterfly gardens keep things humming.

If you're lucky enough to stay the last weekend in April, be sure to check out the Glide Wildflower Show, where hundreds of native wildflowers are on display. Learn more at *thesteamboatinn.com* and *glidewildflowershow.org*.

Abella Garden Inn • **Arroyo Grande, California**

Garden-themed rooms and a setting that includes a running stream and waterfalls make a stay here a relaxing experience. The tearoom offers such flavors as lemon mint, bay leaf and orange leaf, all picked right out of the garden. The owner and chef was born in Italy, and her cooking reflects her heritage. For more information, visit *abellagardeninn.com*.

The Garden Gables Inn • **Lenox, Massachusetts**

The large, late-blooming kousa dogwood on the grounds is one of the summer attractions here. The innkeepers promise it's quite a sight to see.

The landscape is alive with perennial beds, container gardens, stretches of burning bush and an organic veggie garden that furnishes part of the breakfast menu. As an extra treat, guests are welcome to divide garden plants to take home with them. Learn more at *gardengablesinn.com*.

BERRIES FOR BREAKFAST, HILLCREST HIDE-AWAY: MARVIN EGGERT; BLUE STONE COTTAGE: HEIDI RACIOPPO;
ABELLA GARDEN INN: GINA, ABELLA GARDEN INN; BREWSTER INN: MARK STEPHENS; INN SERENDIPITY: JOHN IVANKO

Brewster Inn

Inn Serendipity

Brewster Inn • Dexter, Maine

If you appreciate hard workers, the owners of the Brewster Inn will impress you. Mark and Judith Stephens are completely reinventing the 2½ acres of gardens surrounding their historic inn. The 1875 home, which was featured on a 2008 segment of HGTV's *If Walls Could Talk*, is on the National Register of Historic Places. So Judith and Mark have made sure that both the indoor and outdoor renovations are in keeping with the property's original character.

One of the couple's current projects is replanting lilac hedgerows like the ones that bloomed decades ago—bushes so fragrant, some people in Dexter say you could smell them all over town. And here's a challenge: With such ambitious landscaping plans ahead, Mark promises a free stay to any guest willing to turn a part of the gardens into something truly special. Learn more at *brewsterinn.com*.

Inn Serendipity • Browntown, Wisconsin

The innkeepers here follow the 100-foot rule: Almost all their breakfast ingredients travel no more than 100 feet from their gardens to your plate.

Guests can also enjoy an extensive tasting tour of the inn's kitchen gardens, as well as a tour of the perennial flower beds. You're welcome to join in on each harvest to get the full experience. Operating on solar energy, Inn Serendipity uses organic growing methods and even has a straw bale greenhouse. For more information, visit *innserendipity.com*.

destination BIRDING

Turn all your vacations into bird excursions with a little creativity and research.

GREAT EGRET, NIGHT-HERON: EILEEN COHEN; EASTERN MEADOWLARK, BRIDGE, BALD EAGLE: WILDLIFESOUTH.COM

BY DANIELLE CALKINS, ASSISTANT EDITOR

Give me a popular vacation spot, and I'll tell you where to find the birds.

As one of the newest members of the *Birds & Blooms* team, I'll admit that I'm a newbie when it comes to birding. But as I began researching the subject, I discovered that memorable birding is everywhere.

Each year I take a break from winter to spend a family vacation in sunny Florida. I can't wait to put my research to the test and use birding as a relaxing way to connect with wildlife and view the area's natural beauty.

Ready to turn your favorite getaway into a birding hot spot? Let's go.

SAN FRANCISCO

Maybe a visit to Alcatraz is in your future, or you're dying to take in one of the country's most vibrant cultural scenes. Either way, if you're headed to San Francisco, pack your binoculars. The city is along the Pacific Flyway, one of the major north-south routes for migrating birds.

Choosing just one local birding location is hard, but one of the most accessible is the Crissy Field Marsh on the San Francisco Bay, which has more than 100 acres to explore. Another perk? You can see the Golden Gate Bridge (above)—giving you an incredible backdrop for your photos.

LAS VEGAS

Birding is probably the last thing you think of when planning a trip to Las Vegas. Flashy lights and endless rows of casinos, yes. Birds, no.

Actually, the Las Vegas area has many spots for wildlife viewing. The Red Rock Canyon National Conservation Area, on the western edge of the Las Vegas Valley, offers a stunning setting for taking photos of songbirds, hawks, woodpeckers and more. For more info, see *redrockcanyonlv.org*.

FLORIDA

Sure, you're aware of the great beaches, the Kennedy Space Center and all

things Disney. But did you know the Sunshine State boasts some of the best birding in North America? Each year 2 million birders take advantage of Florida's diverse avian habitats; this year I was happy to be one of them. I was amazed at how much birding activity is near popular vacation spots.

The Venice Area Audubon Society Rookery, for example, is a hidden gem. Just an hour's drive from Fort Myers, it's a prime area for birds to nest from January to March. (The photos at right are just a few examples, taken at Joe Overstreet Road in Kissimmee and The Venice Area Audubon Society Rookery.) The society sponsors activities like bird walks, identification classes and bird counts. Birders who are more independent can grab a camera and binoculars and explore at their leisure.

Great egret
Eastern meadowlark
Yellow-crowned night-heron
Bald eagle

READY FOR TAKEOFF. This majestic great blue heron was photographed at the Venice Area Audubon Society Rookery in Florida. Photographer Eileen Cohen has been a proud member of the organization for years.

Learn more at *veniceaudubon.org.*

Another Florida hot spot is the Robinson Preserve in Bradenton, less than an hour from Tampa's famous beaches. Open for a few years, this birding paradise offers over 400 acres of marshlands, open water and trails. If that's not appealing enough, the grounds also boast a 500-foot boardwalk, perfect for wildlife viewing.

If you're headed to Florida for some family fun, be sure to look beyond Mickey Mouse. After a day of crowds, you'll be ready for a short, serene break just 25 minutes from the bustling grounds of Walt Disney World. Joe Overstreet Road in Kissimmee is a five-mile dirt path that leads to Lake Kissimmee, where you'll find ample opportunities for birding. You'll return from your getaway not only refreshed, but with a camera full of bald eagle and sandhill crane photos for your vacation scrapbook.

NEW YORK CITY

If you're flying to the Big Apple, here's a must for your itinerary: the New York City Audubon website, *nycaudubon.org.* With the site as your guide, you'll see Manhattan and the surrounding area in a whole new light. The site's online events calendar lists things to do virtually every weekend of the year.

Further afield, rural New York state offers prime birding opportunities. Iroquois National Wildlife Refuge, in the small western New York towns of Alabama and Shelby, lies on the Atlantic Flyway, another major migration route. The preserve's claim to fame is its 21 species of birds of prey. Visit *iroquoisnwr.fws.gov.*

Thousands of places throughout North America offer outstanding opportunities for bird-watching, and your own search can easily find some of those treasures. It's just a matter of taking the time to look.

ROOKERY, NIGHT-HERONS: EILEEN COHEN; ROBINSON PRESERVE, ROSEATE SPOONBILLS, LOGGERHEAD SHRIKE: DOTTY MOTTA; SANDHILL CRANE, WILDLIFESOUTH.COM; BEACH, DORLING KINDERSLEY / GETTY IMAGES

6 steps to finding a birding hot spot while on vacation

1. Find water. When it comes to bird-watching, you can't go wrong by starting with water. Beaches, lakes, streams and more make popular hangouts for birds. So find the nearest splash pool around your destination of choice, and you'll be well on your way to having a successful trip.

2. Talk to your hotel concierge. He or she is trained to be an expert on the area. If you can't get specific advice about birding, ask about the best nature areas. That's a start.

3. Research before you leave. If you do some homework before packing the binoculars, chances are you'll find state or local birding groups that can tell you more about the area.

4. Chat with others on vacation. Fellow vacationers can be good sources of information. Ask them about their travels—maybe they're birders, too!

5. Take advantage of local literature. No matter where you go, your hotel is sure to have a plethora of pamphlets to help you plan your stay. Nature centers, gardens and other natural destinations can all lead to memorable birding.

6. Take a drive. Spend a few hours exploring. Bring a map and stop at any place along the way that offers a lookout. You never know what you'll find!

Northern cardinal
Photo by Maslowski Wildlife

Clark's grebes
Photo by Marie Read

Perrenial garden
Photo by Mark Turner;
Garden owners: Fonda & Ron Downs

Bike among blooms
Photo by Richard Day / Daybreak Imagery

MARY LIZ AUSTIN

CHAPTER 7

Gardening *for nature*

It's easy to create an inviting habitat for birds, butterflies and insects. Learn birdscaping basics, grow a butterfly-shaped garden, attract migratory birds and discover the benefits of planting top shrubs and monarchs' favorite foods.

bird

TERRY WILD STOCK

Make your backyard irresistible with just a few easy tricks.

BY SALLY ROTH, CONTRIBUTING EDITOR

scaping made easy

Put up a feeder, pour in some seed and you'll attract birds. Yes, it really is that simple. Food is the first step to winning the hearts of birds, and keeping a feeder makes you feel good, too.

But a feeder is just the beginning. To really bring in the birds—more birds, of more species—you need to make them feel at home in your yard. And the way to do that is with plants.

"Birdscaping," as some people call it, is a lot simpler than it sounds. All it takes are some common sense and a few lessons from the very best gardener of all, Mother Nature.

Safety First

All birds are sitting ducks when it comes to predators. A stalking cat may rush the robin on the lawn. A hungry hawk may drop from the sky at any moment. Vulnerable nestlings, eggs or even parent birds on the nest may be the target of a prowling raccoon or slithering snake.

Only a few birds, including robins and blackbirds, spend a lot of time out in the open. Most of our friends stay under cover as much as they can to boost their chances of survival.

Here's where nature's lessons come in handy. Just imitate natural wild areas, and you've got it made. You could just let your whole backyard go wild; birds would heartily approve. But most of us like to keep some sense of order, so try these tricks to keep both you and your birds happy:

- Plant shrubs in groups of three or more, to build larger areas of cover.
- Spread a thick layer of mulch beneath and between shrubs. Instantly, you've made an inviting foraging area for towhees, robins, native sparrows and juncos.
- Add a hedge along a boundary or your privacy fence. Include thorny shrubs, such as barberry, roses or flowering quince, to provide tempting nesting places for brown thrashers, gray catbirds, cardinals and others.
- Plant evergreen shrubs and trees such as holly, rhododendron, and spruce to offer shelter from the weather in all seasons.
- Vary the height of your flower beds and boost their bird appeal by planting small trees—flowering crab, dogwood, redbud—right in the beds.

Blooming Bird Feeders

Talk about multitasking—the plants in our yards do it all. They supply vital protective cover, shelter birds in bad weather and serve as nesting places.

And that's not all. Many plants also serve up enough natural food—seeds, fruit, berries and especially bugs—to keep birds coming back day after day.

Insects are the natural food our feathered friends rely on year-round. A big banquet of them will draw in birds of all kinds, just as feeders do.

To boost your bugs—yep, more insects is a good thing, if you want birds—add spring-flowering trees to your yard. Crabapples and other fruit trees bloom at migration time. That makes them an inviting pit stop for traveling wood warblers, vireos, gnatcatchers, tanagers, orioles and other birds that recognize the opportunity for a feast.

Caterpillars are another can't-miss menu item. They're at their peak during nesting season, just in time to stuff down a bunch of gaping beaks. No need to research good plants for caterpillars—just go native. Many native trees, shrubs and other plants serve as hosts for egg-laying butterflies or moths, as well as nurturing a plethora of other insects.

BIRDBATH, CAROL L. EDWARDS; ROBIN, RICHARD DAY / DAYBREAK IMAGERY

the power of water

A reliable source of fresh water can be more powerful than the best-stocked feeder. At migration time and during the long, hot summer, your birdbath is likely to get more traffic than your feeding station.

Style doesn't matter, as long as the basin isn't too slippery for birds to get a grip. Birds will find water, whether it's a puddle of rainwater in your wheelbarrow or a nifty waterfall you spent a weekend setting up.

The key words are reliable and fresh. Keep your birdbath clean and filled, so your friends know they can count on a sip and a splash at your place.

Of course, you'll want to avoid pesticides as much as possible in your bird paradise. Just think of those pesky bugs as bird food, and be patient until the troops arrive. Chickadees, wrens and vireos will help you out with aphids. Cardinals and rose-breasted grosbeaks snap up potato beetles. And starlings are your best friends when it comes to Japanese beetles: They're searching for grubs when they waddle about, stabbing the ground.

Fruits and Berries

Ask any bird lover what plants are best for birds, and the answer is likely to be berry bushes.

Birds somehow know when the fruit crop is ready, and it's quite a thrill when our favorite songbirds—bluebirds, rose-breasted grosbeaks, waxwings and more—start winging their way in from miles around.

Still, it takes only a week or so until the birds have gobbled every berry. The show is over until the next fruit or berry in your yard starts to ripen.

I wouldn't be without berry bushes or fruit trees in my yard. But I look beyond the harvest, and so do the birds. Any fruit or berry we plant is going to be home to bugs. Even if they escape our notice, birds will find them. Plus, like any plant we find a place for, berry bushes will add to the available cover and maybe even cradle a nest come spring.

Home Sweet Home

Some of our favorite birds take to birdhouses, or nest boxes, almost as soon as we hammer them up. Wrens, chickadees, titmice, tree swallows and woodpeckers all readily accept our real estate; bluebirds take a little more coaxing.

Add nest boxes to your birdscape, because it's so heartwarming to watch your bird family grow up. But keep an eye out for other nesters, too—those that build their own cup of twigs in your trees or shrubs, or smack-dab in the middle of your hanging basket of petunias. Some birds nest right on the ground, so be alert for the cheep of alarm that tells you you're trespassing.

The presence of a variety of nesting birds is a sure sign that your birdscaping is working. You have succeeded in making the birds feel at home, and that is cause for celebration. Here's an idea, why not plant another berry bush to mark the occasion?

native or not?

Nearly every native berry is beloved by birds—as long as it's the "unimproved" species of the plant. When breeders get to tinkering with them, aiming for bigger, brighter berries, the bird appeal sometimes gets lost. Crabapples and deciduous hollies, for instance, used to be bona fide bird plants; nowadays, the crop on new, improved varieties often goes uneaten.

best bets for berries

Plant some of these, and get ready to welcome a plethora of winged friends.

American bittersweet
Arrowwood
(and other native viburnums)
Bayberry
Blueberry
Cherries, sweet or sour
Cherry laurel
Dogwood
Elderberry
Flowering dogwood
Hawthorn
Holly
Juniper
Mulberry
Raspberry
Shadblow (serviceberry)
Spicebush
Toyon

SHRUBS WITH BENEFITS. Buttonbush shrubs (left with tiger swallowtail) are host plants for sphinx moths and offer abundant nectar. The highbush cranberry (above) is a type of viburnum that attracts spring azure butterflies.

best shrubs for wildlife

Attract more activity with these top picks.

BY DAVID MIZEJEWSKI, CONTRIBUTING EDITOR

Shrubs are the workhorses of the wildlife garden. They come in all sizes and provide food, cover and places to raise young. Here are just a few of the many species that will attract wildlife. Check with your local garden sources to discover which are native to your area.

Bearberry

(Arctostaphylos uva-ursi)

This evergreen ground cover's bright-red berries are eaten by songbirds, game birds and mammals. Its flowers provide nectar, and it's a host plant for elfin and hairstreak butterflies.

Buttonbush

(Cephalanthus occidentalis)

Naturally found in wetlands, this plant has wonderful globe-shaped flowers that are like a magnet for butterflies. The seeds are also a favorite of waterfowl, and it's the host plant for sphinx moths.

Viburnums (*Viburnum* spp.)

Nutritious berries and nectar-producing flowers make viburnums some of the best shrubs for wildlife. Try varieties like mapleleaf (*V. acerfolium*), arrowwood (*V. dentatum*), mooseberry (*V. edule*), common (*V. ellipticum*), nannyberry (*V. lentago*), possumhaw (*V. nudum*) or American cranberrybush (*V. trilobum*) viburnums. As an added bonus, spring azure butterflies use viburnums as host plants.

Hazelnuts (*Corylus* spp.)

American filbert (*C. americana*) and beaked filbert (*C. cornuta*) are perfect if you don't have room for larger nut trees such as oaks, hickories or pecans. They're also the host plant for hairstreak butterflies.

Hollies (*Ilex* spp.)

Both evergreen and deciduous species provide fine cover and food. Try possumhaw (*I. decidua*), inkberry (*I. glabra*), myrtleleaf (*I. myrtifolia*), winterberry (*I. verticillata*) and yaupon (*I. vomitoria*) hollies. Yaupon holly is a host plant for the Henry's elfin butterfly.

BUTTONBUSH, MARK TURNER; VIBURNUM, BRUCE COLEMAN INC. / ALAMY; SUMAC, TOM UHLMAN / ALAMY; DOGWOOD, GAY BUMGARNER / ALAMY

Dogwood

Dogwoods (*Cornus* spp.)

They provide highly nutritious fruit for migratory birds. Some species offer nectar and some are host plants for spring azure butterflies. Shrub species include alternate-leaf or pagoda (*C. alternifolia*), silky (*C. amomum*), gray (*C. racemosa*), roundleaf (*C. rugosa*) and redosier or redtwig (*C. sericea*) dogwoods.

Bayberries (*Myrica* spp.)

Birds relish berries from these shrubs, including the northern (*M. pensylvanica*), Pacific (*M. californica*) and southern wax myrtle (*M. cerifera*) species. Wax myrtle is a host plant for hairstreak butterflies and the northern bayberry for silkmoth caterpillars.

Roses (*Rosa* spp.)

Roses attract pollinators, produce nutritious rose hips and provide cover with thorny branches. Some are host plants to mourning cloak and gray hairstreak butterflies. Native species include Carolina (*R. carolina*), nootka (*R. nutka*), swamp (*R. palustris*), prairie (*R. setigera*), desert (*R. stellata*) and Virginia (*R. virginiana*).

Sumacs (*Rhus* spp.)

Sumacs are surefire draws for wildlife, including skunkbush (*R. trilobata*), fragrant (*R. aromatica*), smooth (*R. glabra*) and winged (*R. copallina*) sumacs. Their blooms offer nectar to bees, their berries are an important winter food for birds, and they are host plants for hairstreak butterflies.

Elderberry (*Sambucus* spp.)

Birds like the fruits, whether they are the blue-black berries of the common species (*S. nigra*) or the ruby ones of the red elderberry (*S. racemosa*). The flowers offer nectar to insects and, in the case of red elderberry, hummingbirds. Native bees are also known to nest in hollowed-out elderberry branches.

Blueberries (*Vaccinium* spp.)

They come in different sizes, from lowbush (*V. angustifolium*) to highbush (*V. corymbosum*), and some go by different names such as deerberry (*V. stamineum*). Western varieties are called huckleberries and have red (*V. parvifolium*) or black (*V. membranaceum*, *V. ovatum*) fruits instead of blue.

Sumac

pacific *paradise*

TERRY DONNELLY

In just a few short years, this gardener transformed his hillside retreat into a bird and butterfly haven. BY ANN WILSON, GENEVA, ILLINOIS

When an experienced gardener wields his green thumb in Washington state's temperate climes, the result is amazingly gorgeous views. Dr. Richard Driscoll is such a gardener. In just six years he has converted a lackluster 3-acre site into a lush landscape that not only provides him with a creative respite from a hectic career, but is home to bevies of birds and butterflies.

CRAZY FOR CONTAINERS. To add color and texture to his yard, Richard placed containers like those seen here in walkways and patios.

Richard and his wife, Pam, bought the Vashon Island home as a weekend retreat in 2005 and immediately saw potential in the weedy pasture that sloped steeply away from the hilltop house.

"We had been in a home with a shady yard for 16 years," Richard recalls. "And we were looking for a place with lots of sun for growing perennials. This property offered great views of the harbor and gave me a blank slate for planting."

A Frenzy of Flowers

Before Richard could dig in, excavators terraced the hillsides and contractors installed rocky walls and stone stairways to connect upper terraces to those below.

"We brought in yards and yards of topsoil," Richard says. "Then, working in five phases, I did one garden a year, planting each and every plant myself. I started the gardens with structural plants like flowering shrubs and small trees, and then added perennials.

"I've been gardening for 35 years and have always loved flowers, but now I'm getting into foliage and textures," adds Richard. "I love to use every flower color and mix things up."

He handily combines his favorite plants—hydrangeas, roses, lilacs, flame-leafed heuchera and bright-red dianthus—with sprawling sedums and blue-flowering lithodora in borders that spill over into seating areas and pathways. Vast plantings of purple-leafed heuchera, ornamental grasses and fragrant lavenders ramble across a hillside. Nectar-rich hummingbird magnets, including cape fuchsia, azalea, wisteria, trumpet vine, agastache, lupine and foxglove, pop up across the landscape.

"We have a ton of hummingbirds in our garden," says Richard. "They really like the tubular yellow, red and orange flowers.

There seem to be flowers for them during most of the season."

A Fully Stocked Garden

In addition to his perennial borders, Richard tends a vegetable garden comprising 12 raised planting beds and dozens of raspberry and blueberry bushes, a fruit orchard, and 55 containers that he plants with spring-blooming bulbs, then replants in May with vibrant annuals.

"There's a lot of planting going on at our house," Richard says with a grin. "The pots are really important to the overall design. I think of containers as artwork that supply long-term interest."

He positions the statuesque containers to define entry points to paths and stairways and to enhance courtyards and borders. Along with the weathered structures and whimsical garden ornaments, they ensure that there's something worth seeing at every turn. As he works on new gardens, Richard also tweaks those he planted before—his landscape is always evolving, so garden views shift from year to year.

"I do a lot of re-creating, and I don't necessarily follow all the rules," he notes. "You do the best you can with the time you have, which means I divide and move plants all year long. And I plant things close together because I don't like to see bare spots."

Densely packed gardens keep Pam well stocked with fresh-picked bouquets and a bounty of homegrown produce for meals. Outdoor rooms overlooking watery vistas invite the couple to linger.

"Pam and I relax on the patios, and we occasionally entertain in the garden," says Richard. "I spend most of my weekends cultivating, weeding and planting. Gardening is the only thing I do that is really creative. I love to create areas with a fun look."

OPPOSITE PAGE, BOTTOM RIGHT: MARY LIZ AUSTIN; TOP: TERRY DONNELLY

back to basics

Richard has learned a thing or two about gardening over the past 30-some years. He offers the following tips for getting the most out of your landscape.

USE THE BEST SOIL YOU CAN. Richard plants in a 50-50 mix of compost and soil, which allows roots to spread easily and water to drain quickly.

FERTILIZE STRATEGICALLY. Richard applies Marine Cuisine fertilizer to his gardens once a year and adds it to every new planting hole.

COMPOST RELIGIOUSLY. Make sure your soil has plenty of nutrients by spreading a thick layer of compost around your plantings every spring. Richard brings in 50 to 75 yards of compost every year to nourish his gardens.

a garden for butterflies

Invite butterflies to your backyard with a butterfly-shaped garden plan filled with their favorite eats. BY SALLY ROTH, CONTRIBUTING EDITOR

Butterflies are pretty simple to please.

Just put a few of their favorite plants in your backyard and you'll notice them swarming around, hungry for nectar.

For a fun way to attract them, try planting a butterfly-shaped garden in your backyard. We have two plans to choose from: one, a pairing of perennials composed of host plants and nectar plants, and the other, a feast of nectar-rich annuals. Choose the one right for your backyard, feel free to edit to your liking and plant away! Before you know it, butterflies will be frequent guests at their new dining digs.

Instructions for Building Your Bed

1. A place of honor in your lawn, in full sun, is perfect for your butterfly. To fully appreciate the effect, find a site that gives you a view from above, too.
2. Measure a 10- by 10-foot square or an 18- by 10-foot rectangle. Use garden stakes to mark the corners and tie garden twine to them to outline the garden.
3. Use white flour to draw the butterfly shape. For a guideline to wing placement, divide the area into quarters by sprinkling out two intersecting lines, one vertical and one horizontal. Then draw one wing in each quarter.

Perfect Pairings

Total Size: 18 feet by 10 feet

PLANTING KEY

1. Butterfly bush, dwarf (2)
2. Purple coneflower (2)
3. Tall Brazilian verbena (*Verbena bonariensis*) (2)
4. Autumn Joy or Autumn Fire sedum (6)
5. Bronze fennel (2)
6. *Aster* x *frikartii* 'Mönch' (2)
7. Broccoli (6)
8. Oregano (2)
9. Anise hyssop (3)
10. Lantana (2)
11. Purple annual verbena (6)
12. Pinkish-purple swamp milkweed (2)
13. Annual ageratum (6)
14. White sweet alyssum (about 12)
15. Carpet zinnia (about 12)

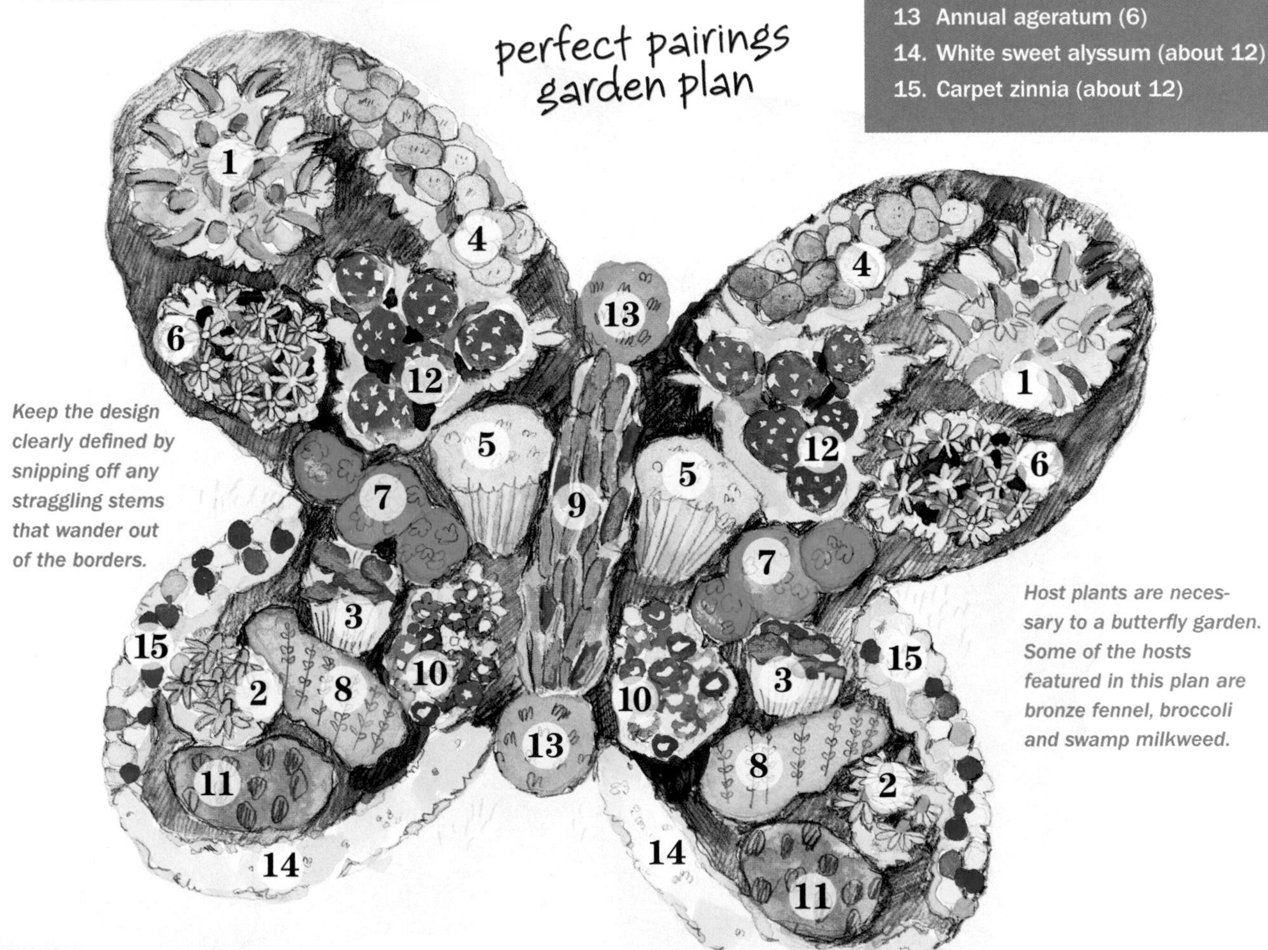

Keep the design clearly defined by snipping off any straggling stems that wander out of the borders.

Host plants are necessary to a butterfly garden. Some of the hosts featured in this plan are bronze fennel, broccoli and swamp milkweed.

ILLUSTRATIONS, MELISSA SWEET

4. Removing lawn grass sounds daunting, but it's actually a quick and satisfying job. First, slice a continuous line about 4 to 5 inches deep all along the butterfly with an edger or spade. Then use a sharp, flat shovel or a manual or power sod cutter to slice through roots. Then roll up the sod like a carpet.
5. See your butterfly? Nice work! Now let's loosen the soil for planting. Turn it with a spade, breaking up clods, and rake it smooth. Add several inches of organic matter to the soil if you need to improve drainage in heavy soil or increase water-holding ability in dry, sandy or rocky soils.
6. Edge your butterfly with a mowing strip to keep the lines clean and make lawn mowing easy.
7. Ready to bring your butterfly to life? Our recommended plants in these two plans are reliable, adaptable and easy to find at garden centers. Set the pots in place, and then plant each one. Finally, sow seeds for the fast-growing annuals, according to the design.
8. Now it's just a matter of time until your fluttery friends arrive. Both designs are overflowing with nectar flowers, and dozens of species, from teeny-tiny blues and hairstreaks to magnificent monarchs and swallowtails, will be drawn to the sweet treats.

No matter which design you choose, you'll have a front-row seat for the whole process, from the first pearly eggs and munching larvae to the final magic—a brand-new crop of fresh, beautiful butterflies for your garden.

Nectar Feast

Total size: 10 feet by 10 feet

PLANTING KEY

1. Annual ageratum (12-14)
2. Purple annual verbena (2)
3. Red annual verbena (2-4)
4. Purple sweet alyssum (about 12)
5. White sweet alyssum (about 20)
6. Parsley (4)
7. Bronze fennel (2)
8. Low-growing or carpet zinnias (2-4 seed packets)
9. Lemon Gem marigolds (4-6 seed packets)
10. Tangerine Gem marigolds (2 seed packets)

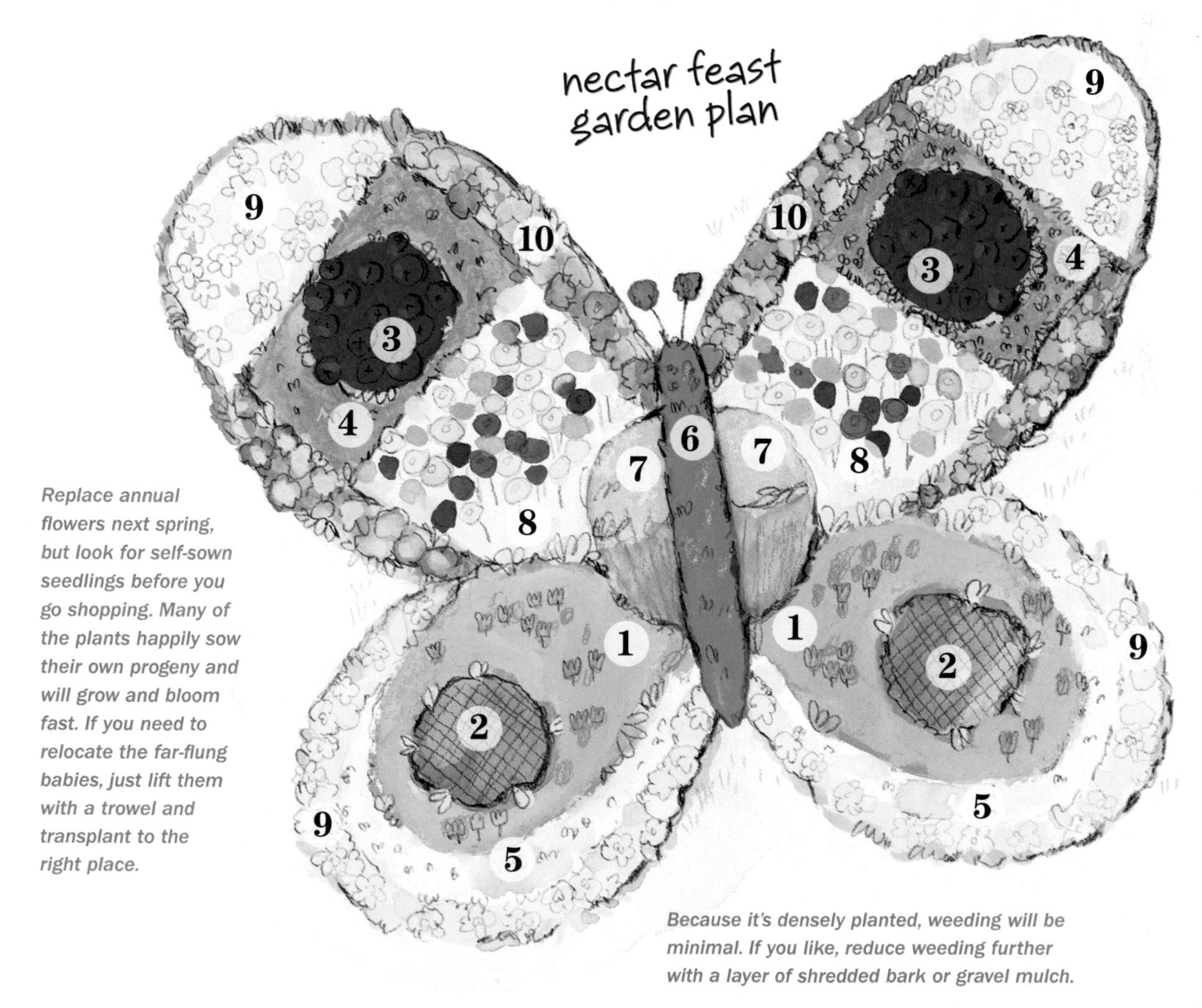

Replace annual flowers next spring, but look for self-sown seedlings before you go shopping. Many of the plants happily sow their own progeny and will grow and bloom fast. If you need to relocate the far-flung babies, just lift them with a trowel and transplant to the right place.

Because it's densely planted, weeding will be minimal. If you like, reduce weeding further with a layer of shredded bark or gravel mulch.

food for FLIGHT

Give migratory birds the fuel they need by making your backyard a stopover habitat.

BY DAVID MIZEJEWSKI, CONTRIBUTING EDITOR

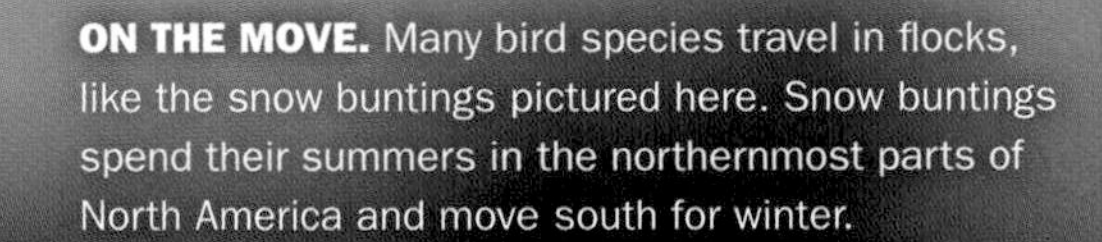

ON THE MOVE. Many bird species travel in flocks, like the snow buntings pictured here. Snow buntings spend their summers in the northernmost parts of North America and move south for winter.

JOHANN SCHUMACHER

As autumn approaches, animals begin to change their behavior in anticipation of the oncoming lean and often harsh winter months. Backyard wildlife like frogs and bats start fattening up for their long winter sleep, while animals that don't hibernate start growing thick coats for protection. Many other species of backyard wildlife, especially birds, simply avoid winter altogether and head for much warmer habitats. With a little planning, your garden can serve as a special stopover habitat for these migratory species.

Give 'em Some Energy

Migratory birds fly many thousands of miles to their winter homes, with some going as far as Central or South America. The journey requires an enormous amount of energy, so one of the best ways to attract migrants is to make sure your garden is fully stocked with native plants that provide food.

Fruit-bearing native trees and shrubs produce their berries at the same time birds are migrating through and need them most. The birds benefit from the energy-rich berries, and the plants benefit by getting the seeds in the berries distributed by the birds.

Similarly, migratory hummingbirds rely on late-blooming native vines, shrubs and perennials to provide them with nectar.

Including a diversity of native plants is also the best way to ensure that your garden is stocked with plenty of protein-rich insects for the birds. It's a fact that native plants support many more insects than exotic ones.

Check with your local native plant society for a list of fall-producing plants in your region. Another great resource is the Lady Bird Johnson Wildflower Center's website, *wildflower.org*.

You can supplement the food provided by these native plants by putting out feeders for seedeaters.

Migratory hummingbirds will also take a much-needed break from their travels to feed at a well-stocked nectar feeder. And don't worry, research shows this doesn't interfere with migration.

FOOD, WATER AND SHELTER. Keep your sugar-water feeders (right) out as long as possible to attract migrants. Above right, a small pond is like a giant welcome sign to birds flying through. If you don't have room for something this big, try a birdbath instead. Above, the juvenile American robin can get both food and shelter from this viburnum.

The Big Picture

After food, migratory birds need two more things, water and cover. A backyard pond or water garden is a great enticement, especially if you include a shallow area that's only an inch or two deep where the birds can land to take a drink and to bathe. A birdbath will do the job nicely, too.

Finally, migratory species need safe places to take a break and regain their strength. Patches of dense vegetation, especially evergreens, will provide this.

Keep in mind that some of the most common backyard birds, including chickadees, cardinals and bluebirds,

ROBIN, MASLOWSKI WILDLIFE; HUMMINGBIRDS, WATER FEATURE: RICHARD DAY / DAYBREAK IMAGERY; DRAGONFLY, LARRY DITTO / KAC PRODCUTIONS

don't migrate and will stick out the winter in your backyard. Other species, such as dark-eyed juncos and snow buntings, breed in the far north and migrate down to the lower 48 for the winter. So the things you're doing to support migratory species will benefit year-round residents, too.

don't forget butterflies and dragonflies!

Monarch butterflies rely on late-season nectar plants to fuel their migration to Mexico or central California. Dragonflies, on the other hand, need plenty of insect prey. When you can, avoid pesticides in your garden to help these beautiful migratory insects on their seasonal journeys.

milkweed: *not*

Learn about the intriguing insects this plant attracts and why it deserves a spot in your yard.

STORY AND PHOTOS BY BILL JOHNSON, MINNEAPOLIS, MINNESOTA

just for monarchs

We all have our favorite foods, and insects are no different. Over time, they've adapted to feed on one or more plants, commonly referred to as host plants.

Milkweed (*Asclepias*) is famous for being the only host plant for monarchs in their caterpillar stage. Without it, this beloved butterfly couldn't survive. But most people don't realize that milkweed is also a host plant for many other insects. So why not add it to your garden? Not only will you help out the monarch population, you'll support other fascinating insects at the same time.

Benefits of Milkweed

Of course, choosing the right kind of milkweed makes a difference. Many options are available, but planting species native to your area is always your best bet. Check with your local nature center, extension office or nursery for more specifics.

Milkweed is easy enough to grow—well-drained soil, a sunny to partly shady spot—and it easily reseeds. In fall, the seedpods burst, sending out copious quantities of seeds. This is a perfect time to gather some for passing on to friends. Or in spring, when you do a little selective thinning of the spreading plants, you can share the new sprouts with others.

So why exactly is milkweed so essential? The sap from the leaves is quite toxic to many insects and other animals, but monarch caterpillars, among others, can safely absorb the toxins. This absorption, in turn, makes the adult butterflies, moths or other insects undesirable to predators.

Other Milkweed Munchers

One of the first insects I think of when it comes to milkweed is the milkweed tussock moth, whose caterpillar is a furry eating machine. Like monarchs, the adult moths absorb the toxins the caterpillars have ingested, keeping predators away.

MONARCHS AREN'T THE ONLY ONES that enjoy the benefits of milkweed. From top, a large milkweed bug, a red milkweed beetle and a milkweed leaf beetle are fans of this plant, too.

TOP RIGHT, LARGE MILKWEED BUG: ELLIOTTE RUSTY HAROLD / SHUTTERSTOCK.COM

The red milkweed beetle and the milkweed leaf beetle, as their names tell you, also feast on these versatile plants. The first is a member of the longhorn wood-boring beetle family. The second looks like an oversized lady beetle, even though it's in an entirely different family known as leaf beetles.

An obscure insect that dines on milkweed, one I've run across only a few times, is the milkweed stem weevil. The weevil feeds on the milkweed stem but doesn't absorb the toxins from the sap. Instead, it girdles the stem, allowing the sap to ooze out; then it proceeds to feed on the leftovers.

Also worth mentioning are the large milkweed bug and the small milkweed bug, members of the family commonly known as seed bugs. These insects nibble the seeds of milkweed flower. The seeds, like the sap, are harmless to the bugs but dangerous to their predators.

Red for a Reason

Different as these milkweed-loving species are, they have at least one other thing in common: Each has bright, distinctive coloring, mostly in shades of red or orange. To many predators, that coloring says, *Don't eat me! I'll make you sick!*

If you already have milkweed in your garden, take a look and see what's chomping on it. And if you don't have any yet, plant some species that are native to your area. You'll be sure to get some interesting visitors.

JUST LIKE MONARCHS, the milkweed tussock moth (main photo) can safely absorb the toxins of the milkweed and ward off predators. Of course, the monarch caterpillar and butterfly (inset photos) rely on milkweed, their sole host plant, for survival, too.

top milkweed picks

To get you started, here are some easy-to-grow species you can add to your backyard.

Common milkweed (*Asclepias syriaca*, Zones 3 to 9)
Showy milkweed (*Asclepias speciosa*, Zones 3 to 9)
Butterfly weed (*Asclepias tuberosa*, Zones 4 to 9)
Tropical milkweed (*Asclepias curassavica*, Zones 9 to 11)
Pine needle milkweed (*Asclepias linaria*, Zones 9 to 11)
Desert milkweed (*Asclepias subulata*, Zones 9 to 11)
Whorled milkweed (*Asclepias verticillata*, Zones 9 to 11)

Interested in a milkweed that's out of your zone? Try growing it as an annual.

Green treefrog on waterlily
Photo by Rolf Nussbaumer

Eastern bluebird
Photo by Maslowski Wildlife

Downy woodpecker on sunflower
Photo by Carol L. Edwards

Giant swallowtail on a butterfly bush
Finalist in our Backyard Photo Contest
Photo by Gary Ward

CHAPTER 8

DIY *backyard*

Why pay someone else when you can make it yourself, save money and have fun doing it? Clever projects include a quaint nesting box, sparkly wind chimes, easy bird feeders, glow-in-the-dark stepping stones and much more.

Materials

- Bluebird house (or wood or recycled material to make your own)
- Plant holder with dish to fit
- Base of your choice
- Roofing material of your choice
- Material for clean-out door, including hinge, handle, etc.
- Paint
- Clear shellac sealer

Tools

- Assorted screws or nails
- Cordless drill
- Jigsaw or coping saw
- Snips
- Drill bits

bluebird bed-and-breakfast

This nesting box doubles as a mealworm feeder.

BY ALISON W. AUTH, RICHMOND, VIRGINIA

This bed-and-breakfast design offers a fun alternative to ordinary bluebird houses. To make it yourself, just buy or build a plain bluebird nest box and dress it up to make an attractive B&B. Pretty soon, you will be singing a little "Zip-a-dee-doo-dah" in your very own backyard.

House Basics

Whether you buy a basic bluebird house or decide to make your own, there are a few necessities. First, make sure it has ventilation holes at the top, drainage holes in the bottom and a clean-out door for annual maintenance.

The house should have a 5-by-5-inch floor, a height of 8 to 12 inches and an entrance hole of 1½ inches placed 6 to 10 inches above the floor. Mount the house 4 to 5 feet above the ground toward an open field on a fence, post, utility pole or tree.

Step 1: The box. I have found that old columns cut to size make for easy birdhouse building. All they need is a roof, a bottom, a door and whatever adornments tickle your fancy. I frequently visit our local architectural salvage yard, where I load my wagon up with a column or two, skeleton keys, old door hardware and cabinet knobs, hooks of all shapes and sizes, orphaned light canopies and other assorted castaways. If you don't have a column lying around, don't fret. Four pieces of wood cut to size and nailed together will put you in business.

Step 2: The roof. As a fan of Dr. Seuss illustrations, I find that many of my box designs are curvy and whimsical. The roof of this house, which uses tin flashing, is an example. Any kind of flexible, water-impervious material can be used to cover a wood substrate. Rubber, Sunbrella fabric scraps, tin, copper and aluminum flashing are all possibilities.

If you have something that will work but you don't like the look of it, paint it with glue and press sheet moss over it. Not only does it provide a gorgeous green roof, the birds love pulling out bits of moss for their nests!

Step 3: The clean-out door. I like to cut out my doors before I put the bottom on the house. I use a jigsaw, but you can also do it with an old-fashioned coping saw. You can hinge the door with a little strip of rubber or fabric, or a little metal hinge, as I've done here.

Step 4: The base. Before I attach my base to the house, I prefer to attach "feet" or a pedestal to the base. Even though I'll be mounting the house on a post, I can never resist adding them anyway. I just like the way they look. If you do, too, you can use anything from old coat hooks (which remind me of bird feet) to sticks from the yard, antique ceiling light canopies, tub faucet handles, candlestick bases or even small discarded lamp bases. Start wandering around your garage or rifle through your junk drawers. You never know what you might find that will work perfectly!

I used an old piano leg for my house here, with the idea that the house could be mounted on the post from the base or the back.

Step 5: Perches and predator guards. Perches right in front of the entrance hole can pose a real threat to baby birdies and eggs. Squirrels and other predators use them to extend their reach into the house. It's much better to have perches on the side of the house. Here, I attached a wrought-iron plant holder to double as a side perch and a convenient place to leave food.

A predator guard can be anything applied to the entrance hole to add depth. I've used radiator and plumbing supply escutcheons, porcelain light sockets and even just a block of wood with the same diameter hole drilled in it and nailed over the existing hole. Anything that makes it harder for a squirrel or raccoon paw to reach inside the house will do.

Step 6: Finishing touches. This is the fun part! Paint and adornments of all kinds can make your house one of a kind. (Whether you paint or not, remember to use a top coat of clear shellac sealer.) The wrought-iron plant holder on the side of my house, for instance, presents several options. You can use it for a live plant, or turn it into a year-round feeder for bluebirds and fill it with mealworms.

Use your imagination, and you'll have a B&B no bluebird could resist!

HEIDI HESS

hip to be SQUARE

Make the most of time and space with this smarter way to plant your patch.

BY DONNA AND TOM KRISCHAN, BIG BEND, WISCONSIN

What do you get when you combine the analytical brain of an engineer, the organizational tactics of an efficiency expert and the passion of a vegetable gardener? A little something called square-foot gardening, that's what! A cutting-edge way to plan and plant, it makes the most of your space and cuts down on work. Sounds like a busy gardener's dream. Developed by Mel Bartholomew after years of work in community gardens, the method is simple and versatile, making it the perfect choice for beginners and experts alike.

Square-Foot Gardening 101

In its most basic form, a square-foot garden is a 4-foot-by-4-foot raised bed garden divided into 16 squares, with each square measuring 12 by 12 inches. You plant a specific crop within each of the 12-inch squares, rather than in rows.

Small-growing crops, such as lettuce or peppers, occupy a single square or two, while larger crops, like tomatoes and corn, can take up multiple squares. Trellises at the end of a bed support vining crops.

Beds can be made any length, but should be kept to no more than 4 feet wide. This allows easier access to the garden. Most people can reach halfway across the bed from either side for easy planting, weeding and harvesting.

If you plan to use multiple beds, it's a good idea to make sure you leave paths between each so you can have access from either side. These paths, and the limited width of each bed, make it unnecessary to step into the beds—thus avoiding two dreaded words no gardener worth his or her green thumb wants to hear: soil compaction.

Let's Begin with the Basics

Planning is a very important part of this system. A well-executed plan can result in a beautiful and productive garden that minimizes time spent on maintenance. Here are a few basics to keep in mind before you break ground.

LOCATION If you're just getting started, place your garden where it'll get at least eight hours of sunlight. If it receives more than eight hours, even better.

SIZE Decide how big you want your garden to be. At this point, a little reality check is beneficial. Are you growing just for your own consumption or are you planning on doing some freezing or canning? If you don't know just yet, start with no more than one 4-foot-by-4-foot bed for each family member.

CONSTRUCTION Build your own raised beds or buy a kit and assemble it. Raised beds put to rest any pre-existing soil issues because it's a cinch to just fill them with a well-draining, premixed growing medium. In addition, raised beds require less bending when weeding or harvesting. The height can vary depending on the crops you plant. It can be as low as 3 inches for a salad garden, although a height of 8 to 12 inches is most common.

For material, naturally long-lasting woods, such as cedar or redwood, are

start with these square-friendly veggies!

This quick list of popular crops suggests the most common planting scenarios within a square.

BEETS, CARROTS, RADISHES
Space 3 inches for a total of 16 per square

BUSH BEANS, ONIONS, SPINACH
Space 4 inches for a total of nine per square

PEAS
Space 3 inches in center two rows for a total of eight per square (train on trellis)

CHARD, LEAF LETTUCE
Space 6 inches for a total of four per square

CUCUMBERS
Space 6 inches in center row for a total of two per square (train on trellis)

BROCCOLI, CAULIFLOWER, EGGPLANT, PEPPERS
Plant one per square

CANTALOUPE, VINING TOMATOES
Plant one per square (train on a trellis)

BUSH TOMATOES
Plant one per four squares

BUSH-TYPE SQUASH
Plant one per nine squares

VINING SQUASH
Space 16 inches for three plants per 4 feet of bed width (train on trellis)

1. Fill the raised bed with blended top soil designed for flower and vegetable gardens.
2. Use wood lath, plastic strips, etc., to build the grid that forms the 12-inch-by-12-inch squares.
3. By following the seeds-per-square guidelines, you eliminate the need to thin seedlings.

RULER, TRINACRIA PHOTO / SHUTTERSTOCK.COM; CARROT, ELENA MOISEEVA / SHUTTERSTOCK.COM; STEPS 1, 2: COURTESY OF SQUARE FOOT GARDENING FOUNDATION; STEP 3, DONNA & TOM KRISCHAN

4. Vegetables grown in square-foot gardens produce better yields because the plants aren't overcrowded and fighting one another for precious resources. Square-foot gardening also reduces water consumption.

5. Vertical-growing plants, such as peas or pole beans, are fine choices for square-foot gardens. It's no problem at all to find room to install a supportive trellis.

fine choices. Other options include plastic lumber, vinyl and pressure-treated wood. The last bit of construction is to create the grid that divides the beds into 12-inch squares.

CROPS Here comes the fun part: deciding which vegetables you'd like to grow! First, create a map that details what crop, including how many plants or seeds, you plan to put in each square. Next, devise a planting timeline based on your area's average last spring and first fall frost dates. If planting seeds, take into account the "days to maturity" date on back of the seed packet.

SPACING To determine how much room your plants need, consider the recommended space between each plant after thinning. You may even want to consider interplanting, which means incorporating fast-growing vegetables (such as radishes and leaf lettuces) among slow-growing varieties, which don't need all of their allocated space right away. But by the time they do need the space, the quick-growing crop will be harvested and out of the way, providing more elbow room for the remaining plants.

PLANTING Here's a key item to remember: Sow seeds one at a time. The extra effort in single-sowing even the tiniest seeds pays big dividends later because there's no need to thin seedlings.

CARE AND MAINTENANCE Compared to traditional methods, square-foot gardening uses a smaller area. This results in less area for weeds to grow and more efficient watering. Use soaker hoses, or hand water with a wand. Ideally, walk by your garden each day to pull any weeds and keep an eye out for pests. If that's not possible, be sure to spend time at least once a week in the garden.

HARVESTING AND REPLANTING Harvest crops as needed or when mature. Once a square is empty, use hand tools to work in a little compost or a pinch of fertilizer before replanting the same crop or trying a new one altogether.

To learn more, check out All New Square Foot Gardening by Mel Bartholomew. The book provides wonderfully detailed crop-by-crop information, including time from planting to harvest, succession planting and more! Or visit the Square Foot Gardening website at *squarefootgardening.com*.

RULER, TRINACRIA PHOTO / SHUTTERSTOCK.COM; STEP 4, DON RICHENS SFG; STEP 5, COURTESY OF SQUARE FOOT GARDENING FOUNDATION

FRUIT IN THE BACKYARD. Melinda says it's simple to add fruit to your garden. These apples were trained to grow up a fence. Another good option is strawberries; they make a fast-spreading ground cover.

fresh from the garden fruit

It's easier than you think to grow your own apples, peaches, citrus and berries.

BY MELINDA MYERS, CONTRIBUTING EDITOR

First of all, throw out your old visions of an orchard or berry patch. The truth is, you don't need a lot of space to grow fruit. All you need to do is look for ways to incorporate these edibles into your garden.

Landscaping with Fruit

Consider using apples, peaches or oranges, for example, as ornamental trees in your landscape. The flowers, fruit and often the fall color will provide seasonal beauty. Choose the most disease-resistant varieties suited to your growing conditions and the space available. You may be surprised at all the dwarf varieties that allow small-space gardeners to grow fruit trees.

Use currants, raspberries and other shrub-type fruits as hedges and dividers in the landscape. Fruit-bearing bushes also create a nice backdrop for other plantings. Just be sure to leave enough space around them for maintaining the plants and harvesting.

Another easy option is to use strawberries as ground cover throughout your yard. These mat-forming plants can produce lots of fruit with minimal space. And the white flowers, red berries and beautiful red fall color will brighten up the landscape at your feet.

Fruit in Small Spaces

For those with limited space, consider growing fruit in a pot. This is another way to bring your harvest right to your back door. Select an all-weather container with drainage holes. Use a well-drained potting mix and care for these the way you tend your other container plants.

In a cold climate, you'll need to provide extra winter protection for container-grown fruit. Insulate the roots from temperature extremes by surrounding them with bales of straw or moving them into an unheated garage. Water overwintering containers thoroughly whenever the soil is thawed and dry.

If you like a challenge, try growing a few things indoors. You'll need a bit of space near a sunny window, supplemented with an artificial light for best results. Consider starting with a Meyer lemon, which takes to the indoors more easily than most fruits. Its fragrant flowers are a plus.

A Healthy Start

Look through garden catalogs and websites that specialize in fruit. Select certified disease-free plants to get your edible landscape off to a healthy start.

Be sure to consult friends who are already growing fruit. They can provide valuable advice pertinent to your area and may even share a plant or two. Many fruit trees and shrubs can be started from cuttings, but you'll need to be patient as you wait years for them to start producing fruit.

Raspberries and blackberries can be started from divisions. A couple of divisions of these plants will quickly spread into a fruiting hedge. And harvest a few of the runners from strawberries to start your own.

As you can see, the possibilities are endless. So go ahead and make fruit a regular part of your garden plan.

APPLE TREE, JUDY WHITE / GARDENPHOTOS.COM

tin cans and
crystals make
a sparkly
combo!

waterfall wind chimes

Reuse tin cans to make this appealing set of dazzling wind chimes. STORY AND PHOTO BY ALISON W. AUTH, RICHMOND, VIRGINIA

There can't possibly be many projects that make tin cans look beautiful. But this one can! This is the ultimate recycling project, because it doesn't require even one new item. It all comes from your kitchen, toolbox, and garage sale and thrift store finds. It's fairly simple to construct, so it's a perfect family project. On top of that, it's customizable. Make a large one, an all-red one or an extra-fancy sparkly one! Start using up some canned food in the kitchen, and get to work!

What You Will Need

- Fishing line
- Split shot fishing weights
- Cans, 3 different sizes (see step 5)
- Finishing nail
- Hammer
- Needle-nose pliers
- Baubles (old chandelier teardrops are charming, but also try beads, forks or anything that dangles)
- Wire
- Old lamp shade

Instructions

1. Punch a hole in the center of the can bottoms with the finishing nail and hammer.

2. Take a length of fishing line long enough to attach three cans with room at the top for hanging, and attach a bauble at one end with either a knot or a split shot.

3. Using the pliers, squeeze a split shot onto the line about 6 to 7 in. above your bauble.

4. Thread your line through the smallest can. Add another split shot a few inches above the small can. Now thread the medium-size can onto the line. Place it so the small can is inside the medium one, and squeeze the split shot tight. Repeat, adding the largest can to the top of the line.

5. Continue making lines of cans until you have as many as you want, varying the spacing of the cans along each line. The wind chimes pictured have seven sets of cans, or 21 total cans.

6. The round upper frame of an old lamp shade will serve as the hanger. In the center of the round frame, attach a wire or another piece of a lamp frame (pictured) for easy hanging.

7. Arrange your cans on a table in the pattern you want them to hang.

8. Attach the cans by looping each line over the frame and squeezing a split shot tight with your pliers. Make sure the loop is snug but not too tight around the frame's wire.

9. If you want to add some more pizzazz, make some extra strings of baubles and attach them as well.

10. Trim any excess fishing line, and let the music begin!

adorning your chimes

INEXPENSIVE CRYSTALS are a shimmery way to give a little life to your wind chimes. Here are a few more ideas.

BEADS. Use thin wiring to string up beads to hang from the edges. They hold up well in weather!

RIBBON. They might not last as long as beads, but strands of fabric ribbon add wonderful color. For a little more life, use the curling ribbon that you often use for wrapping.

SEASHELLS. Finally there's a way to use those shells you gathered from last year's vacation. Adhere them directly to the tin cans or dangle them from string.

SHELF LINER. Give the cans themselves a new look by wrapping them in a decorative shelf liner.

TWIGS. Mix in a little bit of nature by choosing decorative and interesting twigs to hang from your chimes.

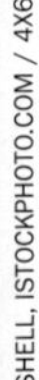
SHELL, ISTOCKPHOTO.COM / 4X6

What You Will Need

- Vent (shanty) cap
- Aluminum pie plate
- ¼-in. eyebolt
- ¼-in. hex head cap screw
- ¼-in. coupling nut
- Exterior primer and paint (optional)
- Superglue
- Twine or wire for hanging

pie tin bird feeder

You don't need a lot of materials or time to put together this good-looking, durable feeder with industrial flair.

BY JENNIFER MANCIER, LYNCHBURG, VIRGINIA

If you're looking for a bird feeder that will stand the test of time, this one is for you. A vent (shanty) cap protects the food while a pie pan presents a picnic for your backyard birds. You can easily obtain all the supplies from a hardware store, but also look for vintage pie tins and cake pans at yard sales and consignment shops. Then each feeder you make will be unique!

Instructions

1. Choose an eyebolt and cap screw that have a combined height of 1/8 in. to 3/4 in. less than the height of the vent cap. That way, there will be just enough room for the coupling nut to hold the two together tightly.

2. Wearing safety glasses, drill a 5/16-in. hole through the center of the vent cap and the pie plate. Cake pans work, too.

3. While you're at it, drill a few small holes through the bottom of the pie plate to allow for water drainage.

4. Leave the vent cap and pie plate bare for an industrial look, or paint them to add a pop of color! I find that a latex-based exterior paint on top of primer adheres best to galvanized metal. Paint the vent cap and pie plate separately before assembling your feeder. Be sure to follow the instructions on your paint can and allow adequate drying time.

5. Place the cap screw through the center hole in the pie plate with the threads facing upward.

6. Give the coupling nut about 3 or 4 turns onto the threads of the cap screw to hold it in place.

7. Next, center the vent cap over the pie plate while holding the cap screw in place.

8. Place the eyebolt through the center hole of the vent cap and turn the eyebolt into the other end of the coupling nut. Using a wrench, hold the nut steady while hand-tightening the eyebolt. Seal the coupling with a few drops of superglue for extra holding power.

9. To hang, slip twine or wire through the eyehole and tie.

10. Hang from a tree branch. Then fill the platform with birdseed and watch the birds gather to enjoy your backyard masterpiece!

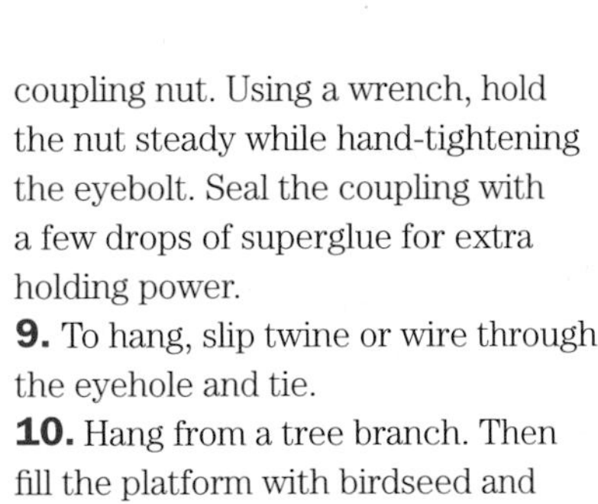

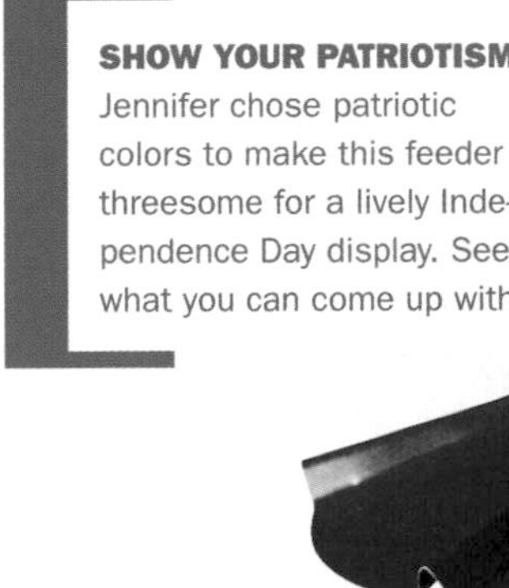

SHOW YOUR PATRIOTISM. Jennifer chose patriotic colors to make this feeder threesome for a lively Independence Day display. See what you can come up with!

light the way

Illuminate your backyard with these easy glow-in-the-dark stepping-stones.

STORY AND PHOTOS BY ALISON W. AUTH, RICHMOND, VIRGINIA

Here's a nifty idea that's both affordable and virtually foolproof. With some concrete and a little glow-in-the-dark paint, you can have an illuminated pathway in nothing flat, perfect for midnight strolls under a full moon.

The beauty of these stepping-stones is that it doesn't matter how long, short, wide or narrow your area is. You have total freedom to design the stones and the pathway you want. And you don't need a mold. Just dig, add concrete and walk away. It really is simple. Take a look!

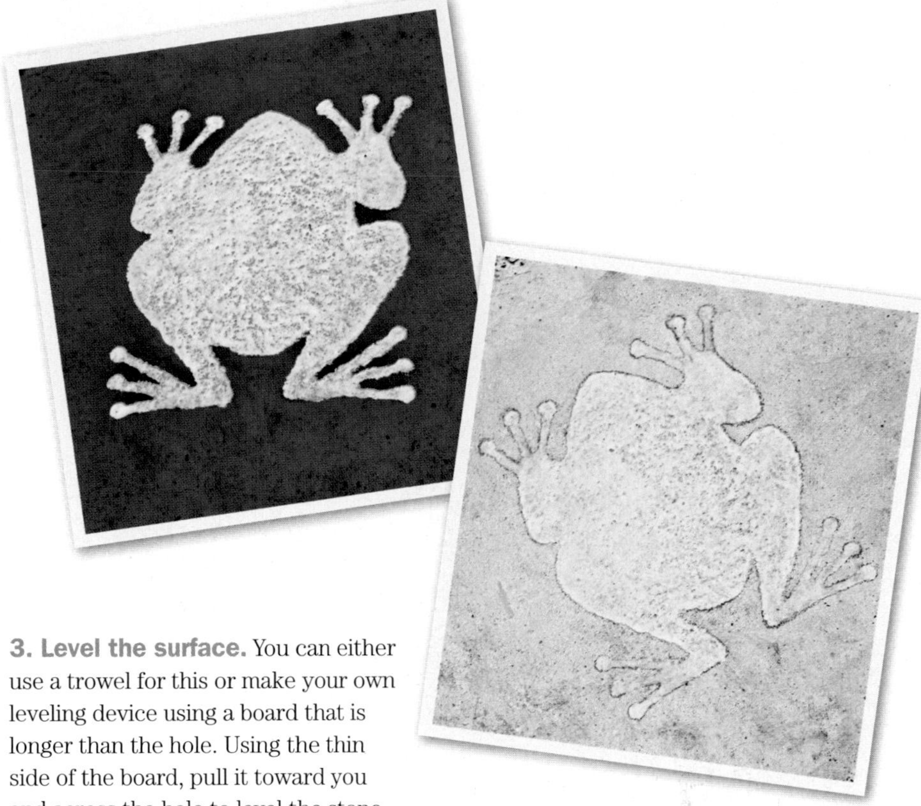

What You Will Need

- Straight-sided spade
- Wheelbarrow
- Shovel or hoe
- Powdered concrete mix
- Water
- Trowel or board
- Glow-in-the-dark paint (powder or premixed)
- Small paintbrush
- Water- or oil-based paint, depending on glow powder you choose

1. Dig your hole. Your earthen hole will be the form for your paver. Just dig about 2 inches or more deep with a straight-sided spade, making sure the sides of the hole are as vertical as possible. You can make the hole the shape and size you like, but I find that a 2- x 3-foot stone, in any shape, is a nice dimension for walking.

2. Mix your mortar. Count on using one 60-pound bag of concrete mix (I use Sakrete) per stepping-stone. Pour the mix into a wheelbarrow and add water according to instructions on the bag. Use a shovel or hoe to mix until smooth, and fill the hole as full and high as possible.

3. Level the surface. You can either use a trowel for this or make your own leveling device using a board that is longer than the hole. Using the thin side of the board, pull it toward you and across the hole to level the stone with the surrounding ground.

4. Wait a little bit. It's a good idea to give your stepping-stones a couple of weeks to set up and cure before you start painting them.

5. Get your glow on. I found glow-in-the-dark paint online at *glowinc.com*, and it works like a champ. I ordered 1 ounce of the Green V10 powder and mixed it myself with a water-based paint in clear gloss. You can also buy it premixed and ready to go. Keep in mind that a little goes a long way, especially with the powder. Just an ounce made more than enough for me to paint several coats on each paver.

For the finishing touch, I found a frog design I liked, cut it out as a stencil, sketched the outline on each rock, then painted it with the glow paint. Several coats intensified the glow.

I love my new stepping-stones. They are virtually invisible in the daylight, which is nice, but at night you can leave your flashlight in the drawer and keep your hands free for dragging up that porch table from the shed.

If you have some paint left over from this project, here are some fun ideas for using it up.

- Paint it on your flashlight in case you drop it in the dark.
- Paint a little on your car keys or house keys to make finding them easy.
- Have a favorite outdoor concrete frog, bird or other ornament? Paint a friendly face that will shine at night.
- Paint the handles of your garden tools, making them easy to round up after a long day in the garden.
- Paint the hands of a clock to keep you on time day or night.
- Paint some small stones and line a garden path.

it's teatime

BY KRIS DRAKE, SANTEE, CALIFORNIA

Repurpose a mismatched or slightly damaged teacup and saucer by turning it into a bird feeder.

You can easily customize this project with the beads or other accessories you choose. It can be as basic or as intricately detailed as you want! It's practical, too. Watch the birds as they perch on the rim of the cup. As a bonus, the saucer catches most of the discarded seed shells.

What You Will Need

- Cup and saucer
- Spoon or fork
- 14- and 19-gauge galvanized wire
- Drill
- Tile drill bit
- Nut and bolt (depends on the size of drill bit you are using)
- Needle-nose pliers
- Beads (about ten 6-10 mm beads and four more beads with a larger hole)
- Hammer
- Safety goggles

Instructions

1. Drill a hole on the side of the teacup opposite the handle. Use the tile drill bit, but drill slowly and apply minimal pressure to avoid cracking the cup. Next, drill a hole in the center of the cup bottom and center of the saucer.

2. Cut two pieces, about 10 in. each, of 19-gauge wire. Fold each piece of wire in half to make a small loop. Hold the loop with the pliers and twist about five times to make a hook at the top. Leave about 4 in. of wire on each side.

3. Insert one of the wire ends into the hole in the cup from the inside out. Make the loop tight so that it rests on the rim. Twist the ends together to close the loop. Coil the excess with the pliers.

4. With the second piece of wire, make another small loop, which will sit on top of the cup's handle. Try to make it about the same height as the other one. Depending on the placement of the handle, you might need to make more twists. Once they're close to the same height, wrap the excess wire around the handle.

5. Take 16 in. of 14-gauge wire and fold it in half to make a V. Using the pliers, coil the ends into swirls, leaving the V about 4 in. on each side stemming from the center.

6. Press the piece by laying the wire on an anvil or hard surface and flatten with a hammer. This will prevent the wire from uncoiling.

7. Add beads to the V by wrapping 19-gauge wire around it, adding a bead every three to five wraps.

8. For the attachment pieces, use three pieces of 19-gauge wire and two beads. Thread one bead and bend two eyehooks on each end. Repeat for the other two wires.

9. Attach one end of each attachment piece to the swirls of the V. Attach the other ends to the hooks at the top of the cup.

10. Attach the saucer to the cup using the nut and bolt. Gently tighten, being careful not to crack the cup or saucer.

11. Flatten the bowl of the spoon using a hammer. To roll the spoon to use it as a hook, gently tap the tip of the bowl. It will start folding or rolling, depending on the material the spoon is made of.

12. Cut a 38-in. length of 14-gauge wire and make a swirl at one end. Press the swirl with a hammer so it doesn't uncurl.

13. Insert the opposite end of the wire into the fold of the spoon. Wrap the wire around the spoon a few times and add beads.

14. When you get to the top of the spoon, there should be about 4 to 8 in. of wire left. At the end, make a hook with the pliers. Start by making a small loop, and then make a U at the end. Press this hook.

15. Connect the spoon hanger to the rest of the feeder using the attachment bead. Now you're ready to add some birdseed!

This versatile planter can also hold a vase or bowl for summer blooms from the garden.

sitting pretty

Old chairs make pleasing containers for flowers and ferns.

STORY AND PHOTOS BY ALISON W. AUTH, RICHMOND, VIRGINIA

I love chairs. Unfortunately, with my modest-size home, I don't always have a place for them, so I dream up other uses. This classic farmhouse spindle-back chair seemed the perfect seat for a lush fern.

1. First, determine the diameter of the hole you need. Measure the circumference of your pot based on where you'd like it to rest in the chair. Also measure the circumference of the largest part of the pot to make certain that it won't hit the back of the chair.
2. Mark the center point of the chair seat. To do this, measure both the width and the depth of the seat, and mark the center of each. The point at which they intersect is the center of the seat.
3. Divide the diameter of your desired hole size in half, and cut a piece of string several inches longer than that measurement. Tie a pencil to the string so that, with the string fully extended, it's half the diameter of the desired hole. Then place the cut end of the string on your center mark and extend the pencil outward, drawing a circle.
4. With your hole drawn, take a large drill bit and drill one or a series of contiguous holes just on the inside of your pencil line. The hole(s) must be large enough for your blade to fit through so you can saw. Using your cutting tool of choice, cut along the circle you've drawn on your chair seat.
5. Depending on the condition of your chair, now's the time to clean, scrape and sand it to prepare it for painting. For wooden chairs that haven't been painted or painted chairs with minimal wear, just lightly sand the entire surface with a fine-grit sandpaper to provide a "tooth," or bonding surface, for your primer.
6. Time to paint! Since this chair will probably live outdoors, the hard enamel-based spray paints provide more protection than their latex cousins. Just be sure to work outside or in a well-ventilated area. Use a gray or rust primer if your final paint color will be dark. If you're going for a bright, light or vibrant color, use a white primer.
7. Once your paint is dry, drop in the plant of your choice and set it by your front door as a seasonal welcome for guests, as a focal point in your foyer or on your summer porch for cottage charm. It won't stain your floor or deck, and it's the perfect height for tending.

What You Will Need

- Chair
- Plant pot
- String and pencil
- Drill and large drill bit
- Jigsaw or small handsaw with fine teeth
- Paint scraper or putty knife (optional)
- Sandpaper, rough and fine (100-200 grit)
- Orbital or palm sander (optional)
- Enamel-based spray primer and spray paint

citronella candles

Banish mosquitoes in style (and for cheap, too) by making your own candles out of soy wax chips.

Every little bit helps when it comes to mosquitoes. Citronella candles are among the easiest and cheapest ways to keep mosquitoes at bay, so when we saw this DIY on Amy Bell's blog, *positivelysplendid.com*, we knew we had to share it with readers. Have fun making your own candles!

What You Will Need

- A few clean, dry glass jars
- Braided candlewick
- Hot glue
- Wooden dowel pieces
- Wooden clothespins
- Natural soy wax chips
- Double boiler
- Old crayons or wax dye
- Citronella essential oil, found at natural food stores (not citronella-scented oil)

1. For each jar, cut a braided wick a few inches longer than the jar's height. (You can find wicks at a craft store or wherever you'd find candle-making supplies.) Carefully dab a bit of hot glue to one end of the wick. Adhere glued end to the bottom center of your jar. When the glue is set, wrap excess wick around the dowel and top with a clothespin to keep it out of the way of the hot wax.
2. Pour wax chips into your double boiler, following the package instructions to melt the wax. As an alternative, you can make quicker work of this project by using microwavable soy wax chips instead. These are fairly inexpensive and are available at many craft stores and a few discount department stores. If you go this route, be sure to use a microwave-safe bowl.
3. To color your candles, peel the paper off the crayons and chop them up. (The more crayons you use, the deeper the candles' color will be.) You can also use a wax dye to get your desired color. Either way, drop the dye pieces into melted wax and stir to incorporate.
4. Depending on the candle's size, add five to 10 drops of citronella essential oil for each candle you're making. Once the oil is stirred in, carefully pour the wax into your jars, being careful not to disturb the wicks.
5. Allow the wax to cool completely before trimming excess wicks and lighting the candles.

DO CITRONELLA CANDLES WORK?
Well, don't expect a single candle on a huge patio to be your golden ticket to eliminating mosquitoes. But in a controlled area, with enough candles, they do make a difference, studies have shown.

ALL PHOTOS, RDA-MKE

license plate **window feeder**

Woodworking duo MingTa Li and Wayne Wiegand of Lyndhurst, New Jersey, make and sell these recycled license plate bird feeders in their Etsy store, CraftyGuys (*etsy.com/shop/craftyguys*). Try your hand at making one! It's easy to create your own as long as you've got an old license plate and some spare wood on hand.

This feeder is about 6 inches wide, 4 inches tall and 6 inches deep.

1. Measure the bend line carefully; license plates are hard to flatten once they're bent. Measure twice and bend once! (Old license plates are thinner than new ones, so they bend more easily.)
2. When bending in half, bend along a straight edge like the corner of a heavy table or something that will not move under the pressure.
3. Attach natural recycled wood as a border to keep the birdseed in the feeder.
4. Make it a window feeder by adding suction cups for easy up-close viewing.

simple suet **cupcakes**

In the winter, birds benefit from a high-energy suet treat. Stacy Tornio, editor of *Birds & Blooms*, developed this recipe with her kids using cupcake liners to stay mess-free. They're happy to report that the birds love it.

1. Melt 1 cup shortening and 2 cups chunky peanut butter over low heat
2. Mix in 5 cups cornmeal.
3. Fill cupcake tins and top with your choice of nuts, birdseed or dried berries.
4. Cool in the refrigerator.
5. To give as a gift, arrange on a plate or stack and then wrap with cellophane. Attach a recipe card so your recipient can make more. Add a bow, and you have an instant gift!

plantable gift tags

Recycle your junk mail and encourage gardening with this easy project.

PROJECT BY KENDRA ZVONIK, ST. PETERSBURG, FLORIDA

For Mary

Isn't it about time your junk mail had a purpose? Now you can turn it into plantable gift tags, using this simple method from Kendra Zvonik. She sells these tags at her Etsy store, *greenpost.etsy.com*, using 100% recycled materials.

Here's what you'll need to start:

- Junk mail
- Paper shredder
- Bucket
- Hand mixer

1. If desired, sort your junk mail into colors. Or mix everything together to make gray. (For this project, do not use newspapers, magazines or other glossy printed material.)
2. Using a shredder, shred paper in batches, then soak pieces in bucket(s) with water for about 24 hours.
3. Remove the shreds and blend with a hand mixer, making a creamy, smooth pulp. If it's too dry, add water. Spread to dry if not using immediately.

Now it's time to turn your pulp into paper. Here's what you'll need:

- 8½-in. x 11-in. mold and deckle (make your own or buy at *carriagehousepaper.com*)
- Recycled paper pulp (above)
- Large plastic tub
- Large sponges
- Felt sheets, approximately 10 in. x 13 in.

4. Add roughly 1/3 lb. dried pulp to 5 gal. clean water in a large plastic tub. (If pulp is still wet, use more than 1/3 lb.) The mixture should be loose, not too watery and not too thick (something like a creamy soup). Mix often with your hand or a hand mixer to keep pulp evenly dispersed in the water.
5. Take your mold and deckle and gently but quickly submerge it in the tub. Enter the tub with the front edge first, scooping the pulp away from you. If you plunge too deeply into the tub, your sheet will be too thick. If you don't go deep enough, the sheet will be uneven or incomplete. It takes practice, so be patient.
6. Drain water from the mold back into the tub. Carefully pull deckle upward and away from the mold and set aside.
7. Place your newly formed sheet on a felt sheet. You can achieve this with a continuous rocking motion from the back edge of the mold to the front edge. Repeat as desired to make more sheets. Set mold aside.

Ready to make your gift tags? Here's what you'll need:

- Cookie cutters
- Seeds
- Plastic squeeze bottle
- Large sponge
- Felt sheet
- Flat clothes-drying rack
- Hole punch
- String

8. While your newly formed sheet of paper is still wet on the felt, firmly press a cookie cutter into the pulp and then spread approximately 1/8 tsp. seeds inside the shape.
9. Next, fill your squeeze bottle with pulp mixture from the tub. Using the bottle, fill the inside of the cookie cutter about halfway, covering the seeds. Let the pulp settle. Repeat Steps 8 and 9 to form more tags.
10. Remove the cookie cutter. Cover the entire paper sheet with a felt sheet and sponge away the excess water.
11. Carefully flip the felt and sponge the back side. Remove the top felt sheet. Pick up the bottom felt sheet with your paper on top and gently flip the felt over onto a drying rack so your tags are facing upward.
12. Peel and remove the final felt to finish air-drying overnight.
13. Once it's dry, you can cut the shapes out, punch the holes and string them up. Done!

Gather paper for recycling.

Place your paper on felt.

Add seeds.

Looking for a quicker way? Place your cookie cutters directly onto your felt sheets. Then, instead of using a mold and deckle to make sheets of paper, use your squeeze bottle to create the layers of pulp.

PHOTO AT LEFT, RDA-MKE; PHOTOS AT RIGHT, KENDRA ZVONIK

JOY BROWN / SHUTTERSTOCK.COM

BONUS CHAPTER 9

easy container Gardens

It's a breeze to learn the basics of container gardening and add color and beauty to balconies, patios, decks and porches. Then follow the no-fuss "recipes" for stunning seasonal arrangements, baskets, flower pots and more.

container gardening 101

Everything you need to know to make a little outdoor magic of your own.

If you haven't tried container gardening, you're missing out on all the fun. And here's a secret: It's easy! Any spot, large or small, is a good space for creative planting: a flower bed, a courtyard, a second-floor balcony—even a patio tabletop. Whether your aim is to plant a small-space garden, cover a bare wall or cheer up a dull patch in a flower border, you'll find that the right plants in the right planter can do the trick without breaking the bank. And you'll most likely develop a year-round, lifelong passion for pots—and plants.

Set the Scene

Before you head to the garden center or flip open a seed catalog, it's important to decide how much effort you're willing to invest. If you want a harmonious yet easygoing garden, consider combining an evergreen shrub with bright, fuss-free perennials or annuals that don't require deadheading.

Also consider the emotion you'd like the container to evoke. To create a relaxing seaside vibe, plant portulaca in a pale-blue pot decorated with starfish or seashells. Or mimic an exotic jungle by filling a weatherbeaten wooden box with elephant's ear, impatiens, begonias and sweet potato vine.

For pure indulgence, consider a romantic container garden where delicate flowers begin to glow as the sun sets. Choose blooms in pastel pinks, blues, yellows and white. Fragrant blossoms tend to be most heavily scented toward the end of the day, so place them near your lounge chairs, fix up some soft lighting and enjoy your backyard retreat each evening.

Love to cook? Plant flowers alongside herbs and vegetables for a decorative yet practical mix. This style of container garden will need regular watering and feeding, but the rewards will make those tasks more than worthwhile. After all, you and your family will enjoy fresh-cut flowers and homegrown salads and vegetables all summer long!

TOP 3 *design* essentials

How do you get that inspiration to take root and grow? Start with form, color and texture.

SEASIDE PLANTER, RDA-GID; ALL OTHER PHOTOS: PROVEN WINNERS, PROVENWINNERS.COM

1. Form

In general, you'll need to include three different styles of plants to ensure that your container arrangement has an attractive shape:

Thriller. The vertical accent in an arrangement is key. If the container will be visible from every angle, plant the thriller in the center. But if the pot is placed against a wall or other large object, position the thriller in the back of the mix.

Filler. This type of plant has a mounding habit or is just plain compact, anchoring the combo and filling in the gaps around neighboring plants. It should be planted in the middle ground of the pot, whether all the way around the thriller, or front and center. Many container designers use multiple fillers.

Spiller. A trailing plant that complements the thriller can make all the difference in a great container arrangement. One or more of this type of plant should be placed close to the edges of the pot to provide interest by draping over the container's sides. Spillers should appear in all of the visible angles of the container.

These rules may not apply to all situations. Depending on the size of the arrangement, a tall filler could step in for a thriller, and a spreading one could serve as the spiller. A plant that is frequently used as a thriller may be paired with something much larger, like a tree, and will take on the filler role. In any case, trust these guides and your instinct for a winning combo!

NO-FAIL *thrillers, fillers and spillers*

Thrillers

Coleus
Fern
Elephant's ear
Angelonia
Fountain grass
Boxwood
Sedge

Fillers

Calibrachoa
Begonia
Coral bells
Impatiens
Petunia
Sedum
Nasturtium

Spillers

Bacopa
Creeping wirevine
Licorice plant
Creeping Jenny
Sweet potato vine
Mecardonia
Ivy

PERFECT COMPLEMENTS: For maximum impact, choose shades that fall into the same range of intensity, rather than pairing a pastel color with a bright one.

2. Color

Once you have plants in mind, start thinking about colors. Remember that a single hue can look stunning on its own. A pot brimming with one type of bloom—known as a monoculture arrangement—has showstopping potential despite its simplicity. Likewise, a monochromatic display, where each component is a similar shade, can also look positively fetching.

When it comes to mixing colors, options abound. Hot tones—reds, oranges and yellows—are top choices for a sizzling mix. A more calming combo could come from a blend of cool greens, blues and violets.

Think back to grammar school art class and you may remember our next concept: complementary colors. These opposites attract by creating eye-popping contrast.

If you're feeling bold, follow the triad method. Here, three colors that are equally spaced on the color wheel play off one another. With this approach, it's wise to stick to the three base colors without accents, or the mix risks looking gaudy.

Last, don't ignore the foliage! With plants in a rainbow of hues, foliage can take the spotlight or play a supporting role. Silver shades work with cool colors, bronze leaves lend a rustic feel and lime ones complement warm tones. Dark foliage can be dramatic or serve as a base for brighter plants.

3. Texture

The third attribute to consider when designing your container garden is the texture of flowers and foliage.

If you want the components in the container to blend together, choose plants that have a similar texture, whether it's smooth and silky or rough and shaggy. Conversely, if your goal is to create contrast and keep the eye moving, opt for a multitextured arrangement.

COLOR WHEEL, CLIMBING PLANT: RDA-GID; GARDEN CENTER, ELENA ELISSEEVA / SHUTTERSTOCK.COM; ALL OTHER PHOTOS: PROVEN WINNERS, PROVENWINNERS.COM

ANNUAL AFFAIR: Like to give your garden a different look each year? Try annual blooms like phlox.

picking plants

Even if two plants look fantastic together, they may not be very good neighbors.

It's vital to use varieties that share the same growing and care requirements. Also be aware of the light, wind and temperature conditions in the spot where you'll display the container. Use varieties that are equally assertive, or fast-growing plants will overtake their more timid companions in the pot.

Last, if you're a beginner or travel a lot, give your plants a fighting chance by picking drought-tolerant types, such as portulaca, lantana, verbena, zinnias and gazanias.

The annuals listed above represent just one facet of the wide world of container plants. These heavy bloomers are a terrific choice if you like to change your garden's look each year.

Longer-lasting perennials, which can boast both color and texture, will return in the future (provided they're hardy in your area). Even so, many container gardeners toss them on the compost heap at the end of the season and dream up something new the following year. If you're in the overwintering camp, see page 233 for tips.

Whether they're perennials or annuals, climbing plants can be just as fuss-free as their shorter counterparts while providing lots of small-space impact.

Fasten a trellis to an adjacent wall or right to the pot. Or place the planter next to a chain-link fence or tie string in a crisscross pattern against a wooden fence You could also build a freestanding structure, such as an obelisk or wigwam. Or take another route and hang a grow bag for your vining plants instead.

Look to shrubs or small trees if you want a focal point that's more substantial and permanent. These offer striking silhouettes that are nearly impossible to achieve with annuals or perennials: a lofty spire, a soft weeping effect or a dramatic branching outline.

Just as they do in the ground, most container-grown trees and shrubs also make an excellent windbreak. And perhaps best of all, many provide yearlong interest.

getting STARTED

We can't stress it enough: Choose a pot that's large enough for the plants you have in mind. It will hold more moisture and allow for better root growth. But even more important is what you put inside your container.

DIY PLANTING MIX:

1. Combine 1⁄3 each peat moss, perlite or vermiculite and garden soil. If you have compost, you can substitute it for peat moss.
2. Mix it thoroughly.
3. If needed, add more peat moss or vermiculite to improve drainage.

Soil

Containers require a special planting mix because the drainage, water retention and growing conditions differ drastically from those in your garden. Most ready-to-use mixes contain materials like perlite and/or vermiculite for drainage, and peat moss or other organic material to help retain moisture. Some also include fertilizer, and many have water-holding polymers, a great addition that helps reduce watering needs. (See page 232 for more ideas.)

A planting mix with good drainage and water retention will minimize the amount of regular care required. Ask the staff at your local garden center what they would recommend.

Drainage

Being waterlogged will eventually kill plants, so make sure your pot has plenty of holes in the base: Water will escape more freely this way. Then add a layer of drainage material in the base to prevent blockage. Try pottery shards or coarse gravel, or, if those are too heavy for your planter, foam packing peanuts. Whatever you use, fill the container to one-tenth of its total height.

Next, set the container on bricks, pot feet or anything else that keeps the drainage holes open. Protective saucers are popular, too, but watch out for standing water (unless you're headed out of town).

POT WALL, JOY BROWN / SHUTTERSTOCK.COM; ALL OTHER PHOTOS: RDA-GID

Planting

It's the moment you've been waiting for. You've read all about what makes a truly spectacular container combo, and it's finally time to pull out that trowel!

Start with your well-draining planter, filled with drainage material. Next, scoop planting mix into the container, allowing enough space to accommodate the plants' root balls. Then, nestle the plants inside. Try to space them evenly throughout the pot, leaving a little room around the edge so they can expand and thrive. Fill around them with potting mix.

There's no need to pat down the soil. A hearty drink of water will help it settle and will perk up the plants. If there's a lot of space from the soil to the top of the pot (also known as headspace), sprinkle in more soil. Small pots should have about a half-inch of headspace; larger ones need one to two inches. This helps keep the soil and water inside the container.

Mulch

Because potted plants dry out more quickly than their ground-dwelling counterparts, it's smart to add a little mulch. A thin layer of something that's permeable yet helps keep the planting mix moist is best.

If the mulch also looks nice, so much the better! Some casual-looking choices include moss, bark, pinecones and wood chips. For a fancier pot, try pebbles, seashells or cocoa hulls (which smell delightful).

how many plants will fit?

There are two approaches to filling containers:

1. **Living flower arrangement.** Packed with as many plants as the pot can handle, it looks wonderful immediately after planting. But crowding increases the risk of disease and reduces longevity.
2. **Traditional planting.** The plants are initially spaced apart so they can fill in over time. Proven Winners typically suggests three or four plants for a 10- to 12-inch pot, four to six in a 14- to 16-inch planter, six to eight for a 16- to 20-inch pot and so forth.

In either case, consider the size of the seedling. The larger its original pot, the fewer plants you'll need. When in doubt, check the plant's tag. Most of them include spacing info, but if not, ask at your garden center.

taking good care

With a container garden, you have complete control over the level of maintenance. No heavy digging or weeding is involved, just the manageable tasks of watering, feeding and occasional pruning and deadheading.

Water

Perhaps the most time-consuming aspect of container gardening, watering is a must. The key is to be generous so moisture and nutrients easily reach the roots. Give plants a morning drink to keep them from drying out during the midday heat or wind. Plants are more susceptible to mildew if they're watered after sunset because moisture remains on the leaves. On summer's hottest days, you may need to water each pot twice; early evening—while the sun is still up—is a good time for a second go-round.

There are a few ways to get around such frequent watering. One popular choice is a self-watering container, which has a false bottom with a reservoir beneath. When the soil starts to dry out, water is drawn up into the pot. Another option is water-retaining crystals. Added to the planting mix, these granules absorb many times their own volume of water, releasing moisture as soil dries. Last, if you have many pots or travel frequently, consider an automatic watering system. Turned on manually or by a timer, these drip water into pots through small tubes.

Fertilize

To reach their full potential, plants need a regular source of nutrients—especially important

how do i help keep plants disease-free?

- Scour containers (and treat wooden ones) before planting
- Never reuse old planting mix
- Remove dirt and algae from walls and concrete near containers
- Sanitize garden tools
- Water regularly
- Deadhead and snip off withered leaves
- Use fertilizers that are high in phosphates and potash for strong root systems

for those growing in containers. There are several forms to choose from, including liquids, powders, spikes, foliar sprays and capsules. Some are fast-acting and others release their nutrients gradually.

For container cultivation, a balanced, slow-release fertilizer is a good choice. In a planting mix, this fertilizer generally peters out after a few months. Six weeks to two months after planting, start using a water-soluble fertilizer regularly, or poke a few slow-release spikes into the soil to keep the plants at their best. No matter what fertilizing method you choose, always follow the package instructions: Overdosing is potentially toxic.

Deadhead, Prune & Repot

When they need it, deadhead plants throughout the season. It keeps containers looking neat, and many flowers require this for continued blooms.

Pruning is a quick way to revive a sluggish plant or to keep a vigorous one from taking over a container. Shrubs often require pruning in the early spring or after the blooms fade. Ask about the specifics at your nursery.

After a few years, shrubs, perennials and trees may need to be repotted to encourage bushy new growth. Prevent plant shock by always selecting a pot that can comfortably accommodate the root ball.

how can I protect hardy container plants in winter?

Most hardy plants need no special preparation for winter as long as they are in containers large enough to insulate the roots in very cold weather. Get extra peace of mind by selecting plants that are two hardiness zones lower than the one in which you live. For example, if you live in Zone 6, look for plants that are hardy in Zone 4. If you want to add protection, envelop the pot in bubble wrap (as in photo below), layered cardboard or a piece of old carpet. You can also bury the pot in the garden, top it with mulch and pull it out again when the weather warms. Protect foliage with a couple of layers of a lightweight garden fabric or burlap.

ALL PHOTOS: RDA-GID; SPECIAL THANKS TO MELINDA MYERS, BRENDA HOUGHTON, TERI DUNN AND PROVEN WINNERS FOR THEIR CONTRIBUTIONS

type casting

What kind of planter works best in your space? Read on to find out!

When you hear the phrase "container garden," does your mind's eye flash to a group of terra-cotta pots on a concrete slab? If so, that's OK: This image certainly fits that category. But container gardening can be so much more!

Consider the dull parts of your outdoor living space. No matter what their features, you can find containers to enhance them. A front entry might call for a hanging basket to provide color and fragrance at eye level, while a backyard deck offers space for a variety of colorful container vignettes. Plain aluminum siding will get new life thanks to a window box, and a patio table will look all the more inviting if it's topped by a lush living centerpiece.

Your choices are vast when it comes to containers. Over the next few pages, we'll help you decide which will perfectly fit your gardening needs and your personal style.

Upright Containers

A pot is a natural choice to adorn most outdoor spaces. A lone planter full of shade-loving plants perks up a dim corner, and a few pots along a front walk make guests feel doubly welcome. For a bold effect, place a large, colorful urn in the lawn or within a row of plain shrubs. You'll find that upright containers can truly look at home anywhere.

Though they've certainly stood the test of time, pots do present a couple of gardening challenges. A large planter, because it holds more soil, is ideal for growing an interesting plant combo. Once filled with flowers and foliage, however, it will be difficult to move. To lighten the load, fill the base with foam packing peanuts or broken polystyrene plant trays. This is also important if you plan to display your containers on a balcony, where you'll want to keep weight to a minimum. A pot's stability is also crucial, especially if it's holding tall or top-heavy plants. The most stable shapes are square pots, taller containers with wide shoulders and wide bases, and large, low bowls.

Window Boxes

A window box sitting snugly on a sill or secured to the wall beneath a window offers the chance to change your outlook with every season and to boost your home's curb appeal. Long, thin and usually rather shallow, a window box needs water and nutrients regularly. Try to attach it before you plant; a full one is heavy. If you're adding a planter below a window that opens outward, be careful to position the box low enough so that you can still open the window after the plants mature. And last, install a drip tray so if you live above other people or if the window box hangs over a sidewalk, no one will be "rained on" when you water the flowers.

WINDOW BOX AND TERRA-COTTA POT WALL ON OPPOSITE PAGE, WINDOW BOX AND WHITE POT: RDA-GID;
ALL OTHER PHOTOS: PROVEN WINNERS, PROVENWINNERS.COM

Hanging Baskets

Suspended anywhere from a door to a tree, a basket full of flowers offers plenty of old-fashioned appeal. But with the right plants and container, the hanging basket can have a place in even the most modern of settings. There are many different styles of wire baskets and liners available. If plants will fill in to cover the basket, a plain one will do, but if the basket will show, go the decorative route.

A hanging basket doesn't hold much soil and dries out quickly, so it should be watered each day. Moss and coco fiber baskets have particularly good air circulation (which causes dry soil), so if you like the look, pick one with a plastic liner to help retain some moisture.

Living Centerpieces

A planter needn't be large to make a big impression. A short, sweet living centerpiece is often the perfect finishing touch to a backyard picnic table, an entryway console or an outdoor bar.

Remember one thing, though: When seated, folks must be able to see one another over the top of your arrangement. Consider this when selecting the plants as well as the pot. Whether you choose a basket or a bowl, living centerpieces tend to be shallow and need daily watering. Set the planter in a saucer to keep it from soaking the tabletop, and be sure to drain it regularly.

TABLETOP BASKET AND ILLUSTRATIONS: RDA-GID; ALL OTHER PHOTOS: PROVEN WINNERS, PROVENWINNERS.COM

MATERIAL *witness*

Great plants deserve great containers. But not every planter material suits every arrangement and location. Consider these options as you decide what kind of container works best for your plants—and for you!

Terra-Cotta

PROS: This all-time classic adapts to almost any landscape design, and it looks good holding practically any sort of plant.

CONS: Terra-cotta absorbs moisture and often cracks in freezing temperatures.

STYLE NOTE: Spruce up the color while keeping the classic shape: Slick on a coat of exterior house paint to coordinate with your home, the garden surroundings or the flowers inside.

Metal

PROS: Metal is durable, intriguing and often colorful.

CONS: Metal rusts and can get very hot, harming the plants within.

STYLE NOTE: Get witty and grow herbs in an olive oil tin. Or go minimalist and plant a line or cluster of sleek metal tubs with spiky plants.

Wood

PROS: The natural look fits with many types of plants.

CONS: It can split and, over time, rot. (Though more expensive, cedar and teak are quite durable.)

STYLE NOTE: Capitalize on the rustic look: Fill planters with woodland plants, lush herbs or spring-flowering bulbs. A large wooden container, such as a whiskey barrel, can hold a small tree or, with a plastic liner, aquatic plants.

Stone

PROS: Great at insulating against heat and cold, one of these sturdy pots can look quite antique or thoroughly modern.

CONS: Its weight restricts possibilities for relocation, drainage can be problematic and price is often prohibitive.

STYLE NOTE: If you want a mobile planter, find one made from volcanic rock. Already have a boulder lodged in your lawn? Plant succulents such as hens-and-chicks—which have shallow root systems—in the crevices.

Glazed Pottery

PROS: These pretty pots have the heft of clay, plus there's a wide variety of styles on the market.

CONS: Exposure to sunlight and the elements often leads to fading or, eventually, to breaking down.

STYLE NOTE: Instead of trying to find flowers that match the pot colors, fill glazed pottery with foliage or less-flashy plants so the container can be the star.

Resin & Fiberglass

PROS: There's a color and design to fit every locale, so these lightweight wonders will match your personal style and space.

CON: Single-walled ones crack easily in subzero temperatures.

STYLE NOTE: Get the appearance of stone without the bulk with a fiberstone planter, made of a limestone-fiberglass compound.

Plastic

PROS: This material is economical and lightweight.

CONS: Plastic can fade in the sun, shatter in the cold and holds in moisture (which is fine for some plants, but damaging to others).

STYLE NOTE: While green, white and faux terra-cotta pots have become staples in the landscaping world, seek out solid colors or containers with stripes, patterns or whimsical designs.

TOP 10 tricks
for unique containers

It's true: Classic container gardens often look absolutely gorgeous. But why not make sure yours is in a class of its own with these innovative ideas?

1. COMBINE THE UNEXPECTED

Ensure an eye-catching combo by mixing dramatic colors, such as black and white or blue and silver. Or go for a neon display with coleus. Pop it in a coordinated pot for an unforgettable mix.

2. GO SOLO

A single-plant display, also called monobotanic, creates enormous impact. Lantana, twinspur, coral bells, calibrachoa and many others look fetching all by themselves. The same goes for plants of similar hues.

3. BRANCH OUT

Just as they do in flower beds, shrubs add another dimension in planters. Many cultivars are available in compact or dwarf versions that are happy in contained environments. For interest through several seasons, consider conifers, redosier dogwood or flowering shrubs, such as weigela (shown above) or hydrangea.

4. INCORPORATE EDIBLES

Many fruits, veggies and herbs make fantastic container residents. Take advantage of their textural foliage; sage, thyme and chard are fabulous choices. And don't forget the produce! Tomatoes pair well with marigolds, peppers get along with nasturtiums and blueberries pop among asters. Many edibles bloom beautifully, too, including chives and rosemary.

5. HAVE A GATHERING

Pack complementary pots with identical combos, or group those that share similar plants. Fill a painted stepladder, line them up on a short wall or arrange them along a stairway.

1, 2, 3: PROVEN WINNERS, PROVENWINNERS.COM; 4, 5, 6: RDA-GID; 7, TERRANCE KLASSEN / ALAMY; 8, JOY BROWN / SHUTTERSTOCK.COM; 9, SARAH JONES; 10, LINDA BELL

6. PLAY DRESS-UP

A little paint can work wonders on plain old pots. Personalize one for a special gardener in your life, or have the kids do the honors and include their handprints. Try stencils and other crafting techniques, too. (See below left).

7. GIVE IT A PLACE OF HONOR

Remember to think about your planter's environment. Fill window boxes with plants that echo the color of your home (above right), nestle a brightly colored arrangement in a foliage-only bed or hang baskets of blooms from shepherd's hooks along your front walk.

8. ADORN IT

Consider adding a birdhouse, a brightly colored whirligig, a clay toadstool or a cast-iron critter. Use attractive mulch, such as sea glass, acorns, pinecones or colored stones, for a thoughtful finishing touch.

9. UPCYCLE

Who said that terra-cotta was the only avenue to container success? Plant succulents in worn-out cowboy boots, fill a broken drum with annuals or give new life to a cracked mixing bowl. It's a fun way to show off your personality. Turn the page for a host of other ideas.

10. TAKE THE SILK ROAD

Incorporate a few faux yet realistic plants in a container arrangement to guarantee continual color for the whole growing season. Take care to buy the type that are meant for the outdoors, or they won't blend in for long.

"What's your favorite way to dress up a container garden?"

Birds & Blooms **readers weigh in.**

I place a whimsical stake in the soil. Curling ribbon adds a nice touch, too.
—**SHARON L.**, *Wauseon, Ohio*

Sweet potato vine cascades over the sides and floods the container with bright colors.
—**TOM K.**, *Elizabethtown, Kentucky*

I like to personalize my flowerpots. Right now I'm working on one that will feature a '50s fashion collage.
—**PAULA MARIE H.**, *St. Peters, Missouri*

I use big, white flowers. They show up well and look so pure and clean.
—**PAT H.**, *Greenville, Mississippi*

unconventional containers

1.

Recycling household castaways is the fresh, new trend for unused planters.

4.

8.

11.

15.

19.

Sure, a brand-new store-bought flowerpot or window box will certainly do the trick, but why not take a quirkier approach to choosing a container? Explore your attic, scour local garage sales or rescue something from the curb on trash day. Then turn it into a one-of-a-kind, container-garden masterpiece.

Why You'll Love It

Creating your own planter isn't just fun, it's thrifty. If you're trying to keep your gardening budget in line, this is a great choice, particularly if you need to cover a lot of ground. You have to invest only as much time as you want. Stick to a simple plan and plant the container as is, or go all out and completely revamp it. By salvaging an item that's seen better days, you're doing the environment (not to mention yourself) a favor.

A project like this allows you to achieve exactly the effect you want. If you have a cottage-style garden, fill a rusty mailbox with plants. If you love to run, convert a worn pair of cross-trainers. Want something more modern? Flip a cinder block on its side and grow spiky foliage plants in the two holes.

What You'll Need

You can turn just about anything into a container, but whatever you choose needs to meet a couple requirements. First, it may go without saying, but the planter must hold soil—either on its own or in a smaller, less decorative pot you set inside.

If you're displaying it outside, the planter should also be weatherproof. The weather-beaten look can be charming, but if the item looks likely to rust through or fall apart, either patch it up or pass it by.

Last, like all garden containers, the planter-to-be should have good drainage, so drill holes in the bottom if necessary. If you're concerned about preserving the item's integrity, create a water reservoir in the base by adding a layer of pebbles or broken pottery. If you're worried that the item may leak too much, line it with plastic and poke a few holes through it.

Let's Get Started

Now you have all the know-how you need to give new life to something that was all but forgotten. You'll save money, preserve natural resources and end up with a planter that says "you" through and through. Let the creativity begin!

1, PROVEN WINNERS, PROVENWINNERS.COM; 11, ANGE / ALAMY; 15, KIM MIDDLETON; ALL OTHERS: RDA-GID

22.

25.

29.

32.

36.

39.

50.

43.

46.

50 *container finds*

Not sure what will work? Keep an eye out for items like these.

1. Watering can
2. Colander
3. Piano
4. Curing box
5. Handbag
6. Lunch box
7. Golf bag
8. Fruit crate
9. Chair
10. Gourd
11. Rowboat
12. Birdhouse
13. Lantern
14. Wagon
15. Galvanized tub
16. Hollow log
17. Toy dump truck
18. Pitcher
19. Birdbath
20. Canvas tote bag
21. Canoe
22. Bicycle basket
23. Dresser drawer
24. Shop-Vac
25. Work boots
26. Vintage food tin
27. Chandelier
28. Suitcase
29. Teakettle
30. Wheelbarrow
31. Birdcage
32. Sand pail
33. Burlap sack
34. Sink
35. Guitar
36. Barn trough
37. Conch shell
38. Hat
39. Bathtub
40. Bed frame
41. Toolbox
42. Doggy dish
43. Smokestack
44. Grill
45. Whiskey barrel
46. Tire
47. Tube TV
48. Butter churn
49. Wishing well
50. Lobster pot

22, ER_09 / SHUTTERSTOCK.COM; 25, MARIA DRYFHOUT / SHUTTERSTOCK.COM; 29, ROS DRINKWATER / ALAMY; 32, 43: RDA-GID; 36, SHELLI JENSEN / SHUTTERSTOCK.COM; 39, DAVID WEI / ALAMY; 46, ANDREA JONES / ALAMY; 50, LORRAINE HALEY

designer Q&A

No matter how seasoned their skills, gardeners are always seeking inspiration for spaces large and small. Four amazing designers, all of whom happen to read Birds & Blooms *magazine, share their secrets for surefire container success.*

Christina Salwitz
Renton, Washington

As the "Personal Garden Coach," container gardening guru Christina Salwitz shows clients ways to have fun while saving labor, time and money. Check out some of her best design tricks.

B&B: ***What are the best ways to keep plants happy in a container?***

CS: Here are four musts:

1. Use great potting soil. You usually get what you pay for.
2. Enable good drainage—unless you're trying for a water garden!
3. Ensure compatible light and watering needs for plants within the same container.
4. Follow a consistent watering and fertilizing schedule.

B&B: ***How can novices get started in container gardening?***

CS: Containers are a beginning gardener's best friend. Try plants together that you love. Success and failure are how we learn about plants; some of my best designs were unplanned. Follow my "theory of threes": Simply use three colors, textures and heights.

B&B: ***How can experienced gardeners challenge themselves?***

CS: Try color schemes that may be out of your comfort zone. Also challenge yourself to make any form of planter great: garage sale finds, discount pots in unusual colors and the like. Or experiment with making edibles as attractive as summer annuals.

B&B: ***What's your favorite unconventional container combo?***

CS: When I got a new water heater, I saved the old one's stand. I painted it black and used it as a pedestal in the garden. Then, I found a giant black ceramic bowl and filled it with a monochromatic mix, and set it on the recycled stand. The container arrangement was so lush that you couldn't see the bowl or the stand. It was amazing!

CHRISTINA'S TOP CONTAINER PLANT PICKS

Kalipso wood spurge

Dolce® Blackcurrant coral bells

Graceful Grasses® purple fountain grass

PORTRAIT AND CONTAINERS: CHRISTINA SALWITZ; FIDDLESTICKS GLASS ART BY BARBARA SANDERSON; ALL OTHER PHOTOS: PROVEN WINNERS, PROVENWINNERS.COM

P. Allen Smith
Little Rock, Arkansas

For many gardeners, P. Allen Smith is a celebrity. This lifestyle expert and garden designer hosts three television shows, has written several books and is the pro behind the Proven Winners Platinum Collection. Here Allen shares some of his container gardening wisdom with us.

B&B: ***Where do you look for inspiration when you're designing a container arrangement?***

PAS: The seasons themselves are great inspiration for color palettes, from cool spring pastels to hot summer hues and fiery autumn arrangements. I also look to the home. Both a home's color and its architectural elements can influence container design, from the vessel itself to the plants inside.

B&B: ***What are your tips for incorporating perennials into a container garden?***

PAS: Hostas and coral bells are natural for shade containers, and I love them combined with Rockapulco® double impatiens. Grasses, such as Ice Dance sedge, are also exceptional perennials for containers and combine well with Supertunia® Pretty Much Picasso® or Supertunia® Vista Bubblegum. I even plant daylilies in containers. They're a great old standby that performs well with lantana.

B&B: ***How about bulbs?***

PAS: I love growing bulbs in containers! When I plant spring-flowering bulbs in the fall, I pack them shoulder-to-shoulder for abundant blooms. What's great about containers of spring bulbs is that you can overplant them with cool-season annuals like pansies or violas for continuous color until the bulbs emerge. Summer-blooming bulbs such as elephant's ear, cannas, caladium and lilies make for spectacular arrangements, too.

B&B: ***What are a few ways to make sure that your arrangement is one of a kind?***

PAS: I use the "three-shape rule." The idea is to combine three basic plant forms—tall and spiky; round and full; and trailing and cascading—in each container, which for many people requires looking at plants in a new way. This method takes the focus away from colorful flowers and foliage and places it on the overall silhouette. When you follow this method, you'll find most plants fall into one of the three forms. They complement each other so well that the combination results in a more dynamic and appealing design.

Fan flower

Angelface® Blue angelonia

Diamond Frost® euphorbia

Superbells® Blackberry Punch calibrachoa

PORTRAIT AND CONTAINERS: P. ALLEN SMITH; ALL OTHER PHOTOS: PROVEN WINNERS, PROVENWINNERS.COM

designer Q&A

Patty Sutherland
Apple Valley, Minnesota

Here at *Birds & Blooms* magazine, we have long admired designs submitted by reader Patty Sutherland. But this mom of four isn't a garden professional; she's a flight attendant who, when on land, loves to stay home and observe nature at work. We asked Patty to tell us about her delightful design pastime.

B&B: ***How long have you been creating container gardens, and what got you into this hobby in the first place?***

PS: I have always loved flowers and gardening, something I picked up from my parents. About seven years ago, I started playing with different color combinations and textures of different plants. The choices really are endless, although with containers you obviously have limited space and have to choose wisely.

B&B: ***How have you shared your container gardening talents with others in your community?***

PS: I've designed container arrangements for my neighbors, the local high school and nearby assisted-living homes. It's rewarding to cheer people up and add beauty to their lives.

Lantana

B&B: ***What are some of your all-time favorite outdoor spots to dress up with container gardens?***

PS: Practically anywhere! I have a woodland garden where I love to place containers at random. I put them along paths and tuck some away for a surprise. A splash of color in a front entry always looks welcoming. And I spend a lot of time on my deck, where I like to surround myself with scents such as gardenia and jasmine, as well as vibrant color.

B&B: ***How do you keep your containers going all season?***

PS: I spend time cleaning and deadheading to keep them blooming. Sometimes I have to prune aggressive plants to keep the shape I want. I also fertilize throughout the growing season.

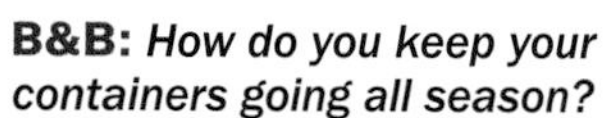

Patty's Top Container Plant Picks

Nonstop® Appleblossom tuberous begonia

Bandana® Cherry lantana

Goldilocks creeping Jenny

PORTRAIT AND CONTAINERS: PATTY SUTHERLAND; ALL OTHER PHOTOS: PROVEN WINNERS, PROVENWINNERS.COM

Sweet potato vine

Lynn Felici-Gallant
Raymond, New Hampshire

In the flower business for the past 15 years, Lynn Felici-Gallant manages marketing for Pleasant View Gardens, one of Proven Winners' founding partners. In her spare time, she heads the garden and container design firm Indigo Gardens. Read on for some of Lynn's top insights.

B&B: ***How did you develop a love of container gardening?***

LFG: My passion for designing outdoor containers is an extension of my love for interior design and flower arranging, two interests that I've had all my life.

B&B: ***What do you think are the keys to a winning combo?***

LFG: The best ones make a statement yet are still easy on the eyes. There's a reason we suggest that a combination include tall, mounding and trailing plants. If the right ones are chosen, this advice works; trying to do too much with too many elements can be very jarring.

Nearly all of my container plantings feature at least one dramatic or dark-leaved foliage plant to anchor or contrast with the flower colors. I like to have at least one striking foliage plant.

B&B: ***When selecting a container for an arrangement, what should you keep in mind?***

LFG: It's important to study the surroundings and decide if you want the container to blend seamlessly into the area or to create drama. The container itself should either complement or completely challenge its environment. The first is easy to do; the second is harder to do properly but more fun.

B&B: ***Do you base your design on the space where it will be displayed, or plant the container first, and then find a spot for it?***

LFG: I typically design a container to complement the space in terms of style and color. I like to pick up a color in the area of the planting, whether it's the trim on a home's windows or a dominant shade in the neighboring gardens.

PORTRAIT AND CONTAINERS: LYNN FELICI-GALLANT; ALL OTHER PHOTOS: PROVEN WINNERS, PROVENWINNERS.COM

ALL TIERED UP: Once each plant has reached its full maturity, Amethyst Tryst will appear to have three distinct layers.

no-fuss container recipes

These easy planting plans add splashes of color to any space.

Amethyst Tryst

Various hues of purple and green combine for a calming effect in this easy-care container for sunny spots.

Light requirements: Part to full sun

Pot size: 14 inches

Ingredients:

A. Artist® Blue floss flower (1)

B. Merlot coleus (1)

C. Lemon Licorice licorice plant (1)

D. Quartz Creek soft rush (1)

E. Supertunia® Bordeaux petunia (1)

Playful Pastels

Spiky plectranthus bursts from a soft bed of Marguerite daisies, petunias and bacopa in this fun, pink-and-purple combo of annuals.

Light requirement: Sun

Pot size: 14 inches

Ingredients:

A. Blue Yonder plectranthus (1)

B. Snowstorm® Blue bacopa (1)

C. Marguerite daisy (1)

D. Supertunia® Cotton Candy petunia (1)

Bacopa

Tropical Treasure

Island-inspired foliage shares the spotlight with vibrant blossoms in this shade-loving arrangement.

Light requirements: Part to full shade

Pot size: 20 inches

Ingredients:

A. Eranthemum (1)

B. Summer Wave® Large Violet wishbone flower (2)

C. Infinity® Scarlet New Guinea impatiens (2)

PROVEN WINNERS, PROVENWINNERS.COM

Soft & Sweet

Lemon-yellow petunias seem to glow among bright flecks of orange and gold in this lush hanging basket.

Light requirement: Sun

Pot size: 12 inches

Ingredients:

A. Flambe® Yellow strawflower (2)

B. Flying Colors® Orange twinspur (1)

C. Supertunia® Citrus petunia (2)

C A
B
C A

Patriot's Party

Give your best to the red, white and blue with this cheerful box of blooms that's colorful all summer long.

Light requirement: Sun

Pot size: 14 inches

Ingredients:

A. Laguna™ Sky Blue lobelia (2)

B. Sunsatia® Cranberry nemesia (1)

C. Tukana® White verbena (1)

C A
A B

Nemesia

Star-Studded

Star-Studded

Invite these distinctive plants to the same mix, and you've got yourself a party.

Light requirement: Sun

Pot size: 24 inches

Ingredients:

A. ColorBlaze® Kingswood Torch coleus (2)

B. Northern Lights tufted hairgrass (2)

C. Gold Mound duranta (2)

D. Lemon Licorice licorice plant (2)

E. Superbells® Pink calibrachoa (2)

Cheerful Collection

These five springtime classics brighten up any dreary day.

Light requirement: Sun

Pot size: 12 inches

Ingredients:

A. Helena's Blush wood spurge (1)

B. White Lace™ evergreen candytuft (1)

C. Chic™ in Yellow primrose (1)

D. Foamflower (1)

E. Pansy (1)

ECHOING HUE:
Tuscan Charm is a perfect example of color echoing: The blooms enhance the yellow tones in the mostly green foliage.

SWAP IT OUT!
Once a perennial outgrows its pot, plant it in your garden for a great show next year.

A B
C C

String of Pearls

These spring-blooming perennials look lovely in any container, from a classic pot to a hanging basket—even a wall sconce.

Light requirement: Sun

Pot size: 14 inches

Ingredients:

A. Variegatus dwarf white striped sweet flag (1)

B. White Sequins™ rock cress (1)

C. Polar™ White English daisy (2)

A B
F C
D E

Sunny Disposition

Spread some cheer with this friendly fall container filled with perennial sunflowers and Shasta daisies.

Light requirement: Sun

Pot size: 24 inches

Ingredients:

A. Northern Lights tufted hairgrass (1)

B. Maple Sugar hibiscus (1)

C. Leatherleaf sedge (1)

D. Tuscan Sun perennial sunflower (1)

E. Broadway Lights™ Shasta daisy (1)

F. Coco Loco™ coleus (1)

Tuscan Charm

A laid-back combination for a sunny spot, this monochromatic container radiates Mediterranean style.

Light requirement: Sun

Pot size: 16 inches

Ingredients:

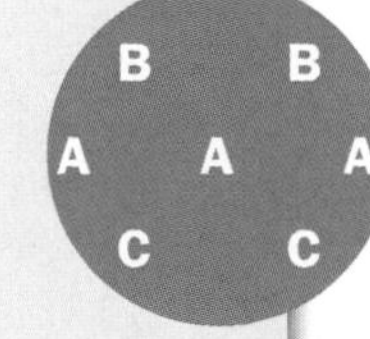

A. Tuscan Sun perennial sunflower (3)

B. Kalipso wood spurge (2)

C. Dolce® Key Lime Pie coral bells (2)

Index

A

B

C

D

E

F

G

H

Index

"There shall be eternal summer
in the grateful heart." —Celia Thaxter